Layman's
BIBLE
Commentary

Psalms thru Song of Songs

Volume
5

Contributing Editors:

DR. STEPHEN LESTON
STEPHEN C. MAGEE, M.DIV
JEFFREY MILLER, Th.M
STAN CAMPBELL, M.A

Consulting Editor:
DR. TREMPER LONGMAN

BARBOUR
PUBLISHING

ISBN 978-1-62029-778-0

Produced with the assistance of Christopher D. Hudson & Associates. Contributing writers include Jane Vogel, Laura Coggin, Carol Smith, Heather Rippetoe, and Jeff Walter

Published by Barbour Publishing, Inc., P.O. Box 719, Uhrichsville, Ohio 44683, www.barbourbooks.com

Our mission is to publish and distribute inspirational products offering exceptional value and biblical encouragement to the masses.

Member of the
Evangelical Christian
Publishers Association

Printed in the United States of America.

TABLE OF CONTENTS

PSALMS

INTRODUCTION TO PSALMS

The book of Psalms has been called the "hymnbook" of the Old Testament. Depending on one's perception of a hymnal, the title can be misleading, or it can be quite accurate. Sometimes the modern church approaches hymns lightly—singing one before the "real" worship service begins and another before going home. Or perhaps old hymns are disregarded altogether. But anyone who closely examines a traditional hymnal and reads the words of Martin Luther, Charles Wesley, Fanny Crosby, and others will find a wealth of biblical truth and weighty theological tenets. The fact that the words are rhymed and set to music may actually disguise their importance to modern ears.

This is the case with the book of Psalms as well. Its poetic format tends to diminish its importance for some people. They turn to Psalms for comfort or for light reading, yet many fail to approach the psalms with the same reverence as other portions of scripture. Yet for those who read closely, the psalms reveal much about God and the impact of His presence during the joys and struggles of human life.

And just as a modern hymnal may contain hymns with updated language in places, or perhaps a newer hymn set to an old familiar tune, so, too, the book of Psalms has revisions. It is believed that in certain instances, psalmists from the exile or later may have adapted much earlier psalms to apply to Israel's current situation.

AUTHOR

The psalms have a variety of authors. Some psalms identify the writer, and others don't. Yet even the people acknowledged as authors may not have actually written the psalm. A psalm attributed to David may have been written *by* David or possibly written *for* David. Or it could have been another psalmist's attempt to write in the style of David. One of the writers, Asaph, was a contemporary of David's, yet some of the psalms of Asaph refer to events of the exile that occurred long after his death. Therefore it is sometimes a challenge to verify authors. Other times the content of the psalm provides a clear indication of the author. In cases where the writer is uncertain (or not identified), it is traditional to refer to "the psalmist" as the author.

Almost half of the psalms (seventy-three) are attributed to David. Asaph (including his descendants, one of the clans of Levites assigned to oversee the music ministry of the temple) is credited with twelve psalms. Another music ministry clan, the sons of Korah, is identified with eleven psalms (although Psalm 43, which is unattributed, may have originally been an extension of Psalm 42 and therefore added to the total). Two psalms are assigned to Solomon. One each is assigned to Moses, Heman, and Ethan. That leaves forty-nine psalms with no designated author.

PURPOSE

The Hebrew title for the book means "praises." (The word *psalm* comes from the Greek translation rather than the original Hebrew.) Overall, the content of the book is intended for prayer and praise, although there is much variety within those broad categories. Some of the psalms were written as individual laments, some as community laments, some as thanksgiving hymns. Some are classified as penitential—confessional psalms asking God's forgiveness. Others were written as laments that cried for God's mercy on the psalmist and retribution on his enemies. Some were intended as regal celebrations when a new king was crowned.

OCCASION

Some psalms celebrate special occasions in the community, such as annual pilgrimages to Jerusalem, the coronation of a king, and liturgical ceremonies. Other psalms are written in regard to personal experiences. (Of David's seventy-three psalms, fourteen of the introductions refer to specific events in his life.) Yet the poetic nature of the psalms leads to their use on many occasions. Jesus and numerous New Testament writers naturally referred to the psalms to emphasize what they were trying to say. Jesus even quoted from the psalms as He hung on the cross (see Psalm 22:1 and Matthew 27:46; Psalm 31:5 and Luke 23:46).

THEMES

Unlike most of the biblical books that precede it, Psalms is not written in chronological order or any linear fashion. It is a collection of poetry written by numerous people over a long period of time. Yet regardless of the author, time period, or specific situation, the author invariably acknowledges the presence of—and humanity's total dependence on—God. Whether describing the wonders of creation, expressing a personal and painful trauma, recounting the history of the nation, bemoaning life in exile, or detailing any other experience, the psalmist's words are directed toward God. Some psalms express more faith than others, but they all appeal to God's strength, mercy, forgiveness, deliverance, and other qualities that are exclusively His.

HISTORICAL CONTEXT

With one psalm attributed to Moses and others to psalmists during and after the exile, the content of the psalms covers centuries of Israel's history. The scope of the psalms covers times when individuals and the nation were close to God and basking in His blessings as well as times when the people had drifted away from the will of God, and they were suffering as a result. In addition, some of the psalms have messianic applications, so the context is future as well as past and present.

CONTRIBUTION TO THE BIBLE

No collection of ancient lyrical poetry is more extensive than the book of Psalms. Hebrew poetry was not known for rhyme and meter but rather for repetition of thoughts and a style of parallelism that reemphasized or contrasted a concept in adjoining lines. The psalms also introduce some words that have never been clearly defined—words such as *sheminith* (Psalms 6, 12), *shiggaion*, (Psalm 7), *gittith* (Psalm 8, 81, 84), *alamoth* (Psalm 46), *mahalath* (Psalm 53), *mahalath leannoth* (Psalm 88), *miktam* and *maskil* (various psalms), and *selah* (found seventy-one times in thirty-nine psalms). Most are believed to be musical or perhaps historical references.

OUTLINE

The collection we know as the book of Psalms is actually a series of collections—five books in all. Books I and II are thought to be early collections, dating from the era of the kings. Book I may even have been compiled by David himself. The latter three books were probably compiled after the exile.

Book I	Psalms 1–41
Book II	Psalms 42–72
Book III	Psalms 73–89
Book IV	Psalms 90–106
Book V	Psalms 107–150

PSALMS: BOOK I

PSALMS 1–19

Setting Up the Section

The first "book" within Psalms is the earliest of the five compilations. It is widely associated with David's life and reign. This section contains the first nineteen (of forty-one) psalms from the first book.

PSALM 1

The placement of Psalm 1 does not appear to be coincidental. The work of editors seems clear from the fact that each book within the book of Psalms ends with a doxology. Similarly, Psalm 1 seems well chosen to emphasize a theme that will be ongoing. Throughout scripture God calls His people to set their standards higher than those of the world in general. People who commit themselves to God and are obedient to His clear instructions are promised rewards; those who reject Him can expect judgment. The first psalm reflects this ongoing biblical theme, as will others throughout the book.

In verse 1, the word *blessed* describes the status of someone who has placed trust in the Lord and lives according to His commands. This desirable state is one of inner joy more than financial prosperity, although the two are sometimes intertwined (1:3). Blessedness results from committing to certain activities while avoiding others (1:1–2).

Those desiring God's blessing must be careful of their worldly associations, according to the opening of this psalm. While being a light to the world, they must not allow themselves to linger too long around ungodly influences, lest they be seduced. They are not to walk among the wicked, and they are to remain focused at all times on God's Word (1:1–2).

According to verses 3–6, the reward for doing so is significant. The image of the wicked is that of chaff being blown away by a breeze (1:4). Those who devote themselves to righteousness, however, are portrayed as a fruitful tree, soundly rooted beside streams of water (1:3). No matter how great the thrill of various tantalizing sins might appear, it will not compare to being able to stand in (withstand) the judgment of God (1:5).

The wicked may appear to prosper, but their success is always temporary. Those [who] remain committed to the Lord and in His care will endure forever (1:6).

PSALM 2

Psalm 2:2 refers to the anointed one of God. The Hebrew for "anointed one" is the source of the English word *messiah*. New Testament references make it clear that the writers applied the psalm to Jesus (Acts 13:32–33). The original readers, however, would have considered it a reference to one of God's chosen kings in the Davidic line.

Critical Observation

Like Psalm 1, the author and date of Psalm 2 are not known. The leaders of the early New Testament church attributed Psalm 2 to David (Acts 4:25), although their intent may simply have been to give him credit as the primary author of Psalms.

The psalmist doesn't expect an answer to his opening question in verse 1. He is simply pointing out that by resisting the one anointed by God, the nations are resisting the authority of God Himself—a futile effort. The psalmist's original readers would have been familiar with the political turbulence that frequently took place surrounding the rise of a new leader. Perhaps they recalled that, in spite of David's credentials, the supporters of King Saul were still slow to accept him as their leader. Later, when Solomon's son (and successor) Rehoboam attempts to assert himself as a new king, the people strongly resist, and the kingdom is divided from that point onward (1 Kings 12:1–24).

The people whom the psalmist describes in Psalm 2:2–3 are not at all cooperative. They consider service to their king the equivalent of slavery. Such treason would have had harsh consequences from a human king, but this group is resisting God.

The Lord does not need these people or their cooperation. Their attempted resistance is laughable. He will carry out His plans, installing the one He has chosen to be the reigning king (2:4–6). How others respond does not impede His plans.

In verse 6, *Zion* is a term that often indicates Jerusalem in the Psalms. Zion appears to have originally been only one *section* of Jerusalem—a southern hill on which a Jebusite fortification was established until David conquered it (2 Samuel 5:6–7). In time, however, Zion became synonymous with Jerusalem.

The first-person comments in Psalm 2:7–9 are the affirmation of the one being anointed, directed to the sitting king. Today the psalm points out a clear messianic truth. Originally, however, it would not have been unusual for a king to be referred to in a fatherly position over other leaders who were subject to him. And in Israel, where it was understood that God was the king, any earthly figurehead was only a son in comparison. The great authority of the "father" king was therefore bestowed upon the "son."

In verses 10–11, the psalmist turns his attention back to the kings of the earth, who are gathered against the Lord's anointed one. Their arrogant and conspiratorial attitude is inappropriate. If they are wise they will acknowledge the Lord and devote themselves

hey will also honor the son to prevent incurring his wrath (2:12).
...nted one are formidable enemies. But as allies, all who turn to Him
...blessed.

This is the ... the seventy-three psalms designated "of David." And in this case, the occasion of writing is included as well: when David fled from his son Absalom. The story of David fleeing from Absalom is told in 2 Samuel 15–18, but the sentiment expressed in the psalm is appropriate for anyone who has been betrayed or turned upon by a close friend or family member.

Demystifying Psalms

Psalms is divided into five books. Some people feel that each successive book is a compilation of songs assembled sometime after the previous collection. Book I may have been compiled during the time of David, so it isn't surprising to discover that all but four of the first forty-one psalms are attributed to him.

According to verses 1–2, David's numerous foes are not only rebellious and defiant but are also attempting to undermine his faith in God. But David realizes that God's presence in his life is the one thing that will enable him to endure. The Bible's frequent usage of a shield as an image of God (3:3) may not entirely register with today's readers. While being shielded from something harmful is understood, it's a different matter altogether to hold a shield in front of one's body for protection during hand-to-hand combat, feeling the shield absorb blows that might otherwise prove fatal. David's ongoing trust in God makes a very real difference in his life.

David's confidence in God is evident in his ability to sleep at night (3:4–6). Insomnia is one of the first side effects of worry. But rather than fretting and losing sleep, David talks to God, enabling him to have peace of mind and decent rest.

Throughout the psalms, the language of the writers will at times be quite harsh, as in verse 7. This is an expression of David's confidence in God, so it is in terms that a warrior might relate to. God will not merely defeat His enemies; He will utterly crush them.

But despite the indelicate language, David's intent is clear. God is always able to deliver His people (3:8). Even in the midst of persecution and troubled times, God's people can look to their Lord for help and hope.

Demystifying Psalms

The term *Selah* accompanies verses 2, 4, and 8, and will be used seventy-one times throughout the book of Psalms. The term may refer to "lifting up," but its precise significance is unclear. Most believe it is a musical cue of some sort, or perhaps a call for a congregational response. However, no one can be sure.

PSALM 4

Psalm 4 is another psalm of David, and scholars frequently detect a connection between this poem and the previous one. Perhaps David wrote them at approximately the same time. If so, this one may also pertain to David's feelings about Absalom's betrayal.

In verse 1, the psalmist again confesses a mindset of distress, yet he expresses the expectation of relief available only from a merciful God. According to the next verse, he is beset by other people who have not only turned away from him but also turned away from God to pursue delusions. David emphasizes that he has kept himself removed from such behavior, and he expects God to respond to him (4:3). Aside from a few well-known exceptions, David is usually faithful in consulting God during both the good and bad experiences of his life.

Another similarity between Psalms 3 and 4 is David's expression of how his faith in God allows him to sleep at night in spite of life's circumstances (3:5; 4:8). But one difference is David's attitude toward those who oppose him. He had previously prayed for God to "shatter the teeth of the wicked" (3:7 NLT). Here in Psalm 4, David's request is much warmer. He appeals to his opponents to not allow their anger to lead to sin, and he urges them to repent before God—to offer right sacrifices (4:4–5). Perhaps David's mind was indeed on Absalom as he wrote this, for it sounds like the plea of a parent worried that a grown child is in danger of harming himself.

In verse 7, David acknowledges that the joy God provides is greater than even the most festive times of regular life. He speaks from experience, but he hopes that others will discover the same truth.

Critical Observation

The superscript at the beginning of Psalm 4 explains that the song is to be accompanied by stringed instruments, which would have included lyres, harps, and similar traditional instruments of the time. Psalm 5 calls for flutes. The Hebrew word is used nowhere else in the Old Testament, so the exact nature of the instrument is unknown.

PSALM 5

Psalm 5 is apparently a morning prayer of David, perhaps to accompany a regular morning sacrifice (Exodus 29:38–39). David had learned that it is always a good idea to present one's requests to God in the morning and then wait in expectation—especially on days that begin with sighing and cries for help, as described in verses 1–3.

David can take consolation because he understands the character of God. The Lord cannot tolerate evil, so He does not respond to people who willingly participate in arrogance, lies, and deceit (5:4–6). Some people begin their mornings proud of what they feel they have achieved or scheming to acquire more through less-than-honorable methods. David, however, expresses his feelings to God and waits for a response.

David is a successful warrior and king, but he doesn't attempt to draw on his accomplishments to curry God's favor. As verse 7 indicates, he realizes it is only by God's mercy that anyone is able to approach the Lord, and he maintains an attitude of reverence and humility. Consequently, he acknowledges in verse 8 that even the assaults of his enemies make him stronger because they drive him to seek God's strength.

David's closeness to God allows him to see his enemies for what they are. They are corrupt throughout: their mouths, their hearts, their throats, and their tongues (5:9). They can expect a harsh downfall because of their rejection of God and their many offenses against others (5:10).

In contrast, verses 11–12 describe those who seek God and take refuge in Him. They experience God's protection, which allows them to be glad, sing, and rejoice. While on the run from King Saul, David had many times felt the surrounding protection of God. He knows for certain that the Lord's shield of favor is available to all who love and serve Him (5:11–12).

PSALM 6

The phrase in the opening superscription of Psalm 6, "according to sheminith," is not fully understood. The same phrase is used in association with Psalm 12 and in 1 Chronicles 15:21. It appears to be a musical term relating to the number *eight*—perhaps a reference to an octave or possibly an eight-stringed musical instrument.

Throughout scripture there are accounts of people who commit sin and, as a consequence, experience physical suffering as God's means of chastening (Miriam [Numbers 12]; Elisha's servant, Gehazi [2 Kings 5:26–27]; King Asa [2 Chronicles 16:10–12]; King Jehoram [2 Chronicles 21:18–19]; King Uzziah [2 Chronicles 26:16–21]; the sorcerer Bar-Jesus [Acts 13:6–12]). In this psalm David speaks of a similar instance, although it is unclear about what specific occurrence to which he refers.

Whatever David had done, he is penitent at this point. Psalm 6 is one of seven psalms that are sometimes classified as *penitential*. The others are Psalms 32, 38, 51, 102, 130, and 143.

Psalm 6 reflects travail on many fronts. On a spiritual level, David has done something that has resulted in God's anger (6:1). Physically, his whole body is afflicted with pain (6:2).

Demystifying Psalms

A common technique in psalm writing was to place the psalm's theme in the center. In this case, David's emphasis is expressed in verse 6.

David is sick of being sick—worn out from groaning and weeping. With his bones in agony and soul in anguish, his whole being is in pain and he knows that only God can heal him. His question in verse 3, "How long?" is asked frequently throughout the psalms.

To make things worse, verses 7–10 reveal that his enemies are taking advantage of his vulnerable position to taunt him. In light of such distress, he makes no effort to put up a

PSALM 8

brave front. His appeal to God is heartfelt and honest.

In verse 4, David expresses his hope for healing because of God's unfailing love. He appeals to God, reasoning that he can continue to acknowledge God as long as he is living, but death will put an end to any praise he might offer (6:5). He concludes the psalm with the confident expectation that God will indeed act on his behalf (6:9–10).

PSALM 7

The introduction to Psalm 7 includes more than one confusing reference. The term *shiggaion* is used only twice in the Bible, here and in Habakkuk 3:1. It appears to be a musical term but has an undetermined meaning. In addition, the man named *Cush*, to whom David refers, is not known elsewhere in scripture. However, the additional note that he is from the tribe of Benjamin makes it likely that he might have been an associate of Saul. This makes sense in light of the psalm's description of being pursued by relentless enemies.

In David's previous psalm, he is painfully enduring his enemies' nasty comments because he realizes he has done something to displease God. Here, however, his approach is entirely different. His enemies are again out to get him, but this time he is able to repeatedly affirm his innocence (7:3–5, 8, 10).

David has great confidence in the Lord, but that doesn't make the attacks of his enemies any less unsettling. According to verse 6, encountering the rage of one who has the capability of tearing someone to pieces like a lion requires no small amount of faith (7:1–2).

According to 1 Samuel, David twice had the opportunity to bring Saul's pursuit of him to an end (1 Samuel 24; 26), but both times he refused to kill Saul, whom he acknowledged as "the LORD's anointed." David chose not to act in vengeance, but rather left justice up to God, as he describes here in Psalm 7:6. By doing so, he allows God to examine his motives as he asks for divine help (7:3–9).

David has also witnessed the wrath of God. In verses 8–9, he realizes that God's wrath is in direct relation to his righteousness. Any conscientious judge, in the interest of justice, must occasionally pass harsh sentences when the guilty party shows neither concern nor remorse. David describes God as a warrior preparing for battle: sharpening His sword, stringing His bow, and lighting His arrows with fire (7:11–13).

According to verse 9, the targets of God's wrath are the wicked; righteous people are secure. Some people show blatant disregard for God and no desire for holy living. Such people are "pregnant with evil" (7:14 NIV), but their time will come. Those who choose such a life cannot prevent trouble in their own lives (7:14–16).

Despite the very real threat David is feeling from his enemies, in verse 17 he concludes this psalm, as psalmists so frequently do, with praise to God—and an advance acknowledgement of God's willingness to act on behalf of His faithful people.

PSALM 8

The introduction to Psalm 8 includes yet another ancient term: *gittith* (also found in the superscriptions of Psalms 81 and 84). The Hebrew word might be a reference to a winepress or to Gath, a Philistine city where David had spent some time (1 Samuel 21:10–15; 27:1–4). Its significance as a musical cue, however, is unknown.

Who hasn't stared into the heavens on a clear night and wondered about the nature of God, the origin of humanity, and other weighty questions? This psalm reflects David's musings about such things. David begins with an acknowledgment that the earth is God's. When God's presence is not considered, people come up with distorted answers to the question, "What is man?" (Psalm 8:4).

According to verse 1, those who are observant see the majesty of God. The expanse and the order of the solar system reflect the design of a Creator. And even the awe of small children as they encounter the wonders of the world gives praise to God (8:2).

When one ponders the vast extent of the universe, it is easy to feel small and insignificant. But verses 3–5 reveal that God has bestowed much significance on humankind. In fact, the word translated as *angels* or *heavenly beings* in verse 5 is *elohim*—one of the Hebrew names for God. It would be just as acceptable to translate the sentence, "You made him a little lower than God." Either way, human beings have certainly been crowned with glory and honor (8:5).

From the beginning, God had designated humankind to be the overseers of the earth (Genesis 1:28). People are privileged to rule over the other animals of the land, the sea, and the air. And this privilege is not to be taken lightly. It is still God's creation, and the people report to a higher master (Psalms 6–8).

The psalm begins and ends with the same verbatim statement (8:1, 9). "O LORD, our Lord" is not a repetition as it might appear to be when translated. The readers of the psalm would have realized that the first *Lord*—the one in small caps in most Bible translations—is a name for God (Jehovah). The second *Lord* is a different word that indicates a title for God. It's the equivalent of President George Washington or King Henry VIII, except the name and the title translate into the same English word.

Both the name and the title of God are majestic. Nothing on earth can compare. As David realizes, those observations are well worth repeating.

PSALM 9

Like several of the preceding psalms of David, Psalm 9 also deals with his struggles to endure the persecution of his enemies. In this case, however, David is eager to sing and rejoice because God has dealt with David's foes. They have not only been defeated but also rebuked, destroyed, and blotted out (9:3–5). Their ruin is endless, and soon there would not even be a memory of them (9:6).

So in verses 7–9, David begins to extol the character of God. He affirms that the Lord is an eternal king, a righteous judge, and a stronghold and refuge for those needing help. People who seek God can count on Him to come through for them (9:10).

Consequently, then, God deserves our praise (9:11–12). When God acts on our behalf, we should be quick to tell others what He has done. When people are afflicted, they cry out to Him (9:12). After God delivers them or administers justice, people should then voluntarily speak out in praise of Him.

Since, according to verse 12, God does not ignore the cries of the afflicted, David begins to voice his affliction (9:13). But rather than dwell on the current persecution he is facing, he quickly turns his attention to the future. He envisions himself already delivered, safe, and rejoicing once more in Jerusalem ("the gates of the Daughter of Zion").

As for the nations, they will reap what they have sown. What they plotted against others will be their own downfall (9:15–17). The justice of God will not allow them to prevail. God will remember and restore the needy, even as He humbles those who are filled with pride and power (9:18–20).

Critical Observation

A case can be made that Psalms 9 and 10 were originally a single psalm. Some dispute this possibility because the two divisions have quite different themes and each section holds up on its own. However, in the span of Psalms 3 to 32, Psalm 10 is the only one lacking a superscription. And if the two are combined, they create an acrostic poem (a poem where each unit begins with a successive letter of the Hebrew alphabet), albeit roughly. Perhaps they were two songs meant to relate to each other, or maybe a single psalm was divided at a point in church history to facilitate its use in worship.

PSALM 10

In Psalm 10, the psalmist (presumably David) goes into great detail about wicked people, describing both their attitudes and their actions. The people he writes about in verses 2–11 are arrogant, covetous, proud, self-centered, haughty, dishonest, and cruel. Their time is spent scheming, sneering, cursing, murdering innocent people, and otherwise preying on helpless victims. They scoff at God.

It looked as if the evil people were going to succeed in all their corrupt activities. So in verse 1 the psalmist questions God, wanting to know why He doesn't get more involved. Later he calls for God to arise and take action (10:12).

The psalmist knew cognitively that God saw what was going on; but speaking on behalf of the victims, he wants God to take immediate action (10:14–15). In brutal honesty, he wants those who regularly take advantage of innocent people to suffer. The broken arms mentioned in verse 15 would have brought an end to the dominance of the oppressors.

Like many other psalms, this one concludes with eager anticipation that God would indeed take action and would respond to the pleas of the writer. The psalmist verifies that God is in control and will continue to act on behalf of those who cannot help themselves (10:16–18).

PSALM 11

David is both a courageously faithful man and a practical one. He had been the one who matter-of-factly volunteered to go up against Goliath when every single soldier in Israel's army had been afraid to do so, even after forty days of opportunity (1 Samuel 17). But sometimes David also demonstrated that discretion is the better part of valor. After

King Saul would not give up pursuit, David had negotiated with the Philistines to obtain a town of his own outside Israel's borders (1 Samuel 27:1–7). So David possesses a good understanding of when to flee and when to stand firm—the topic of Psalm 11.

If Psalm 11 is based on an actual event in David's life, we don't know exactly what it is. However, there are probably numerous times when he appeared to be in imminent danger and was urged by those around him to flee to the mountains for safety (11:1). Fear initiates panic, and at the first sign of potential danger, some people overreact and take drastic action. Soon an accompanying sense of hopelessness develops as well (11:3).

But David will have nothing to do with their negative thinking. The opening statement of Psalm 11 is his theme: "In the LORD I take refuge." Even though earthly events may seem to be more chaotic and turbulent than usual, one's spiritual condition is as reliable as ever. God is still on His throne (11:4). Nothing has changed. He sees what is going on, He will judge what He sees, and it won't be pleasant for those who have defied Him (11:5–6).

Psalm 11 ends with encouragement for the righteous—they may be shaken by the evil in the world, but they have nothing to fear from the Lord (11:7). Many believers comprehend that on a cognitive level. But what made David so special was that he truly believed it and acted in faith that his righteous Lord would always be there for him. In David's case, God is not just a vague presence but a refuge in the truest sense of the word.

PSALM 12

In Psalm 12 David describes the all-too-common feeling of looking around and seeing that one's world has deteriorated into a sorry state. The superscription comments for this psalm, "according to sheminith" are the same as for Psalm 6.

David is feeling somewhat alone in his commitment to God. The situation he describes in verses 1–2 is not unlike that of Elijah a few decades later (1 Kings 19:9–18)—a sense of loneliness sometimes experienced by those faithful to the Lord. It appears to David that all other righteous people have disappeared. Everywhere he looks he sees shallow people lying, boasting, and flattering one another (12:1–2).

In a short prayer inserted into the psalm, David asks God to deal with the widespread problem (12:3–4). He realizes the verbal outpourings are reflections of proud and callous hearts. People with any regard for God (or others, for that matter) would not speak in such a manner. Such people believe they are their own masters.

God's reply in verse 5 is immediate. He is preparing to arise, and He will certainly protect those who are being maligned. So although David's perception had been that the faithful and godly people had vanished, they are still around. It will not be the last time that the weak and needy appear to be invisible in society.

God's promise to take action in verse 5 is all that is needed. While the oppressing majority of people spout words that can't be trusted, God's words are never in doubt. According to verse 6, they are flawless and comparable to silver that had been refined and re-refined seven times (a number indicating perfection).

As the detestable people of earth "strut about" (12:8 NLT), it may seem that they are in control. But God will surely protect His faithful followers from such people forever (12:7–8).

PSALM 13

In Psalm 13, David expresses yet another complaint common to many people—the feeling that God has forgotten him. David cannot detect God's presence. He is distraught with sorrow and discomfiting thoughts. He is at the mercy of his enemies. So in verses 1-2, he repeatedly asks the haunting question: How long will this go on?

Perhaps David is seriously ill, which would have given his enemies an additional cause to celebrate. His words in verse 3, "Enlighten my eyes" (NASB) might have been a plea for healing, since references to failing eyesight were often indicative of a more widespread physical problem (see 6:7). If this is the case, the illness must have been quite severe because David is contemplating death (13:4). Then again, his words could have been a desire to acquire God's perspective on his situation rather than his own limited outlook.

Yet in spite of the somewhat bleak opening to the psalm, it concludes (like so many others) in verses 5-6 with the psalmist's expression of complete trust in God. The Lord may appear to be distant, but He isn't. David's enemies may have seemed triumphant, but they aren't. The fear of death may have been weighing on David's mind, but he is still alive and able to reach out in faith.

David's steadfast God is still the source of unfailing love, salvation, and goodness (13:5-6). The circumstances of life might change, but the grace and mercy of God never will.

PSALM 14

Psalm 14 builds on several of the themes from previous psalms, particularly the contrast between the holiness of God and the foolishness of wicked people. Psalm 14 places more emphasis on the fools who ignore God. In contrast will be Psalm 15, which focuses on the benefits of being among the righteous.

David begins in verse 1 with a perceptive observation: Foolish people assume that God does not exist. That inner presumption, although entirely wrong, then results in corrupt and even vile outward actions. As those who *do* believe in God look on, they are disturbed and even horrified by such behavior.

In Psalm 12, David wanted to call God's attention to the dearth of godly people. Here, in verses 2-3, God takes the initiative in seeking out anyone who might have any degree of spiritual sensitivity. Previously the godly had been far outnumbered by evildoers. But in this case, all are corrupt. Not even one can be found who is good.

The actions of the wicked people appear to be cold and calculated. They devour God's people like eating bread (14:4)—the modern equivalent might be "chewing someone up and spitting him out." And they never call on God.

However, in verse 5 such people are also portrayed as unsettled. While they won't personally acknowledge God, they can't help but see that He makes a significant difference in the lives of the righteous people. Consequently, the evildoers are left with a sinking sense of dread.

David struggles with the tension between the two groups of people. He hates to see poor and defenseless individuals taken advantage of by those who are powerful enough to do so. But in verse 6 he realizes that God will be there for those who are otherwise powerless. Still, David dreams of justice on a much larger scale. He longs for the day when God's salvation will influence the entire nation (14:7). When that time comes, God's people will truly be joyous.

PSALM 15

With so many of the previous psalms expressing the writer's confusion, despair, and outrage over the fact that ungodly people seem to be running rampant while believers in God struggle to get by, Psalm 15 is a simple but powerful reminder of what is really important. In verse 1, the psalmist (presumably David) opens with a simple question: What does it take to find favor with God? What kind of people may approach Him and spend time with Him?

The answer may have surprised early readers of the psalm. A specific list is provided, but nowhere on the list is the mandate to participate in tabernacle worship services or offer sacrifices. Several items on the list have to do with control of the tongue, which is always a challenge (James 3:2), and all the behaviors stand in bold contrast to the previously described actions of the wicked who oppress God's people.

The simple answer to the question is found in verse 2: "He whose walk is blameless and who does what is righteous" (NIV). Jesus later issues a similar challenge to His listeners in Matthew 5:48: "Be perfect. . .as your heavenly Father is perfect" (NIV).

The psalmist provides a breakdown of what blamelessness and righteousness entails:

- *Speaking truth from the heart* (15:2). Evildoers are easily identified by their lies. God's people should be known for their truthfulness.
- *Avoiding slander* (15:3). It's easy to bad-mouth someone else. Many people become so accustomed to it that they don't even realize what they are doing. But God hears and notices slanderous words.
- *Treating neighbors properly* (15:3). Sometimes it's easier to be kind to strangers than to be consistently decent to those we are closest to, yet believers are called to do both.
- *Refusing to cast slurs on other people* (15:3). For today's believers, this requirement would include issues such as ethnic jokes, road rage, gossip, and other verbal slurs.
- *Despising evil people while honoring those who fear God* (15:4). Believers are challenged to differentiate between evil people and those struggling to follow the Lord, and to treat each group accordingly.
- *Keeping oaths even when it hurts to do so* (15:4). The underlying assumption is that sometimes it will hurt to keep one's promises. The mark of a devoted follower of God is complete trustworthiness at all times.
- *Lending money without usury* (15:5). When able to help others financially, God's people should be willing to do so. Outright gifts are a preferable option when possible, but even loans should be offered without the expectation of extreme interest payments in return.
- *Refusal to take bribes* (15:5). People who use money and power to manipulate others are certainly not on the list of those who can dwell in God's sanctuary. But neither are those who accept money to look the other way when helpless people are being threatened.

It is no easy matter to do all these things consistently. Yet according to verse 5, those who do will stand firm forever.

PSALM 16

The superscription of Psalm 16 includes the first mention of a *miktam*, another presumed but undeterminable musical term. The word appears in later psalms (56–60) where David describes himself in personal peril. In this case, David may be experiencing a threat of some sort (16:1), although throughout most of the psalm he expresses overwhelming confidence and optimism.

In the opening verses of this psalm, David affirms God as his refuge, an image he frequently uses (2:12; 7:1; 9:9). God is his solitary source of comfort and safety. David also relishes the opportunity to see other believers throughout the land (16:3).

Idolatry was a persistent threat to Israel, and David had witnessed people in the land pursuing other gods (16:4). It is a sad sight to see fellow Israelites make sacrifices to false gods while turning their backs on the true Lord and Savior of Israel. The sorrows of such people will only increase.

This is a time in David's life when he feels particularly close to God. Using the imagery of what someone might be served at a meal (a portion and cup), in verse 5 David expresses satisfaction with the blessings God has given him. Then, shifting to a geographic image in verse 6, David expresses pleasure that his life is not a rocky wasteland or a dusty wilderness. Instead, his boundaries are pleasant and his inheritance delightful (16:5–6).

According to verse 7, David is receiving guidance from God throughout the day and into the night. With the ongoing sensation of God being so close, David's response is praise, and the result is that he is not shaken by the undesired circumstances of life (16:8). With his sense of security, David can rejoice and be glad.

David doesn't have the same perspective of resurrection and eternal life as modern believers. Even so, he is assured and positive as he thinks about death. David is expectant that his close connection with God will endure with ongoing joy and eternal pleasures (16:9–11).

Critical Observation

David's expression of faithful confidence in Psalm 16 is so powerful that the psalm is later quoted by both Peter (Acts 2:25–28) and Paul (Acts 13:35). After the life, death, and resurrection of Jesus, David's words about death take on a surprising new significance.

PSALM 17

Psalm 17 is sometimes compared to Psalm 16. Although David doesn't express his specific complaint for some time, he is again besieged by his enemies (17:9–12) and is beseeching God's help. He desperately wants God's attention: He opens the psalm by asking three different times for God to listen to him.

Verse 2 indicates David wants vindication in God's eyes. He affirms that his words come as a righteous request from honest lips (17:1). It takes a person of real integrity to be able to challenge God to probe and test him, convinced that God will find no charge against him (17:3). In particular, David's resolve to control his mouth is reflective of Psalm 15.

According to verse 5, David keeps on the narrow path to God and therefore feels comfortable calling on Him (17:6). David's situation may have been too much for him to handle on his own, but he knew he could turn to God for both love and deliverance (17:7).

David uses a couple of now-familiar poetic images to help describe his perception of how God has protected him. First he asks to be kept as "the apple of [God's] eye" (17:8 NIV). He likely knew the phrase from the Books of Law (Deuteronomy 32:10). *Apple* is apparently a reference to the eye's pupil, which destroys one's vision if damaged. Protecting it is a natural instinct.

David uses a second image in verse 8: the shadow of God's wings. Someone might rest from the summer heat by lingering in the shadow of a tree or building. Similarly, God is an ever-present source of protection to diminish (if not eliminate) the oppressive forces of life. Additionally, the image suggests a mother bird caring for her brood. It is a soft and tender portrayal of God's loving care—one that is missed by many who presume the Old Testament God to be consistently harsh and demanding.

The enemies surrounding David are serious threats: callous, arrogant, and compared to a lion crouching to spring at its prey (17:9–12). David is wise to turn to God for shelter in verse 8, but he also prays that God will confront and deal with his wicked oppressors (17:13–14). Such people live only for what they can accumulate in this world. The righteous, however, know that God provides more than enough (17:14).

The psalm's closing statement in verse 15 sounds almost like a New Testament affirmation of resurrection and eternal life, but David would not have had this perspective. His confidence is that God will eventually remove the problem with the evildoers, allowing David to awaken to a new day, able to fully enjoy his relationship with the Lord.

PSALM 18

This is another psalm about David's praise to God in gratitude for His help in dealing with aggressive enemies. Longer than any of the psalms that precede it, Psalm 18 opens with an introductory overture of praise containing a long string of terms to describe God: strength, rock, fortress, deliverer, shield, horn of salvation, and stronghold (18:1–2). These are all images of power, yet the God they describe is both accessible and personal (18:3).

In contrast, David is in a desperate situation, writing of distress, destruction, and the likelihood of death in verses 4–6. But rather than allow fear and panic to overwhelm him, David calls on God for help.

God hears David's cries. The description in verses 7–15 is vivid and includes imagery of God responding through the forces of nature, the intensity of an angry and powerful animal, and the accuracy of a soldier armed with arrows and bolts of lightning. The mention of cherubim (angels) in biblical texts is frequently an indication of the presence of God (18:10).

David's foes had been too much to handle on his own, but his faith in God is not in vain (18:17). According to verse 7, the Lord is angry and mighty; and He rescues David and delivers him to safety (18:16–19).

Based on the fearful description of God, one might think David would be afraid of Him. But David had a firm conviction that he had been living in obedience and faithfulness to God (18:20–24). The awesome power of God is directed against those who oppose Him, but it works in favor of those committed to living a righteous life.

David doesn't consider himself a special case to receive God's help and protection. In verses 15–27, he affirms that anyone who is faithful will witness God's faithfulness in return, and everyone who is blameless, pure, and humble stands to benefit from the righteous character of the Lord. But those who display deceit or arrogance will view God in a vastly different manner. God's presence provides David assistance and abilities he cannot get anywhere else: light in darkness, strength, courage, and more (18:28–29).

Critical Observation

Psalm 18 is also found in its entirety (with only slight changes in wording) in 2 Samuel 22 as David's song of praise after being delivered from his enemies, including King Saul.

Verses 30–50 are David's personal testimony to the difference God has made in his life. David acknowledges the perfection of God and the fact that the Lord is a unique entity who cannot be compared to anyone or anything else (18:30–31). It is God who empowered and sustained David to be victorious in battle (18:32–42). It is God who designated David to be king in spite of initial resistance he received from Saul and others (18:43–45). And in response, David enthusiastically praises his Lord as savior, avenger, and benefactor (18:46–50).

PSALM 19

God reveals Himself to humankind in numerous ways. In Psalm 19, David begins by giving attention to the natural world that reflects God's glory and then moves on to the revealed Word of God—the source of many various potential blessings.

Verse 1 says the heavens speak in their own way of the glory of God. Humankind has always had a fascination with looking into the skies for weather forecasts, for getting one's bearings, for observation, for warning signs, and simply out of a sense of wonder. The message of the heavens is heard throughout the world (19:3–4).

Verses 2–3 describe the simple repetition of day following night and the soothing sense of rhythm and regularity it provides, reflecting the concept that God is eternal, consistent, and can be relied on. In verses 4–6, the creative description of the sun is that of a bridegroom arriving at his wedding and of a gleeful runner on track across the sky. David's viewpoint would have stood out from most others during his time. He credits God as being in control of the sun, while many other pagan religions held that the sun *was* a god.

After looking into the heavens to witness the glory of God, David looks into the Word of God: its laws, statutes, precepts, commands, and ordinances (19:7–11). His experience is that an awareness of God's Word results both in practical help (wisdom, righteousness, and warning) and in positive, pleasant feelings (joy, enlightenment).

By regularly examining the wonders of nature, someone can come to a broad and general belief that a creator must have designed the world. But to stop there can lead to much speculation and potentially erroneous theology. The living God responsible for creation is revealed throughout the pages of scripture. David knew to consult both sources for an accurate and more complete understanding of God.

David's knowledge of God, in fact, inspires him to excel in his devotion to his Lord. In verses 12–13, David wants to rid his life of willful sins as well as hidden faults. In an often-quoted verse (19:14), David ends this psalm with a prayer that not only his words but his inner thoughts as well would be pleasing to God, whom he acknowledges as both rock and redeemer.

Take It Home

At almost halfway through the first book within the biblical book of Psalms, stop to consider the psalmists' honesty with God. In most cases, that honesty is accompanied by passionate feelings, both positive and negative. How do the psalmists' cries to God compare to your own prayers? What can you learn from the psalms (so far) that might strengthen your current relationship with God?

PSALMS: BOOK I, CONTINUED

PSALMS 20–41

Setting Up the Section

This section continues and completes Book I, the compilation that opens the biblical book of Psalms. Essentially all of the psalms in this section are attributed to David. It is the section that contains perhaps the most beloved and widely known psalm: Psalm 23.

PSALM 20

In the opening verses of Psalm 20, it may appear that the psalmist is offering blessings upon his readers, but in verse 5 it becomes evident that the voice is plural, and the message is being addressed to a singular subject. The psalm is actually written for an assembled group to join the king in prayer preceding a battle.

Significant spiritual preparation has already taken place. The king's prayers have been offered to God, along with sacrifices at the tabernacle (sanctuary) (20:1–3, 5). Battle plans have been made and David is mentally ready (20:4), but he wants to ensure that God is with him and that he has the support of the people. And indeed, the people are anticipating a joyous victory (20:5).

The singular voice in verse 6 may be that of David, the king. Or possibly it is a response assigned to a designated Levite participating in the worship ceremony. Even though the crowd is expecting victory, the credit goes to God even before the battle begins.

At this point, Israel's army stands out among the surrounding nations. Most kings strategize based on their number of chariots and horses (20:7). But faith in God frees one from depending on numbers. As Jonathan had wisely realized when opposing the Philistines, "Nothing can hinder the LORD from saving, whether by many or by few" (1 Samuel 14:6 NIV). Putting one's trust in the name of the Lord is to place faith in His character and known qualities. And doing so enables His people to stand up against trouble (Psalm 20:8).

Verse 9 concludes this psalm in the same way it began, with a united prayer of the people for God to answer and to save their king.

PSALM 21

Psalm 21 is similar in form and purpose to Psalm 20. Some people even feel it may be a follow-up psalm to the previous one, with Psalm 20 recited prior to a crucial battle and Psalm 21 used during the triumphant celebration of victory.

The first section of verses (21:1-6) is either a congregational recitation or the words of the king, expressed in third person. There is no suggestion of distress, as was evident in the previous psalm (20:1). Here is only rejoicing and thanksgiving offered for God's strength, victory in battle, answered prayer, and other blessings (21:1-3).

The crown of pure gold in verse 3 sounds like a metaphor for all of God's blessings. At least once, however, it is a literal truth. After a battle with the Ammonites, David wore the crown of their king—a 75-pound headpiece made of gold and set with precious stones (2 Samuel 12:29-31).

The wish for a king to live forever in verse 4 is a standard figure of speech (see Daniel 6:21). In David's case, however, he had received God's promise that one of his descendants would establish a kingdom and rule forever (1 Chronicles 17:11-14). Victory in battle, splendor, and majesty are three blessings David had already received, yet the expectation is for eternal blessings—an ongoing assurance of God's presence with him (Psalm 21:6).

The crucial theme of the psalm is located in verse 7, the center of Psalm 21: David's trust in God, in conjunction with God's love for David, creates a secure foundation for the psalmist. And his relationship with the Lord is the basis for all the other joy and blessings described throughout the psalm.

The second half of the psalm is a response by the assembled people in acknowledgment and gratitude of God's deliverance. In verse 9, the king is recognized for his strength and success, but ultimately it is God's wrath and judgment that is responsible for the fall of Israel's enemies. By destroying the descendants of enemy leaders, a leader greatly minimizes the likelihood of that opposing nation becoming a danger anytime soon (21:10). Their continued plots and threats would be in vain (21:11-12).

And yet again a psalm ends with an echo of its beginning, this time with an affirmation of God's strength and praise for His power (21:13).

PSALM 22

After two psalms that dwell on the strength of God and the victories experienced by David, Psalm 22 captures quite a different, more somber, mood. According to the superscription, the psalm is intended to be set to an already established tune: "The Doe of the Morning."

Psalm 22 opens with a familiar ring, because Jesus quotes its opening line while hanging on the cross. As will soon become evident, David's words in this psalm are surprisingly descriptive of Jesus' crucifixion.

In verses 3-5, David expresses a cognitive understanding that God is present, as He always had been, and that He had always come through for His people throughout their history. However, David also writes, in verse 1, of a personal experience of suffering during which his feelings did not mirror his cognitive faith. He felt abandoned by God and, like so many people throughout the ages, asked the question, "Why?" He cried out to God around the clock but could detect no response (22:2). He was a target of scorn and ridicule, forced to listen to his enemies mock his faith, yet he tenaciously held to what he knew to be true (22:6-11).

The next scene that David portrays sounds hauntingly like Jesus' crucifixion (22:12-18). According to verses 12-13, David was surrounded by strong bulls and roaring lions, two different symbols for powerful enemies. He describes complete exhaustion, disheartenment, weakness, and thirst (22:14-15). The picture is of someone surrounded by evil men who pierce his hands and feet and cast lots to see who gets his clothing (22:16-18). It's a scene we associate with Jesus, not David.

Jesus endured not only the physical agony of crucifixion but also the spiritual despair of taking on the sins of humankind. David, however, anticipates God's rescue from his own situation (22:19-21). Even before he detects God's deliverance, he is quick to praise God and affirm His faithfulness. Despite appearances, David knows God is fully aware of his situation and concerned about his safety (22:22, 24).

Consequently, in verse 23 David challenges his fellow Israelites to praise and revere God. He wants to set a good example (fulfill his vows) for them (22:25-26). Then he expands his scope to include the ends of the earth and the nations (22:27-29). David hopes the entire world will respond when they hear how God has helped him (22:30-31). And if David does indeed foretell the crucifixion of his most famous descendant in this psalm, the news of God's deliverance and salvation would be heard by the entire world as generation after generation continue to proclaim His righteousness. Of all the psalms, this one is quoted more than any other in the New Testament.

PSALM 23

In what is undoubtedly the best known of the psalms, David uses the imagery of a shepherd to highlight God's blessings and protection of His people. It was rather common for kings of the time to be compared to shepherds. Although King David had firsthand experience in the role (1 Samuel 16:11–13; 17:34–35), in this psalm he is only one of the sheep in the fold of God.

The prophets will later describe the distress of the people by using an absent-shepherd or bad-shepherd analogy (Isaiah 56:9–12; Jeremiah 25:34–38; Ezekiel 34:1–11; Zechariah 11:15–17). However, David's description of God is the epitome of a good shepherd—a title Jesus will later apply to Himself (John 10:11).

As a shepherd, God provides for every need of His sheep (Psalm 23:1). The green pastures and quiet waters are basic physical needs, but God also restores the soul, attending to the inner spiritual needs of humankind (23:2–3).

Guidance is another essential role of ancient shepherds. In a land where many of the paths were rocky and treacherous, the safety of the sheep reflected on the reputation of the shepherd. God keeps David on paths of righteousness (23:3).

David acknowledges God's calming companionship even as he walks through the valley of the shadow of death (23:4). David has had his share of potentially deadly situations: confronting fierce animals as a shepherd, facing off against Philistine giants, a long string of battles, and more. But God's presence dispels fear. The shepherd's rod and staff are comforting symbols to David.

Critical Observation

A shepherd used his staff for support. The rod is frequently perceived as a punishing tool, which it was at times. But that same rod of correction was also an instrument of protection when the sheep were threatened. And more often, it was used for gentle guidance: A tap on the side could prevent a wayward sheep from straying off the safe path. If the adage to "Spare the rod and spoil the child" (based on Proverbs 13:24) means to impose harsh punishment, it is unlikely that David (or anyone else) would have perceived the rod as a comfort.

Verse 5 reveals that even when surrounded by enemies, David is able to function normally and enjoy his life because he is under God's care. Spreading an abundant dinner table and anointing a guest with oil were common amenities of a gracious host. In response, David realizes that his life is overflowing with God's blessings.

In spite of life's other dangers, David has reached the point where God's goodness and love far outweigh those concerns (23:6). He is determined to continue his relationship with God at the tabernacle for the rest of his life.

PSALM 24

David's military victories had expanded the boundaries of Israel, and the spoils from his enemies had greatly added to Israel's treasury. But, as the opening verses of Psalm 24 reveal, David also realizes that his many successes are all the result of God's strength and direction. So from David's experience and perception, he can declare with certainty that the earth is the Lord's, as well as everything in it. The people are His also, although many times throughout their history they didn't seem to realize it.

A painter is acknowledged for the portraits she does, and a sculptor gets credit for the shapes he forms. Similarly, the Creator of the world is the rightful owner of what He has founded and established (24:2).

David's musings on the sovereignty of God lead him to a logical question in verse 3: Who is worthy to stand before such a Lord? The hill of the Lord is probably in reference to the mountain on which Jerusalem, and eventually the temple, was found.

David realizes that God welcomes people whose actions (hands) as well as thoughts (heart) are pure (24:4). Such people will avoid the ever-present opportunity to worship idols, and they will be truthful. In return, God will bless them (24:5–6).

Demystifying Psalms

Portions of Psalms 96, 105, and 106 were used in conjunction with the return of the ark of the covenant to Jerusalem (1 Chronicles 15:1–16:36). It is possible that Psalm 24 was also used on that occasion. If so, the personification of the gates and ancient doors could have been references to the structures of that ancient city.

Any king who approaches a city will receive a magnificent welcome; how much more should the nearness of the King of glory inspire a response (24:7). Even the gates and doors of the city are perceived as responding to the magnitude of the event.

Lest there be any doubt as to who the King of glory is, David repeats the fact for emphasis in verses 7–10. The Lord is strong and mighty in battle—impressive credentials for any king. God is indeed the King of glory.

PSALM 25

In Psalm 25, as in many of his others, David expresses a desire for greater closeness to God. In the original language, the psalm is an acrostic poem. The first verse begins with the first letter, and following verses continue with successive letters throughout the Hebrew alphabet.

Again it seems in verses 1–2 that David's desire is driven by the lurking of his enemies. If David's enemies are to triumph over him, they will interpret their victory as a failure of Israel's God. David wants to avoid that potential shame by all means. Instead, he prefers to put to shame those who cause trouble for no good reason (25:3).

In verses 4–5, David requests both knowledge and guidance from God. His understanding of God as Savior is just as accurate, though not quite as robust, as those referring to the New Testament concept of salvation. The Lord is David's *deliverer* and his sole source of confidence and hope.

As he recalls his imperfections in verse 7, David also calls upon God's mercy and love. He understands that God does not hold people forever responsible for their sins, but He both forgives them and forgets them. As a professed sinner, David needs God's instruction and guidance in order to discover God's way, which includes goodness, upright behavior, humility, love, and faithfulness (25:8–10). David doesn't attempt to hide or downplay his sin (25:11).

According to verses 12–14, God's forgiveness will open the door to numerous blessings, including clear instruction throughout life, prosperity, a decent inheritance for descendants, and awareness of God's covenant promises. David's afflictions and anguish have heightened his awareness of the need for God's direction (25:15–21). Again in verse 20, David uses one of his favorite symbols for God: his *refuge*. The forces of life are pressing in on him, but he can still feel secure and protected.

David's final thought in this psalm builds on his personal request and expands it to include all of Israel (25:22). His problems are Israel's problems. As David seeks God's presence in his own life, he also prays for God to redeem Israel from her troubles.

PSALM 26

Psalm 26 is David's prayer for vindication. In tone it is not unlike Paul's defense of his ministry in 2 Corinthians 11, when the apostle attempts to distance himself from unrighteous peers and their false accusations. He doesn't want it to sound like he is boasting (2 Corinthians 11:10, 16–18, 21), but he needs to state some truths about himself strongly and clearly. So, too, David feels it necessary to defend himself.

David's appeal in verse 1 is directed to God, so any misstatements or exaggerations will be quickly refuted. His claim to a blameless life doesn't suggest that he is sinless but rather that he has not intentionally taken advantage of others—one result of his unwavering faith in God. David invites God to examine his thoughts and feelings because he attempts to *continually* be aware of God's love and truth (26:2–3).

His actions also reflect his mindset. He states in verses 4–5 that he avoids contact with those who are deceitful, hypocritical, or otherwise wicked. Rather than lingering with such people, David cleanses himself externally as well as inwardly and goes to spend time in God's tabernacle. As he meets people along the way, he shares with them what he knows of God's wonders (26:6–8).

In verses 9–11, David declares he doesn't want to be lumped in with the host of unrepentant sinners. Such people tend to eventually suffer for their deeds, if not have their lives divinely abbreviated. Instead, David seeks redemption and mercy. He is on the "straight and narrow," so to speak, and he promises to continue to praise the Lord from whom he expects his vindication (26:12).

PSALM 27

Fear is a universal emotion that frequently triggers a "fight or flight" response in people. When afraid, some people muster all the courage they can and stand their ground, whether or not it's a wise choice. At the first sign of trouble, others flee so they can live to fight another day. David begins Psalm 27 with his own questions about fear and concludes it with another option for responding to fear that involves neither fighting nor fleeing.

David has given the matter of fear more thought than most people because he has already determined that God is his light, salvation, and stronghold (27:1). He will not stumble in the darkness, as many do. He has a deliverer and security, even during the times that are most alarming.

It isn't that David has nothing to be afraid of; if anything, as verses 2–3 point out, his troubles are worse than most. Enemies are approaching with evil intent, and he is at war against powerful armies; yet he is able to remain confident while his foes fall. (Some people suspect that this psalm was written with Absalom's revolt in mind. If so, David would have felt the added stress of being betrayed by a beloved son.)

When faced with fear, David keeps his priorities straight. Verse 4 reveals his priority— a lifetime relationship with God at the tabernacle. His eyes aren't directed toward the approaching enemy but rather toward the beauty of the Lord (27:4). Consequently, he has confidence that when trouble does come, God will protect and sustain him. Rather than panic, he can respond with songs and shouts of joy (27:5–6). He prays that God will continue to be merciful and available, and he believes that God will be there during the worst of times, when even those closest to him might forsake him (27:7–12).

With his steadfast trust in God's goodness, David expects to remain safe and alive. Even though his enemies are still numerous and powerful, he will not run. He will not hastily go into battle but will choose to do something that is often harder than either of those options: wait (27:13–14). His is no idle passing of time, however. To wait on the Lord when things are going badly takes both courage and inner strength. Yet during turbulent circumstances, it is always the best course of action.

PSALM 28

It is a powerful assurance to realize that God hears us when we pray. In the opening verse of Psalm 28, David begins by calling on God and entreating Him to listen. The *pit* is a synonym for the grave, so David is saying that he may as well be dead if God doesn't hear and respond to him. He emphasizes his desire by lifting his hands toward the Most Holy Place—the place in the tabernacle designed specifically to reflect the presence of God (28:2).

David makes a point not to associate with the wicked, and he purposefully attempts to distance himself from them in this prayer. He wants God to provide retribution for all the harm they have done. They seem particularly despicable because they will feign kindness toward others while they inwardly seethe with malice (28:3–4).

With little doubt that the actions of the wicked people will bring about their judgment, David begins to praise God (28:5–6). At this point David is convinced that God has indeed heard him.

In verse 7, David acknowledges his appreciation of God's strength and protection on a personal level. It is a source of joy and consolation for him, prompting songs of thanksgiving. Then David proclaims the benefits of God's strength on the nation as a whole. David is the anointed one who enjoys the fortress of salvation that God has provided. But God Himself is the shepherd over the people. Only He can deliver them from danger and ensure their future (28:8–9).

PSALM 29

Many of David's psalms to this point have been pleas for help, concerns about his enemies, responses to the accusations of the wicked, and so forth. In Psalm 29, however, David's focus begins and remains on the power of God. As the psalmist watches a powerful storm approach and roll through his location, he records his thoughts.

The power of the approaching storm reminds David of the power of the Lord. He begins in verses 1–2 by challenging the *mighty ones* to attribute glory and strength to God. Most likely this is a reference to the angels who attend to the Lord. Possibly the comment is directed toward people who consider themselves "high and mighty," and who need to humble themselves before God.

In verses 3–9, the storm is referred to as the voice of the Lord. First it thunders over the waters (29:3), which from David's perspective would have been the Mediterranean Sea. Then, in power and majesty, the storm blows into Lebanon, where it shatters mighty cedar trees (29:4–5). The earth appears to move beneath the fury of the storm. (Sirion is another name for Mount Hermon. Lebanon is also a mountain.) Meanwhile, lightning flashes overhead (29:7).

Deserts and forests are both affected by the storm (29:8–9). The Desert of Kadesh, approximately seventy-five miles north of Damascus, is shaken as the trees of the neighboring forests are stripped bare. This is a storm of impressive magnitude.

Demystifying Psalms

The original Hebrew of the initial phrase of Psalm 29:9 allows for two rather diverse translations. One likely option is that the oak trees were twisted as a result of the storm. Another possibility is that the deer gave birth (presumably prematurely) out of fright.

Greater still, however, is God whose power far exceeds any storm on earth. He is to be glorified (29:9). His ruling over the floodwaters in verse 10 may be a reference to how He oversaw the creation of the world, or perhaps a reference to the flood of Noah's day. Earthly weather conditions, no matter how severe, don't change the fact that God will always reign as King.

As a pleasant end to a somewhat frightening psalm, David assures his readers in verse 11 that the all-powerful God gives strength to His people. Realizing that God is omnipotent should cause believers to rest in a consoling assurance of peace.

PSALM 30

Even though the superscription of Psalm 30 indicates that it is for the dedication of the temple, it is difficult to target exactly when it was first used. Some people speculate that the superscription was added at some point after the psalm had been written, and that the psalm was used for dedications of later buildings (such as the reconstructed temple after the Babylonians destroyed the first one).

In verses 2–3, the psalmist (presumed to be David) mentions some kind of physical ailment and in verse 6 confesses to a temporary sense of arrogance. So one likely possibility, assuming that David is the author, is that he is referring to his census of fighting men, evidently conducted out of a sense of pride (1 Chronicles 21). God had given David some options for his punishment. David's choice had resulted in the deaths of seventy thousand people and, had it not been for God's mercy, would have included the divine destruction of Jerusalem. Immediately afterward, David provides great amounts of materials that were needed to build Solomon's temple (1 Chronicles 22:2–5). Perhaps this is the incident David has in mind as he writes Psalm 30.

Regardless of the origin of the psalm, it is a powerful reminder of the difference God can make in a person's life when things are going badly. The psalmist writes of being in the depths, of enemies eager to gloat over his vulnerable position, and perhaps even a near-death experience (30:1–3). Yet God had responded with deliverance, healing, and life.

David's experience had given him great insight into the character of God, which he shares with the people in verse 5. God's anger lasts but a moment, but His favor lasts for a lifetime. Consequently, people should be quick to offer songs and praise to Him (30:4).

David's confession in verses 6–10 is true for many people. When life is going well and we are feeling secure, we lose the pressing need to turn to God. Then, when we discover that we have lost touch with God, we become dismayed.

Yet God's mercy is abundant. David's wailing in sackcloth quickly turns to dancing for joy (30:11–12). He senses that God prefers songs and praise to the silence that accompanies mourning. And in response to the fresh start that God has allowed him, David will be forever thankful.

PSALM 31

This is yet another of David's psalms that describes his feelings of rejection and isolation, even though his emotions are offset by the actions of God to revive and restore him. Although David opens the psalm by asking for deliverance in verse 1, it takes a while to determine what is wrong. He requests rescue and speaks of a trap set for him (31:2, 4), but the source of these comments is not identified until verses 11–13, where we discover that David's persecution by his enemies has resulted in the desertion of all his friends.

Critical Observation

Psalm 31, along with Psalm 22, appears to have been on Jesus' mind as He hung on the cross. He quotes verse 5 as one of His final statements before dying.

In spite of his condition, David continues to turn to God, who is consistently his refuge, rock, and fortress (31:1–3). He is left with only God to turn to, and God is the only One who can alleviate his suffering at this point. David is a brilliant fighter and strategist, yet he realizes he can do no better in this situation than to commit himself into God's hands to avoid potential harm (31:4–5).

When in affliction and anguish, many turn to idols, whether the false gods of Canaan or more contemporary idols of wealth, reputation, and pleasure. But David will not be distracted from his pursuit of God, and he is rewarded for his efforts (31:6–8).

When David gets specific about his situation in verses 9–13, it is heart-wrenching to realize the depth of his suffering. He is distressed, in grief and anguish, weak, sick, hated by his enemies, avoided by his friends, broken off from any kind of human support system, and terrified. From time to time he can hear slander and conspiracies against him.

And yet his trust in God is not shaken. David realizes that if God delivers him, then it discredits his enemies. Their lies and contempt will be silenced (31:14–18).

In verses 19–24, David concludes his psalm, as he frequently does, with confidence in God's deliverance. He uses his personal experience as grounds to exhort all God's saints to be faithful as well. They will do well to follow David's example of strength (31:24).

PSALM 32

Psalm 32 is the first of thirteen psalms identified in the superscript as a *maskil*. (The others are 42, 44–45, 52–55, 74, 78, 88–89, and 142.) Like many of the other introductory terms, the meaning of the word has been lost. It is frequently assumed that a maskil is a poem intended for instruction or meditation.

Additional speculation about this psalm is that it was originally a follow-up to Psalm 51, David's confession of his adultery with Bathsheba. If true, Psalm 32 celebrates the relief that David feels after experiencing the forgiveness of God.

The apostle Paul will later make it clear that everyone has sinned (Romans 3:23), yet David here makes it just as clear that forgiveness is readily available, after which God no longer holds the person accountable for his or her sins (Psalm 32:1–2). In response to God's forgiveness, the pardoned sinner should have a renewed, pure spirit.

In verses 3–5, David points out that awareness of one's sin that has not yet been confessed to God can create miserable feelings. If this psalm is indeed a reference to David and Bathsheba, it is worthwhile to note that David allowed his unconfessed sexual indiscretion to escalate into deceit (attempts to fool Bathsheba's husband) and from there to premeditated murder (2 Samuel 11). Bathsheba's child was born before God sent a prophet to confront David, so many months passed before David confessed his actions to God.

Therefore, David writes from experience as he describes the terrible weight people can feel before finally confessing to God (Psalm 32:3–5). Fortunately, he also speaks from experience of the unfailing love of God that follows repentance and confession (32:10). It is far better to voluntarily turn to God during such times than to react like a horse or mule, stubbornly resisting until being forced to respond because of a bit and bridle (32:6–9).

Unrepentant wicked people are left with many woes, but God always provides a better option. After sin, repentance, and confession, God restores one's state of righteousness, enabling the person to once again be pure in heart. Because of God's mercy and forgiveness, the person is once again eager to rejoice (32:11).

PSALM 33

This is the first psalm since Psalm 10 that isn't specifically credited to David.

Psalm 33 is a beautiful acknowledgement of the sovereignty of God, who deserves worship and praise from His people because they can always count on His faithfulness, righteousness, justice, and love (33:1–5). He is the Creator, who spoke the stars and heavens into existence. In verse 7, the psalmist portrays God as placing the world's seas into jars, as a homeowner might keep jars of fruit or olives.

Just as God spoke to create the universe, His word continues to have power. As people begin to comprehend the unlimited power of God, they should respond with deep reverence (33:8–9).

People and nations have plans that don't always agree with those of the Lord. But God's plans will endure. When people are foolish and presumptuous enough to oppose God, He has no trouble countermanding their plans (33:10–11).

Rather than resisting God, it is far better to yield to Him and receive His blessing. God sees all. The Creator is aware of the actions and inner thoughts of those He created (33:13–15). Only God is capable of sure protection and safety, even though the people of the time looked to other things for security (33:16–17).

In a setting of frequent wars and famines, God is a constant hope for those who trust in Him. Because He sees all, He does not miss the faith and prayers of the righteous. For these He is a shield against calamity. They can learn to rejoice and receive His unfailing love, knowing they will receive His help whenever it is needed (33:18–22).

PSALM 34

The introduction to Psalm 34 explains that it is written with a specific incident in mind. When David was running from King Saul and hiding out in Philistine territory, he began to feel threatened. As a diversion, he pretended to be insane, doodling on the city gate and drooling. The Philistines insisted that he leave, but he apparently posed no threat, so his life was not threatened (1 Samuel 21:10–15). What isn't clear, however, is the name variation of the Philistine king. In the superscription of Psalm 34, he is called Abimelech; in the 1 Samuel account, his name is Achish. However, it isn't unusual for kings of the time to have various names and titles.

In verses 1–3, David opens the psalm with lavish praise to God. David had been afraid, but God had alleviated his fears (34:4). After David's personal expression of exaltation, he enlists others to join him in glorifying God.

Those with no other recourse can always call on God and be heard. And those who seek and receive God's help may even have a different look about them—they avoid the shame experienced by so many others, and their faces radiate with joy (34:5–6).

In verse 7, David affirms that the angel of the Lord will encircle and deliver those who trust God. It is interesting to note that in several stories of the Old Testament, the angel of the Lord turns out to be God Himself. But any of God's messengers are equipped to protect God's people.

Perhaps some people are on the verge of becoming more devoted to God. For them to go on about their lives without making that decision is like walking past an enormous feast without stopping to sample the food. In verse 8, David urges his readers to taste and see that the Lord is good. The lions of the world have no guarantee of success, but those who faithfully seek the Lord will find all they need and more (34:9–10).

In verses 11–18, David provides a number of specific exhortations, but his basic advice for success and long life is to avoid evil in all its forms and to devote oneself to God. A commitment to righteousness does not guarantee a problem-free life (34:19–21), but God responds to His people in their times of distress.

God's redemption and lack of condemnation of His people would have been emphasized for those hearing this psalm in the original Hebrew (34:22). The psalm is an acrostic. With one exception, the first letters of each stanza go through the Hebrew alphabet, a pattern that ends at verse 21. The additional final verse, then, would have drawn much attention to the psalmist's final statement in verse 22—a promise well worth remembering.

PSALM 35

Few experiences in life are as distressing as being in a vulnerable state and having other people take advantage of you while you're helpless. This is the position David finds himself in as he writes Psalm 35. Unable to personally retaliate or achieve justice, he calls out to God for help.

In verses 1–3, David enlists the power of God, speaking to the Lord as a heavenly warrior and asking Him to prepare to fight. Any good soldier would anticipate conflict by fitting himself with the appropriate uniform and weapons, so David appeals for God to dress for battle, so to speak.

David then identifies his problem in verse 4: People want him dead, or at the very least disgraced and ruined. He wants to see his enemies blown away like chaff in the wind, driven away by the angel of the Lord down a dark and slippery path (35:5–6). His is a prayer for a taste of their own medicine. When evil people go to the trouble to trap someone, it is sweet irony if they are to accidentally be caught in their own traps (35:7–8). David has done nothing wrong to evoke their actions, yet those actions reveal their corrupt intent.

His enemies had initiated conflict by ruthlessly repaying David's good with evil, which disheartened him. When *they* got sick, however, David fasted and mourned for them in all sincerity, as if for a close relative. Still, when David faced his next difficult situation, they again gathered to mock him, slander him, and make his life as difficult as possible (35:11–16). So to be rescued from such people would delight David, and he would be quick to rejoice and thank God (35:9–10).

David has had enough. In verse 17, he asks God to stop merely observing and do something. These people have no reason to detest him. And it isn't just David whom they bother; they create havoc for other peaceful people in the land (35:19–21).

Aware that he isn't telling God anything He doesn't already know, in verse 23 David asks Him to take action. David has remained faithful and righteous, and he wants God's public vindication. Not only will David then praise God and tell of what He has done but also others will see for themselves how God cares for those who love and serve Him (35:22–28).

PSALM 36

David is associated with a lot of psalms that feature a contrast between the behavior of the wicked (and the consequences of their actions) and the righteousness of those who seek the Lord (and the rewards for their faithfulness). In Psalm 36, however, David credits his insight on the matter to an oracle—a command or revelation from God. The prophets are usually associated with oracles, but in this case David had a clear epiphany on the subject that he had written so much about.

The crux of the matter is that wicked people have no fear of the Lord. In this case, the root word for *fear* is less suggestive of fright than of anxiety or trepidation. Some people commit grievous injustices that apparently don't trigger any sense of dread or accountability to God. Instead, such people couch the severity of their sin with flattering and deceitful speech. They detect no reason to stop their evil actions, and the problem intensifies to the point where they can lie in bed and dream up new offenses to commit (36:1–4).

In contrast, God has vast amounts of love and faithfulness. In David's imagery in verses 5–6, God has mountains of righteousness and oceans of justice. It's no wonder that self-centered, coldhearted wicked people cannot connect with Him.

Still, many people do indeed seek and find the Lord—people of all different statuses. Their relationship is like a feast, and God provides them both light and life (36:7–9).

In David's continued clarity, he sees that the evildoers will meet defeat (36:12). In the meantime, he prays in verse 11 that he will not be confronted by the proud and the wicked. His wish is for God to continue to love and uphold the righteous people who know Him (36:10).

PSALM 37

Psalm 37 is similar in theme to Psalm 36 in its comparisons between righteous and wicked segments of humanity. But as the psalm opens, David makes a crucial observation about wicked people that will make a critical difference in how people view them. Whatever seems to be in their favor now won't be true for long, because they will soon wither like grass (37:1–2).

In verse 3, David points out that those who trust in the Lord have the opportunity and privilege of a much more lasting result of their actions. And in the meantime, their relationship with God assures them of rewards that have real value. They have a good place to live, in secure surroundings. They have the desires of their heart because the source of their delight is God (37:4).

Critical Observation

Several times within Psalm 37 "the land" is mentioned as a reward for the faithful. After God delivered Israel from Egypt and slavery, He guided them to the land that had been promised to Abraham. Under David's rule, the boundaries of that land continued to expand. The people's homes and surroundings were the result of God's direct blessing. And God's previous faithfulness in escorting them to the land was an assurance of His ongoing presence and involvement among them.

In verse 6, God's righteousness and justice are compared to sunshine. When we consider life in a Middle Eastern locale centuries before the introduction of air conditioning, the noonday sun was something that would get everyone's attention.

In verse 7 it seems that wicked people are getting away with lies, cheating, and deceit. When witnessing such injustice, God's people have one of two choices: They can worry and respond with great anger (a natural response), but that will only lead to more evil; or they can realize that God is aware of the problem and wait for Him to act (37:7–8). Only then will true justice be ensured (37:9–11).

In verses 12–22, David lists a series of contrasts between righteous and wicked people. In each specific instance, given enough time, the apparent success of evildoers comes to a crashing end. The lasting effect of all that wickedness will never last (37:20). For the righteous, however, the blessings of God are both plentiful and eternal (38:18–19).

So, according to verses 23–40, it is far better to focus one's energies on living a righteous life than to fret over the wicked. It's easy to get distracted by personal offenses, but it is much more beneficial to watch blameless and upright people and learn from their example (37:37). Then, when looking back over one's life, the love and faithfulness of God is more readily apparent (37:25–26).

PSALM 38

Psalm 38 fits in the "penitential" category (along with 6, 32, 51, 102, 130, and 143) and recounts David's inner turbulence while dealing with God's disfavor. (The exact nature of David's offense is unknown.)

David quickly confesses to "foolish sins" in verse 5 (NLT). Still, the description of his physical and emotional misery is moving. The hand of God is heavy on him, and God's dealings with David are described in verse 2 as piercing arrows. He is overcome with both guilt and illness, including festering wounds and searing pain (38:5–8).

The situation might not have been quite as bad if it had been between only David and the Lord. But David's suffering leads to his friends deserting him and his enemies taking the offensive against him, both of which add to his agony (38:11–12).

Yet David does not respond to criticism. He may not have literally placed his hands over his ears, but he describes himself in verse 13 as deaf and silent, unwilling to hear or reply to the malicious chatter of his enemies. Even in his defenseless position, he realizes his best option is to wait for God to answer, forgive, and reestablish his physical and spiritual health (38:14–16).

David had sinned, but he confessed and is now dealing with the aftereffects of what he has done (38:17–18). His enemies have also sinned, yet they continue in their iniquity. Their sin is more disturbing because they are persecuting David as he strives to do what is right (38:19–20). So David continues to beseech the Lord, seeking help in the one place he knows he can find it (38:21–22).

PSALM 39

After David had established himself as king over Israel and many of his battles were behind him, he spent considerable time organizing the military and spiritual leadership of Israel. He assigned three clans to oversee the music ministry, one of which was Jeduthun, also known as Ethan (1 Chronicles 25:1), who is mentioned in the superscription of Psalm 39.

Similar to the previous psalm, David again confesses to sin in verse 8. Realizing that God has every right to judge and discipline him, David determines to keep silent (39:9). However, his self-imposed silence only causes additional inner turbulence (39:1–2). He continues to see wicked people around him, and he begins to burn with anger (39:1–3).

But in verses 4–5, David comes to the realization that life is short. The days pass quickly, which should challenge people to put the events of life into a proper context. David realizes that the annoyance and anger he feels toward the wicked is fleeting, so he determines to personally focus on what he can accomplish while he has time (39:6).

Turning his attention back to God, David affirms his hope in the Lord while asking to avoid being ridiculed by foolish people (39:7–8). Because each person's life is brief, David wants to restore his relationship with God as quickly as possible (39:10–11). From David's perspective, death is quickly approaching, so his desire is to rediscover the joy of the Lord as quickly as possible (39:12–13).

PSALM 40

In Psalm 40, David describes several of the same elements as in many previous psalms: his sin, the troubles he is facing, and numerous enemies (40:12–15). In Psalm 39, for example, he is struggling to make sense of his troubles and to regain God's favor. In this psalm, however, God has answered his prayer, and David's personal tribulations seem to pale in comparison to his joy.

In verses 1–3, we see that David's patience has been rewarded. God has heard him and responded. David's new song is one not of questioning and confusion but of faith and praise. He has regained his spiritual footing.

When people stop long enough to ponder what God has done for them, they discover it's impossible to think of everything. Therefore, to envy proud and irreligious people, or to pursue false gods, is all the more foolish (40:4–5).

God is not impressed by the outward practice of one's religion—sacrifices, offerings, and such. David realizes that the Lord far prefers a strong relationship where His Word motivates an ongoing desire to obey and respond to Him (40:6–8).

Demystifying Psalms

The reference to God's piercing of David's ears in verse 6 can be interpreted a couple of different ways. Some people believe it recalls the Israelite practice of piercing the ear of a willing servant with an awl to signify his desire for lifetime service (Exodus 21:2–6). But the word for *pierced* also allows for the possibility of God cleaning out David's ears (in a spiritual sense), permitting him to hear God more clearly and respond more quickly.

God's forgiveness and restoration don't stop with David. In response to what the Lord has done for him, the psalmist is motivated to speak up and tell others (40:9–10). He wants to continue to be surrounded with the love, truth, and mercy of God (40:11).

It isn't that David's problems are over, but quite the contrary: He faces too many troubles to number (40:12). They continue to have a negative effect on him. Among his problems is the ongoing persecution of his enemies who want to take his life, and in the meantime hound him verbally (40:13–15).

In verse 17, David counts himself among the poor and needy. Still, the renewed presence of God in his life makes all the difference. He is able to rejoice and encourage others as he waits for God to deliver him (40:16–17).

PSALM 41

Psalm 41 concludes the first section of the book of Psalms. In this section David is credited with thirty-seven of the forty-one psalms, but in following sections David's influence is less pronounced. This final psalm of the section opens as the first one had, with a definition of what makes a person blessed (1:1; 41:1).

David is again writing from personal experience. The psalm contains a personal confession of sin, the mention of an illness connected to the sin, the derision of enemies while David is physically impaired, and the faithful expectation of God to act.

From his sickbed, David expresses great confidence that God will heal him, deliver him from his enemies, and once again bless him (41:1–3). According to verses 4–6, David's enemies aren't all military foes. Some actually came to visit him while sick, offered insincere words of comfort, and then left to slander him and wish that he were dead. While David lay suffering, his enemies gather to fantasize about bad things happening to him (41:7–8). Their coldhearted attitudes must have been contagious; even those who had been David's trusted friends begin to forsake him (41:9).

Critical Observation

David's honest and uncensored description of being deserted and betrayed by so-called friends strikes a chord with many people. Indeed, as Jesus predicts His betrayal, He quotes David's words from Psalm 41:9 (see John 13:18).

Yet David continues to look to the future. He has confessed to God (41:4) and reestablished his spiritual integrity (41:12). He fully expects God to raise him back up and enable him to confront those who hope to take advantage of him (41:10–12).

This section of Psalms concludes in verse 13 with emphatic praise to the eternal Lord, the God of Israel. The other sections end with similar doxologies.

Take It Home

After perusing the first book within the book of Psalms, the reader gets a varied story of a life—ecstatic joys, traumatic struggles, and all points in between. In this case it is David's life, although untold numbers of people throughout the centuries have related to his genuine expressions. Not everyone is a poet, but anyone can express honest feelings. When you get a quiet moment, try composing a psalm of your own. If possible, try to do so on a regular basis. It won't take long before you, too, will be able to look back over the various events of your life and see how God has been present throughout good times and bad.

PSALMS: BOOK II

PSALMS 42–57

Setting Up the Section

As Book II of the biblical book of Psalms begins, new authors begin to be identified. In Book I, all but four of the psalms are attributed to David, and those four have no designated author. David will continue to contribute to the book of Psalms, but his name will be joined by several others from here on.

PSALM 42

What we know as Psalms 42 and 43 may have formed a single psalm in its original writing. They flow together well and even share a chorus (42:5, 11; 43:5). Psalm 42 is a *maskil*, as is Psalm 32 and others that will follow.

The sons of Korah mentioned in the superscription are one of three divisions of musicians in charge of leading music. One of the three leaders is Jeduthun, previously mentioned in the introduction to Psalm 39. Another is Asaph, whose first mention in Psalms will be in Psalm 50. The leader of the sons of Korah is a man named Heman (1 Chronicles 6:33; 25:1).

Demystifying Psalms

A psalm of Asaph, or psalm of the Sons of Korah, doesn't necessarily indicate that the designated person is the *author*. It is just as likely that the named individual was delegated to see to the performance of the psalm in the community worship ceremony. Therefore, the writers of these psalms are frequently referred to more generically as the psalmist.

In verses 1–2, the psalmist compares his thirst for God to that of a deer panting for water. Perhaps he envisions a deer desperate for a drink after being pursued by predators, because he immediately writes of a long procession of people insulting and making fun of him. No doubt he refers to a spiritual thirst, intensified by his recent diet of salty tears (42:3).

To make his situation worse, verse 4 points out that the psalmist has been prevented not only from attending worship services but also from taking part in his regular ministry there. Isolation and weeping have replaced fellowship, joy, and thanksgiving. Yet in the first of three identical choruses, he chides himself to overcome his negative mindset (some scholars accuse him of self-pity) and instead place his hope in God (42:5).

In verses 6–7, mountains and waters are the images used to portray the psalmist's feelings. He appears to be in a mountainous area, yet his desire is to be in the mountains around Jerusalem. That geographic region is also noted for waterfalls, so the psalmist uses the image to describe surging tides of trouble pouring over him (42:7).

He is lonely, sick, and filled with questions about why he is suffering (42:9–10). Yet he can still feel God's love, and he continues to pray, hope, and praise his Lord (42:8, 11).

PSALM 43

In what is likely an extension of the previous psalm, the psalmist continues to attempt to make sense of his depressing situation in Psalm 43. He has grown weary of the many accusations of his enemies (42:3, 10; 43:1), and he seeks vindication from God. He is holding to his conviction that God is his stronghold, yet he finds it difficult to comprehend why he continues to be rejected, mournful, and persecuted (43:2).

According to verses 3–4, the psalmist has been unable to travel to Jerusalem to worship as he had done in the past, and it is his ongoing desire to go there. He can pray to God wherever he is, of course, but the altar in Jerusalem is a place to worship publicly and enlist the participation of others in praise and music. His is not an unusual yearning. Regular pilgrimages to the temple in Jerusalem were expected from all those able to make the journey, and those trips were usually joyful times for the travelers.

The psalmist concludes in verse 5 with the refrain he has already used twice (42:5, 11). He continues to question his disturbed state of mind, but more importantly, he expresses his expectation that his hope in God will continue to result in praise as he waits for God to act.

PSALM 44

It is always difficult to try to understand why bad things happen, especially to people who don't seem to deserve it. But for the early Israelites, the issue was even more poignant. Their covenant relationship with God is based on His promise that if they follow His instruction they will be blessed. For them to think they are being obedient and yet still experience signs of God's displeasure is indeed a dilemma. The psalmist addresses the situation in Psalm 44.

The opening verse points out that the stories of God's provision and protection of His people have been passed from generation to generation as inspiration and encouragement. As Israel had been faithful, God had led them in driving away their enemies and establishing themselves in the promised land. They realize that their success isn't a result of their military skill but of God's power and love (44:2-3).

Notice the psalmist goes back and forth between singular and plural tense as he refers to Israel. Sometimes he uses us and we to indicate the collective voices; other times he uses I and my to portray a singular national identity. The people had acknowledged God and had offered Him praise. They realize He is solely responsible for their victories (44:4-8).

The fact that God is responsible for every victory is where the psalmist's confusion began. For some reason Israel's enemies have begun to be victorious. Israel has to retreat and is being plundered. The people feel that God has rejected them (44:9-10). It is a miserable feeling, like defenseless sheep being devoured by predators or worthless slaves being sold for almost nothing (44:11-12).

Verses 13-16 point out that surrounding nations have certainly taken notice, which is both embarrassing and potentially dangerous. For any neighboring countries out for revenge, Israel's vulnerable state is the ideal time to attack. It is easier to accept this vulnerable position if the people had been responsible for wrongdoing, but that is not the case. The psalmist affirms in verses 17-18 that Israel has not forgotten God or been unfaithful to Him. They realize God knows when they have strayed, and He cannot be fooled. So they would not attempt to do so (44:20-21).

The people are bewildered, crushed, depressed, and helpless (44:19, 22). In verses 23-26, they cry out to God, pleading with Him to show Himself and see their suffering. They still have confidence in His unfailing love, even during their times of sorrow and confusion.

PSALM 45

Psalm 45 was written to celebrate the wedding of a king. The kings of Judah came from the line of David, which seems to be the case in this instance. The psalm may have been used for numerous kings. In fact, the author of Hebrews later uses this psalm in reference to Christ (45:6-7; Hebrews 1:8-9).

The psalmist's praise for the king is profuse. He is moved by the event taking place, and he wants to put forth his best effort (45:1). In verses 2-5, he extols both the character of the king (grace, truth, humility, righteousness) and the impressive and valiant actions of the king (victory, conquest, splendor, majesty) (45:2-5).

Ideally, the king is anointed by God to rule over the land. Saul, David, and Solomon had all been designated by God to rule. Later, the line of kings included many who had no love for God and little, if any, spiritual awareness. Here, however, the king is not only acknowledged as blessed by God (45:2) but is even temporarily *addressed* as God (45:6). The very next verse, however, reestablishes the clear distinction between God and God's servant, the king (45:7). The reference to his throne lasting forever in verse 6 affirms God's own promise that a descendant of David will always be on the throne (1 Chronicles 17:11–14). A number of David's descendants will rule before the promise is ultimately fulfilled by Jesus Christ.

Critical Observation

Israel's God and Israel's king had similar roles in terms of overseeing the people, protecting the nation against its enemies, administering justice tempered with mercy, and so forth. The glory and majesty of the human king also reflected, to a much lesser degree, the throne of heaven. So to address the king as *God* (45:6) is, in a sense, a compliment that indicates he is doing the things he should.

The king's reputation for justice and righteousness sets him apart from others in similar positions—many of whom may have been attending the ceremony (45:7). A number of special fragrances are used on this wedding day, including myrrh, aloes, and cassia (an aromatic root), but the groom's joy has a prominent aroma because it is from God (45:7–8).

According to verse 9, the king stands beside his bride, dressed in gold. Ophir is thought to have been located in western Arabia. At this point the psalmist turns his attention to addressing the bride, advising her to shift her strongest loyalties from her family to her new husband. The king is stricken with her beauty, and she should honor him in return (45:10–11). The psalmist's description of the bridal court in verses 12–15 emphasizes not only its splendor but also the atmosphere of joy that prevails.

Turning back to the king in verse 16, the psalmist points out that his fathers had come before him and eventually his sons will succeed him in the royal line. And then the psalmist makes a bold promise to help people of all generations remember the king and his wedding (45:17). Since his tribute has been recorded in scripture for centuries, it seems he was true to his word.

PSALM 46

The introduction to this psalm contains an obscure term used only here and in 1 Chronicles 15:20: *according to alamoth.* Based on its usage, it is most likely a musical term. It may have to do with music in a higher register, such as high-pitched flutes, soprano voices, or young maidens with tambourines (68:25).

This psalm, with its focus on the power and sovereignty of God, is similar to some of the previous psalms of David. But where David's are frequently intensely personal, this one is written with the nation of Israel in mind (*our* [46:1, 11]; *us* [46:7, 11]).

Israel may have been facing some troublesome situations, but the psalmist envisions catastrophes to the extreme in verses 2–3. Even if the mountains are to fall and the oceans are to rise, God will be there with His people, and they need not fear. Therefore, the Lord will surely see them through lesser problems.

Nations may have been in turmoil, falling all around, but Israel can be secure in the knowledge of God's presence (46:4–7). Unlike many important cities, Jerusalem had no river. The river and streams mentioned by the psalmist in verse 4 are his poetic terminology to describe God's ever-present influence and blessing on His people.

The reference to the break of day in verse 5 could refer to a distressing time. For those coming out of a long, dark, troubling night, it is a time of insecurity and fatigue. And for a city it is when attacks tend to take place. But God is there to help His people at dawn and throughout the day. The city offers the people a certain degree of protection, but God is their true fortress (46:7).

The psalmist's final verses offer additional consolation. He invites the people to pay special attention to God's work in the world. God can bring peace, but it first requires the destruction of the nations that want to dominate others through force (46:8–9).

In the original language, the instruction to "Be still, and know that I am God" is less a suggestion than an emphatic command (46:10). The intent is not, "Quiet down and you'll discover God's presence," but rather, "Quit what you're doing right now and acknowledge who God is."

The last verse is a repetition of 46:7, likely a response by those in the worship ceremony. It is a closing reminder of God's ongoing presence and protection.

PSALM 47

Few ceremonies in the ancient world were as spectacular as the enthronement of a king. Each nation had its own traditions. A number of psalms are sometimes classified as enthronement psalms, which are those that acknowledge God as the great King. Most are found in a later section of the Psalms (scattered throughout Psalms 92 to 100). This one, however, seems to fit with the preceding and following psalms that highlight the sovereignty of Israel's God. Some people speculate that Israel may have used such psalms for the coronation of their own kings, but no proof yet exists.

While Psalm 46 focuses exclusively on Israel, Psalm 47 immediately makes clear in the opening verse that God is to be acknowledged by *all* the nations. Indeed, Israel's God is both the Lord Most High and the great King over all the earth (47:2). Both of these titles were at times bestowed on human kings of other nations, but those nations will rise and fall while God continues to be sovereign not only over Israel but over the entire world.

The subdued nations of Israel's history include some of the great powers of the world, not least among them the Egyptians and the Philistines (47:3). Israel's inheritance—the promised land—had been populated with many nations, some living in walled cities such as Jericho (47:4). Yet God overcame those peoples and fulfilled His promise to Israel.

Just as other nations celebrate the coronation of a new king, Israel should rejoice over the ascent of their God (47:5). The emphasis on joy is not to be missed: The command to sing praises is found four times in verse 6 alone.

Joy should continue with the awareness that God is King of all the earth (47:7). Israel still has enemies and will fight more battles, yet the truth remains that God is in control (47:8). The other nations might not be ready to concede that fact, but as long as Israel believes it they can look forward to a time when the truth of the statement will at last be realized.

PSALM 48

Psalm 48 is the third consecutive psalm to emphasize the sovereignty of God. In this case, however, God's power is demonstrated in the unequalled security of the city of Zion (Jerusalem).

Verses 1–2 point out that Jerusalem is both lofty and beautiful—appropriate for what is considered the dwelling place of God. Many times a mountain setting is associated with a nation's gods. Mount Olympus is perhaps the best-known example, where the Greek gods were believed to reside. The psalmist's mention of Zaphon in verse 2 might have been in reference to a Phoenician mountain where their primary god (Baal) supposedly lived. But Israel's God does not rely on the protection of the city of Jerusalem. Instead, Israel's God is the fortress that protects the city (48:3).

The city was thought to have been impregnable before it had belonged to Israel. But David had the faith and skill to conquer and claim it, and he made it the capital city of a united Judah and Israel in 2 Samuel 5:6–10. Now, with God's temple there and the blessings of God on the city, it is even more impenetrable. Nations can band together and make an assault, but God's protection will send them fleeing in terror (48:4–7).

Critical Observation

The ships of Tarshish in verse 7 were a noted fleet that sailed the Mediterranean Sea, transporting goods from faraway places. Occasionally one of the ships would encounter a gale and experience an untimely end. The psalmist compares the destruction of Israel's enemies to the shattering and sinking of one of these mighty ships.

God's reputation for protecting His people has long been part of Israel's oral tradition. But with the ability to visit Jerusalem, the people have a visual element to help increase their faith (48:8). The presence of God is even more personal within the temple (48:9). In such an intimate setting, the people are able to meditate on God's love and praise Him (48:9–10). The joy that results spreads from Jerusalem to surrounding villages (48:11).

In verse 12, the psalmist challenges the people to take a close look at the city of Jerusalem. As they do, they will see a well-constructed fortress of towers, ramparts, and citadels. Such defenses should remind them of their eternal God's protection, and they should be eager to share their confidence and enthusiasm with the generations to follow (48:13–14).

PSALM 49

Psalm 49 addresses a recurring theme: the apparent injustice of life as the rich domi-nate the poor. The psalmist will put things in perspective, however, by explaining that death is the great equalizer. No matter how rich or wise a person might be, there is no escaping the same inevitable end as the poor and the foolish.

The psalmist begins in verses 1-2 by summoning all to listen, both low (poor) and high (rich). What he has to say will be a warning to some and an encouragement to others. He will be pronouncing wisdom and understanding, yet his message will also be something of a riddle (49:3-4). The musical accompaniment adds an element of importance to his words.

In verses 5-6, he refers to people who count on their money to get by and boast of all they have. This is no small problem, because he describes being surrounded by such people. And then comes the brutal truth in verses 7-9: No redeemer has enough influ-ence and no amount of money is ever enough to ransom one's life and avoid the grave.

What the psalmist is saying would have been evident to everyone. Upon death, riches are worthless. Accumulated wealth remains for the living. Some people may be remem-bered longer than others if they prearrange for elaborate tombs or spend some of their money on something (such as land) that will bear their name (49:10-11). Still, the donor is left with a tomb for a house. He will never know when others see his fancy grave or hear his name connected with land or other possessions.

The psalmist points out in verse 12 that people have no advantage over animals when it comes to life cycles. Human beings see beasts of burden live and die, thinking little about it, but then seek fruitless ways to avoid the same end (49:13-14). A common im-age of the time was of death (personified) devouring the living (49:14; see Job 18:13; 24:19). In some cultures the perception of death was that of a ravenous monster always on the prowl.

The point of this psalm is to challenge people to not allow themselves to become enamored by wealth and splendor. The privilege of the wealthy will not endure. Those who count on their riches have a common end (49:16-20). The upright, however, have a different outlook (49:15). Death is still a certainty, yet they can maintain the hope that God will not leave them in the grave.

PSALM 50

Psalm 50 is the first psalm attributed to Asaph, one of the three men from whose families the temple musicians were assigned (1 Chronicles 25:1). A few of the psalms have already been associated with the other two men: Heman (connected with the sons of Korah) and Jeduthun. Asaph may not have actually written this and other psalms that bear his name (73-83). The wording allows for the possibility that the psalm was written *for* him, or even for use by his descendants.

This psalm has a different tone than many of the others. Rather than portraying the psalmist crying out to God about a personal matter, in Psalm 50 God does most of the speaking about a spiritual matter. In fact, God summons the people of the earth for a judgment of sorts.

The gravity of what is to come is suggested in the opening phrase, where three separate titles for God are used to verify the unique qualifications of the heavenly judge. The description continues as the psalmist portrays God coming from His city, perfect and radiant, and surrounded by fire (50:2–3). The people over whom He will preside are supposed to be consecrated (devoted to God and obedient) and aware of the covenant between God and His people (50:4–6).

The initial pronouncement is not bad. In verse 8, God acknowledges the many offerings that have been made to Him. However, the people have the wrong idea about sacrifice. First, they aren't actually giving God anything because every creature on earth already belongs to Him (50:9–11). Second, their offerings are not like sacrifices made in other religions—attempts to satisfy the cravings of a god. Unlike those gods, Israel's God does not hunger or thirst; He is complete and perfect, without need for material things (50:12–13).

The people are encouraged to bring offering of thanks to God (50:14–15; see Leviticus 7:11–15). Burnt offerings were sometimes offered routinely, perhaps with little thought. But a thanks offering was made in response to something God had done (healing, consolation, deliverance). The offering of thanks requires acknowledgment of God's involvement in one's life and sincere gratitude in response.

After correcting the worship habits of those who conscientiously want to honor God, in verses 16–17 the Lord addresses those who aren't so genuine in their motives. Some people worship along with the rest, but have no regard for God's law. Their unrighteous acts are listed in verses 18–20 and include stealing, adultery, deceit, and slander. Because God has not yet taken action against them, this wicked bunch has the audacity to presume that silence gives consent. Not so, declares the Lord. This is the occasion for Him to refute their sinful actions personally and publicly (50:21).

Psalm 50 closes with an opportunity for those who have just heard God's pronouncement to consider what He has said and correct their attitudes and behavior. They have two options. Those who continue to oppose God will eventually face His judgment, and there will be no one able to rescue them. Far better off are those who choose to honor God and experience His salvation (50:22–23).

PSALM 51

This is the first of the psalms of David in the second book within Psalms (42–72) and is one of seven sometimes categorized as penitential. Its deeply personal and confessional tone is explained in the introduction. It was composed after David was confronted about his adultery with Bathsheba (2 Samuel 12:1–25). David has avoided God for many months (considering that the baby he had conceived was already born). But when faced with the severity of his sin, his confession is unabashed.

David makes no attempt to deny his sin or excuse his behavior. He readily admits in verses 1–3 that his actions were rebellious and sinful. Yet he is also confident that God is a source of mercy, unfailing love, compassion, and cleansing. David had gotten a married woman pregnant and then arranged to have her husband killed in battle, yet he realizes that his sin is against God (51:4). His propensity to sin reminds him of his sinful nature (51:5).

When he finally acknowledges his sin, David immediately wants to be forgiven. Realizing that inner truth and wisdom had ceased to influence his actions, David asks God for cleansing in verses 6–7. After God forgives him, David can again experience the joy and gladness that he has been missing (51:8). And after God has blotted out David's terrible offense, then David can renew his heart for God. David prays not only for a pure heart but also for a steadfast spirit and ongoing awareness of God's presence. After his grievous sin, he desires the joy of salvation and a renewal of his willingness to serve God (51:9–11).

Critical Observation

Hyssop (51:7) was a plant with a hairy stem. When immersed in water, the liquid clung well to the stem, so the plant was used in purification ceremonies. Hyssop was also used to apply blood to the doors of Hebrew homes just prior to the exodus from Egypt (Exodus 12:22) and to offer Jesus a drink while He was on the cross (John 19:29).

David wants to be a good example for God in both teaching others and demonstrating praise (51:13–15). He has good insight into what God wants from him. Rather than animal sacrifices, God much prefers the sacrifice of a submissive spirit and humbled heart (51:16–17).

David also seems to comprehend that the king's behavior and spiritual integrity (or lack of such) can affect God's perception of the nation as a whole. In verses 18–19, he closes his psalm with a prayer for the prosperity of Jerusalem and a time when the people's sacrifices will once again be righteous and pleasing to God. Some scholars have suggested that the last two verses may have been added to David's psalm at a later date, during Israel's exile. After a period away from home during which sacrifices were suspended, the desire to rebuild Jerusalem and reinstitute offerings would have been strong indeed.

PSALM 52

In many of David's psalms, it is difficult to match his comments with a specific biblical event. But beginning with Psalm 51, several of the superscriptions throughout this section describe what is taking place in David's life as he writes the psalm.

In the case of Psalm 52, David had been trying to hide from Saul and had sought shelter among a city of priests. He had been seen by one of Saul's shepherds named Doeg. Saul is irate to hear that the priests had assisted David and ordered them killed, but none of Israel's soldiers would respond. Doeg volunteered for the vile assignment and slaughtered not only eighty-five priests but also the entire population of the city where they lived—men, women, and children (1 Samuel 21:1–9; 22:6–19).

David may have had Doeg specifically in mind, but the opening description in verses 1–4 can apply to any number of people. Most believers attempting to live godly lives can identify with the type—oppressors who boast of evil, plot destruction, practice deceit, and love falsehood rather than speak the truth. They are good at what they do;

unfortunately, what they do is evil.

Such people may appear to be securely entrenched in a community, and it may seem that no one is able to reason with them. But God is also affected by their actions, and righteous people can count on Him to act. According to verse 5, He will have no trouble uprooting the wicked, who aren't as entrenched as they think. Those who watch will have the last laugh (52:6). The observers will have renewed reverence for God after witnessing the end of those who get ahead by putting others down (52:7).

In the story of Doeg, David is the one on the run. Yet in contrast to the wicked, who will be uprooted, in verse 8 David compares himself to an olive tree—securely rooted, produc- tive, and anticipating long life. (Olive trees can live for centuries.) More importantly, he is flourishing in his relationship with God. His trust in God makes all the difference, and he promises to continue to praise the Lord and place his hope in Him (52:8–9).

PSALM 53

The introduction of Psalm 53 contains a new distinctive term: *mahalath*. The word may pertain to illness or suffering, used here in the psalm in regard to hardship or persecution. A *maskil*, first noted in Psalm 32, may have been intended as an instructive writing.

If Psalm 53 sounds familiar, it may be because of its similarity to Psalm 14. Some schol- ars believe its (re)location between Psalms 52 and 54, both of which have introductions that tie them to events in David's life, suggests a similar (though unstated) association with David. It is possible that the reference to *fool* in verse 1 could recall David's frustrat- ing experience with Nabal, the husband of Abigail (1 Samuel 25).

Demystifying Psalms

Throughout the first book within Psalms, the word used for God is almost always *Yahweh*. In the second book, however, the preferred word changes to *Elohim*. Despite all the similarities between Psalms 14 and 53, the word used to refer to God is changed.

Compared to Psalm 14, the only verse with significantly changed content is 53:5, re- placing 14:5–6. Here David writes of foolish evildoers who are overcome with dread even though there is no good reason for it. Biblical examples abound of instances when God's people are threatened but where God delivers them by creating panic within the enemy camp (Judges 7:19–22; 1 Samuel 7:10–11; 14:13–15). Yet it seems that wicked people never learn (Psalm 53:4).

Another change from Psalm 14 includes the reference to the scattered bones of the ones who had attacked God's people (53:5). The image is one of the aftermath of a large battle that has left vast numbers of unburied dead as the result of an utter defeat—quite a grim outlook for those who oppose God and His people.

PSALM 54

The superscription of Psalm 54 mentions the Ziphites, inhabitants of the Desert of Zith, south of Hebron. David had hidden from Saul in that desert, but the Ziphites operated as Saul's spies, monitoring David's movements and reporting back to the king (1 Samuel 23:15-25). However, such specifics aren't included in the psalm, and it can be applied and appreciated by people in various situations.

As is typical of his psalms, David opens in verses 1-2 with a cry to God, asking for deliverance and vindication. Then in verse 3, he voices his complaint: Ruthless, ungodly, aggressive men are trying to kill him. The Ziphites were little more than informants, but by the time of David's encounter with them, he had been on the run from Saul for a long time. During those years he had undergone some periods of great faith and some other trying times, but God had sustained him through them all (54:4).

As usual, David asks God in verse 5 to address the problem of the evil people in pursuit of him. David had shown unusual patience and self-control in refusing to personally kill King Saul, even when he had ideal opportunities, opting rather to wait for God to act. Yet he had full confidence that God would eventually deliver him. He could speak as if his deliverance had already taken place, even as he continued to be oppressed (54:6-7).

PSALM 55

The introduction does not provide specifics about the event that inspired this psalm, but the psalm itself reveals a painful betrayal by someone who had been a close friend. The psalm may have been inspired by Absalom's revolt, during which several of David's trusted associates deserted him. One of note is Ahithophel (2 Samuel 15:12), perhaps the wisest advisor in the nation who, after Absalom fails to take his advice, realizes David will eventually regain the throne and commits suicide (2 Samuel 16:20-17:13, 23). However, no proof exists of this possibility, and scholars are left to speculate.

David's appeal to God in verses 1-5 includes an account of both the treatment he is receiving from others and the inner turmoil it is creating within him. He describes a progression from anguish, to fear and trembling, to horror. Given the opportunity, he would escape to the desert for some peace and solitude, leaving his tormentors behind him (55:6-7). The word translated *shelter* in verse 8 means "place of escape," and this is its sole appearance in the Old Testament. But apparently the option of escape is not available to him, and David will be forced to weather his emotional storm.

So again David turns the matter over to God. The offenses of the wicked people are mentioned in verses 9-11: violence, strife, malice, abuse, threats, and lies. The extent of their actions had reached the point where David not only prays for them to become confounded and confused but even that they would be surprised by their sudden deaths (55:15). What makes this situation particularly painful for David is the involvement of someone he had considered a close friend and had spent a lot of time with. They had even worshiped together (15:12-14).

In the wake of such emotional trauma, David cries out to God evening, morning, and midday (55:16-17). Without God's support, David would feel vastly outnumbered (55:18-19), yet he remains unharmed. He knows his enemies have no fear of God, and he is no doubt distraught as he realizes that his former friend is now included among them (55:19-21).

Critical Observation

David's regular prayer times, mentioned in verses 16–17, are reminiscent of Daniel's faithfulness and commitment to pray three times a day (Daniel 6:10). We might say, "Morning, noon, and night," but David cites "evening, morning, and noon" because the Jewish day started at sundown.

Yet David's response—and advice to others—is wise and appropriate (55:22). Those who cast their concerns on God will not be disappointed. God will simultaneously take care of the righteous while short-circuiting the work (if not the lives) of the wicked (55:23).

PSALM 56

Psalm 56 is another of David's psalms where the superscription provides a clue to the source of his emotions. Gath was a Philistine city where David went to hide while trying to keep from being captured by King Saul. Though he eventually made a tentative alliance with the King of Gath (1 Samuel 27:1–7), an earlier visit hadn't been so amiable. When the people identified him as the one who had killed Goliath and many more of their soldiers, he quickly became persona non grata and even began to fear for his life. To extricate himself from the situation, he feigned madness. The Philistines forced him out of the city but did not harm him (1 Samuel 21:10–22:1).

If this psalm is a true reflection of David's experience in Gath, then he would have been both pursued by Saul's army and slandered by his Philistine hosts (56:1–2). In addition, he would be running out of places to hide, so his fear is understandable (56:3). Still, he is able to maintain trust in God and realize that the Lord's protection is sufficient.

His enemies are insidious and aggressive. They watch him round the clock, looking for opportunities to harm him while conspiring with one another. If he attempts to defend himself or reason with them, they put words in his mouth to alter what he is really attempting to say (56:5–6).

But David wants to ensure that God hears him correctly. After asking God to not let his persecutors escape in verse 7, he wants God to keep track of his sorrows (56:8). In one interpretation of his request, he asks God to put his tears in wineskin. In other words, if God is well aware of David's situation, David trusts that the Lord will act to restrain the influence of his enemies (56:9).

Despite the ongoing onslaught of his persecutors, in verses 10–13 David reaffirms his trust in God. He expects God's deliverance to be certain, so he will move ahead in faith, continuing to praise his Lord.

PSALM 57

Psalm 57 has a number of similarities to Psalm 56. According to the introduction, this time David's mind is focused on the time he had hidden in a cave to escape the pursuit of King Saul. Ironically, it was the very same cave that Saul chose to enter and relieve himself. David and his men could easily have assassinated the king, although they would have been at the mercy of Saul's army (1 Samuel 24).

But as verse 1 shows, David counts on the mercy of God. A cave had turned out to be a less-than-reliable hiding place, but God is a constant refuge. Disasters will come and go, and during the worst of times the best place to be is in the shadow of God's wings (see Psalm 17:8 and commentary). Saul's army is pursuing David, but he is also being followed by God's love and faithfulness (57:3).

In verse 4, David describes his enemies as beasts, with weapons of war rather than sharpened teeth—just as threatening and just as potentially deadly. But unlike lions and other predators of the animal world, these beasts are cunning and set traps for David (57:6). As David continues to praise God, however, he is convinced that his oppressors will eventually fall into the nets and the pits they had constructed for him (57:5, 7).

He might be amongst beasts but, according to verses 7–8, David expects to awaken at dawn with a steadfast heart and a song on his lips. He is eager to praise God and declare to other nations and peoples what God has done for him. God's love and faithfulness are unlimited, reaching to the heavens (57:9–10).

This psalm concludes with a repeat of a previous refrain (57:5, 11). Because of God's character and concern for His people, He should be exalted over heaven and earth.

Take It Home

Perhaps you have begun to note the comments in the superscriptions of many of David's psalms. Most notably, Psalm 51 explains that it concerns David's adultery with Bathsheba, although others were written in regard to situations where David was displaying faith and courage. Can you think of events in your own recent life that might inspire a psalm? If so, express your heartfelt feelings to God, whether in repentance, praise, thankfulness, joy, or whatever motivation is most appropriate. You might want to write out your psalm, but the expression of your prayer is more important than its form.

PSALMS: BOOK II, CONTINUED

PSALMS 58–72

Setting Up the Section

This section continues and concludes the psalms found in Book II of the biblical book of Psalms. Most in this section are psalms of David. Some continue to have superscriptions that refer to specific events in the psalmist's life.

PSALM 58

In the opening verse of this psalm, David asks rhetorical questions. Are the rulers of the nation speaking justly and acting uprightly? Everyone already knew the answer is *no*.

In fact, the propensity for wickedness by such people could be traced back to the womb. So after a lifetime of practice, the injustice dispensed by such people is well orchestrated (58:2–3).

In verses 4–5, David compares the unjust leaders of the nation to snakes that are supposedly under the control of a snake charmer yet are no longer influenced by the music. The result is akin to having venomous cobras on the loose with little likelihood of rounding them up.

So David asks God, in verses 6–8, to do what people seem unable to accomplish: to rid the land of all those who are abusing their positions and meting out violence rather than justice. If they see themselves as lions, may their teeth be broken. If they perceive themselves as soldiers, may they discover their arrows dulled and useless. David wishes them the same end as water evaporating in desert heat, a slug that starts across a hot surface and doesn't make it, or as a stillborn child.

The original Hebrew of verse 9 defies clear interpretation. The underlying thought, however, appears to be that God's judgment on the people David has described will be sudden and swift—less time than it takes for a pot to feel heat when a flame is placed beneath it.

Critical Observation

Psalms such as this one are sometimes classified as *imprecatory*, meaning that the writer calls down curses or asks for utter defeat to come to the ungodly. Sometimes the requests are quite specific and graphic (104:35; 109:4–15; 137:8–9).

The thought of the righteous bathing their feet in the blood of the wicked (58:10) should not necessarily bring to mind a macabre scene like what might be portrayed in a horror film. However, the metaphor does suggest the aftermath of a battle, when the victor's sandals would certainly be splashed with some of the blood of his victims. In this case the battle is the means through which God has judged the earth, and the end result will be the long-awaited reward for those who have remained faithful (58:11).

PSALM 59

The introduction to Psalm 59 refers to the time when King Saul had ordered David's house watched so David could be killed while entering or leaving. But David's wife (Saul's daughter, Michal) warns him, and he escapes through a window during the dark of night (1 Samuel 19:11–18). However, the psalm itself doesn't appear to reflect such events. Some think, therefore, that a different psalmist updated the original psalm to apply to a later time in Israel's history.

Whoever the writer is, he cites a common complaint found in the psalms: persecution by his enemies. In verses 1–2, he opens with an appeal for deliverance from such people, whom he classifies as evildoers and bloodthirsty men. The psalmist proclaims his own innocence in the matter, yet his enemies continue to conspire against him, looking for opportunities to attack (59:3–4). In previous psalms, some of the psalmist's closest friends had joined in the treachery against him. In this case, however, the opposition seems to come from people outside of Israel (59:5).

In verses 6–7 and 14–15, the psalmist describes his enemies as a pack of snarling dogs, prowling around for food and howling when their appetites are not satisfied. It would have been a fright-inducing scene for most people, but not to the psalmist's God who would laugh and scoff at the pretension of such evildoers (59:8). And the knowledge that God feels no threat from the powers of the nations is assuring to the psalmist, who places his trust in God to minimize his fear.

The psalmist points out in verses 9–10 that as long as God goes before him as a fortress, he can remain impervious to the slander of others. He even has the presence of mind to realize that if God is to strike down the loudmouthed enemies all at once, the people of Israel might soon forget God's goodness and power (59:11). The psalmist wants them to suffer the consequences of their evil, to be sure, but far better to bide enough time to let them be "captured by their pride" (59:12 NLT). He doesn't merely want his enemies off his back; he wants God to be glorified as well.

Many gods of the time were praised for their strength, but the psalmist acknowledges both God's strength *and* His love (59:16–17). In spite of personal persecution and uncertainty, he will continue to sing praises to God.

PSALM 60

Of all the psalms with introductory superscriptions, Psalm 60 is the only one specifically designated for teaching. The historic reference in the introduction is to 2 Samuel 8:1–14; 10:14 and 1 Chronicles 18:1–13, passages that describe David's various victories, although there are minor discrepancies in some of the details. (Samuel and Chronicles cite the deaths of eighteen thousand Edomites rather than twelve thousand.)

This psalm expresses confusion in the wake of confidence. Israel had experienced a defeat in battle, usually a sign of God's disfavor. In this case, however, no explanation is given, and the people appear unaware of any reason God should have allowed them to fall to their enemies. Still, as verse 1 points out, they are aware of God's anger. Israel feels as if God has physically shaken the land to the point of fracture, and it is as if they have been given potent wine that causes them to stagger (60:2–3). They have lost all sense of security and are not themselves.

The intended meaning of verse 4 is uncertain. Troops gathered around banners and then followed those banners out into battle. Perhaps the psalmist is asking God to gather His people and lead them to victory. It is also possible, however, that he is expressing frustration that God led them to defeat instead of victory.

Yet from this point on, the psalm is nothing but confident and hopeful. Since God's anger has led to Israel's defeat, nothing but His favor will restore them. God continues to love His people, and in verse 5 the psalmist (presumably David) calls on God to help and deliver them. In response, God speaks and assures victory for His people.

A map would be helpful in comprehending the geographic references that follow in verses 6–8. The first series of places already belong to Israel. The cities of Shechem and Succoth roughly represent east and west, as do Gilead and Manasseh on a larger scale. The centrally located and well-defended Ephraim is like a protective helmet for the nation. Judah, the tribe from which David came, is portrayed as a royal scepter.

The remaining references (Moab, Edom, and Philistia) are all persistent enemies of Israel, yet they are under God's control just as surely as Israel (60:8). In response to God's pronouncement, the psalmist shows faith. He realizes that God will not only provide aid against, but also victory over, Israel's enemies (60:9–12).

Demystifying Psalms

The image of God tossing a shoe onto Edom in verse 8 is similar to a custom involving a legal transfer of property (as in Ruth 4:7–8, where a sandal is handed over to symbolize the official transfer of land). In this case, however, it is a sign of contempt

PSALM 61

Psalms 61–63 have the common theme of yearning for God during a time of trouble, and they all are written from the perspective of the king (presumed to be David). Psalm 61 appears to refer to specific events in David's life, but those specifics are not provided.

If indeed the psalmist is David, this might have been when he was driven from his throne during Absalom's attempted overthrow of the kingdom. In verse 2, David cries to God from "the ends of the earth"—a phrase that could refer to a sense of either geographical or spiritual distance. He is fainthearted and longs for the "towering rock of safety" (NLT). Perhaps this request is for a secure location that he cannot achieve without God's help, or the rock might be a reference to God Himself.

In verse 3, the psalmist is able to trust God during this crisis because God has always been faithful in previous times of trouble. He desires a more permanent sense of closeness to God with the protection of both the sanctuary of God and the Lord's personal presence (61:4). He has made promises to God, and he is counting on God's promises (heritage) to His people (61:5).

His prayer for long life in verse 6 is not a selfish one. With no anticipation of life after death, the psalmist's life on earth would have been his only opportunity to commune with God (61:7–8). He wants the experience to last as long as possible, committing to praise and obey God day after day. It is also a plea for his successors, not only for many generations but forever (see 1 Chronicles 17:11-12).

PSALM 62

The fact that this psalm is positioned between Psalm 61 and Psalm 63, coupled with the observation that opponents are attempting to topple the psalmist (62:4), suggests that it is authored by a king (again presumed to be David). A king has many resources at his disposal, yet David's sole source of help and comfort is God alone (62:1-2). God is his security (rock), deliverance (salvation), and protection (fortress).

Humanity, on the other hand, is a continual source of chaos. People have repeatedly attempted to undermine David. In verse 3, he compares himself to a weak and wobbly fence that could easily be pushed down. The assaults of others are verbal as well. They bless him to his face but curse him and tell lies about him behind his back (62:4). They do not rest from their efforts to put him down.

So again, David turns to God for rest and everything he needs (62:5-7). In verse 8, he challenges the people to do the same—to pour out their hearts and then trust God to take good care of them.

The psalmist's description of human beings in verse 9 is in direct contrast to his image of God. The Lord is a rock and fortress; people are nothing. Even those who perceive themselves as wealthy and entitled will soon be deflated and forgotten.

People tend to pursue riches, and many desperately turn to dishonest means (including stealing and extortion) to acquire wealth (62:10). Yet a person's accumulated possessions provide no long-range security. One's heart should remain on God, not any other substitute.

It is humbling to realize that God is not only strong but also loving. Devotion and obedience to Him will result in rewards that are both desirable and lasting (62:11-12).

PSALM 63

According to the introduction of Psalm 63, David writes it in connection with being in the desert of Judah. It is a vague reference. David had attempted to hide from Saul in the desert (1 Samuel 23:14), although the fact that the psalm is also written from the perspective of a king suggests a later time in David's life. This might be another psalm written during the period when Absalom had forced David to leave Jerusalem (2 Samuel 15:23).

The desert setting plays prominently in the psalm, however. In verse 1, David compares his longing for God to the thirst of a man wandering in a dry wilderness, desperate for water. For many people, the desire for God is a casual and occasional thing; for David, it is a matter of life and death.

David's desire for God is intensified because he knows what he is missing. He had worshiped God in the sanctuary in Jerusalem and knows what it's like to witness God's power and glory (63:2). It had been the spiritual equivalent of the fine foods he used to eat, but now he has to be content with more meager fare (63:3-5).

Still, he has fond memories of how God helped him in the past, and those memories fuel his faith for the future (63:6–8). He trusts God to sustain him now, just as He had done throughout the psalmist's lifetime.

As for the people who oppose David, their dominance will be temporary and short. They have positioned themselves against God's chosen king, so their end is certain. They will go down to the depths of the earth, being given over to the sword, and becoming food for jackals (63:9–10). They are liars who will be silenced once and for all (63:11).

In contrast, verse 11 says everyone who professes faith in God will offer praise, not least among them the king himself.

PSALM 64

As the opening verse points out, this is another psalm where David immediately turns to God after learning of a conspiracy against him. Those who oppose him use words as weapons. In verse 3, David compares their words to sharpened swords, and they aim them as one would point and shoot an arrow. Such people are also guerrilla fighters; they remain hidden as an unsuspecting person walks by and then attack without notice or provocation (64:4).

To make things worse, the evildoers serve as consultants for one another, encouraging each other and discussing their plans for future mayhem (64:5–6). David's observation in verse 6 that the human mind and heart are cunning is an understatement.

However, for all their many harsh and malicious words, these people will not have the last word. God will step in with arrows of His own, and the aggressors will be the ones struck down (64:7–8).

Those who observe God's judgment of the wicked will have two responses. At first they will experience a scornful satisfaction because the evil people have gotten what they deserve. More importantly, though, they will then turn their attention to God, giving much thought to His justice and proclaiming the good things He has done. After realizing that evil does exist, but only for a short time, righteous people can then satisfy themselves with God's protection and learn to rejoice in their relationship with Him (64:9–10).

PSALM 65

Psalms 65–68 have a similarity of thought and theme, as they focus on the gifts of God to His people. Praise and obedience are the appropriate responses to such a God. The vows to be fulfilled in verse 1 are probably promises made to God by people during prayer when seeking His presence and help.

The fact that God hears and responds to prayer draws people to Him (65:2). Foremost among His blessings is His great forgiveness in light of human sinfulness. And after forgiving them, God welcomes His people to come near to Him and spend time in His house (65:3–4). A renewed relationship with God makes temple worship a genuinely joyous and positive experience.

The psalmist also acknowledges God's power over creation. The Lord is Israel's hope, of course, but His works should have been apparent all around the world (65:5). God's control extends to the farthest seas and the mighty mountains of the world, as well as the chaos among the nations. Go far enough in one direction, the psalmist realizes, and the sun is coming up. Face the other direction and go far enough, and the sun is setting. Throughout that entire span, the people should notice and revere the works of God, and they should respond in joy (65:5–8).

The area of Canaan was heavily dependent on rain to sustain life. Drought could be a death sentence. So, in verses 9–11, the psalmist acknowledges God's part in abundantly providing the needed rains. The streams are filled with water, giving life to the land. Thankfulness for water naturally leads into thankfulness for crops and harvest.

Critical Observation

Some people think this psalm may have been used in conjunction with the barley harvest, during which the firstfruits were offered to God (Leviticus 23:9–14). It was an annual event that included both thanksgiving and celebration.

The all-too-rare greenness in the desert terrain is described as the hills being "clothed with gladness" (65:12 NIV). Just as the psalmist had challenged people throughout the world to sing for joy in their knowledge of the Lord, in verse 13 he calls creation itself to join the song.

PSALM 66

After fifteen straight psalms of David, Psalm 66 is not so designated, although the psalmist very well might have been a king. The psalm begins in verses 1–3 with a declaration of God's power and His works, along with a command to praise Him with shouts of joy. Nothing stands in God's presence: Enemies cower and all the earth acknowledges His sovereignty (66:4).

The invitation to "come and see" in verse 5 is to review what God has done for His people in the past. Perhaps the review is to be conducted at the temple (66:13–16). Centuries after the event, Israel is still recalling the power of God that led His people out of Egypt as the Red Sea was turned into dry land to provide them escape. God's great works in their past continue to inspire them. The stories are also reminders that God still rules and serve as warnings that any rebellion will be ultimately futile (66:6–7).

From the faithfulness of God in the distant past, the psalmist moves to the faithfulness of God in the recent past in verses 8–12. His people had been through some difficult times, including prison, defeat, and other trials. But rather than being brought down by such experiences, the psalmist realizes that they have merely been refined, as when precious metal is treated with intense heat in order to remove any impurities (66:10). God is to be praised because He preserved His people through the trying times and eventually led them to abundant land (66:12).

After challenging the people to praise God, in verses 13–15 the psalmist personally commits to sacrifice offerings to God at the temple and to fulfill the vows he had made. His example will motivate others to do the same. His prayer is sincere and confessional, and God responds with abundant love. Therefore, praise is the only appropriate response (66:16–20).

PSALM 67

Following the general theme of the previous two psalms, Psalm 67 also requests God's favor, in this instance as a group prayer. If the opening verses sound a bit like a familiar benediction, that's because they reflect the blessing taught to the priests in Numbers 6:24–26. As God blesses Israel, other nations will take notice and learn of salvation as well (67:1–2).

Ideally, praise will not be confined within Israel. In verses 3–4, the psalmist wants all the nations to praise God, who is a just ruler of people and a guide for all the countries. Those who acknowledge God's role in leading the nations can experience the joy that He provides. And if the psalmist's initial invitation isn't enough, he repeats it again in verse 5.

When the Israelite spies first searched out the promised land, they had been impressed with the produce that grew there (Numbers 13:23–27), and the abundance of the land continued to be of importance to them. In an agrarian society, the blessings of God were usually apparent in a bountiful harvest (Psalm 67:6–7). As God blesses the people and the crops grow, people from far away will revere the God of Israel.

PSALM 68

With an ongoing focus on God, Psalm 68 is a song of triumph. The first half of the psalm contains a number of references to Israel's exodus from Egypt and journey to the promised land. The song was probably used to commemorate Israel's victories throughout its history. Eventually the first-century church will adopt a portion of this psalm as a reference to the resurrection and ascension of Jesus Christ (68:18; Ephesians 4:8).

The psalmist points out in verses 1–3 that while those who love God are joyful as He rises to lead them, those who do not love God have no hope. No one can interfere with the progress of God. His opponents are blown away like a puff of smoke and melt like wax near a flame. The joy of God's people is for good reason because God responds to their needs and hurts. He is Father and defender, provider of fellowship for the lonely and the source of song among prisoners (68:4–6).

Verse 6 says those who rebel against God find themselves in a sun-scorched land. The righteous, however, can be in a wasteland and still experience God's provision through pouring rain and abundant showers (68:7–9). The mention of the shaking earth and Sinai in verse 8 would have reminded the psalmist's listeners of their people's journey through the wilderness. Settling in their inheritance is in reference to the promised land (68:9–10).

Continuing the review of Israel's journey, the next phase was the conquest of the land. Canaan was inhabited with various nations and their kings, but they all fled before Israel (68:11–14). This passage is difficult to interpret, but some believe Israel was God's dove and that the silver and gold probably represent the spoils of Israel's battles (68:13). Others think the dove might have been one of many valuable spoils of war, or that the dove and the colors could have referred to the colorful banners of the Canaanite kings. Either way, God's decisive victory is like white snow covering a dark mountain (the meaning of ZALMON).

The land contained many impressive and majestic mountains. In verses 15–16, the psalmist describes a feeling of jealousy the mountains felt toward Mount Zion because that was where God had established His dwelling place, the temple. In His grand entrance into His city, God is accompanied by a procession of thousands upon thousands of angels, portrayed as riding chariots (68:17). The captives and gifts in verse 18 are associated with victory in battle—submission and tribute even from those who had rebelled and lost.

Enthroned in His city, God is praised by the psalmist. In His sovereignty, God regularly bears the burdens of His people, saves them from death, and allows them to rejoice in the defeat of their enemies (68:19–23). God's procession to the temple was a festive occasion involving the whole nation. The singers and musicians established a celebratory atmosphere, and they were followed by the tribes of the nation. Only four tribes are mentioned by name, but they are representative of large and small, north and south (68:27).

Israel still had powerful enemies, so the psalmist asks God to continue to provide strength for the nation. Israel's enemies would be scattered and humbled (68:28–31). As God displays His sovereignty, the appropriate response of all nations—not just Israel—should be submission and praise (68:31–35).

PSALM 69

After the thrill and exultation of Psalm 68, Psalm 69 goes to the opposite extreme. David has sunk to a point where he can't get much lower. The psalm opens in verses 1–2 with a sequence of metaphors to describe his mood: waters up to his neck, sinking in mud with no foothold, swallowed up in deep waters. He can neither see God nor hear His voice; he receives no answer when he calls (69:3).

Meanwhile, David's enemies have taken full advantage of his desperate situation. He has done nothing to offend them, yet they are out to destroy him. He has to defend himself for things he has not done (69:4).

David admits he has sinned in verse 5, and he even acknowledges a wound from God (69:26). Perhaps he realizes his unenviable condition is God's discipline. Still, as verse 6 points out, he cares about how he carries himself as a believer in the Lord. He doesn't want to do anything that reflects badly on his Lord or impede someone else's spiritual progress. He has wept, fasted, and dressed in sackcloth, yet he continues to suffer painful indignities: scorn, mocking, shame, insults, and even taunting songs from drunkards on the street (69:7–12).

As a young person, already anointed to be the next king and on the run constantly from King Saul, David had learned to wait for God's timing. Here his patience is displayed during his spiritual crisis. He will attempt to stay above water until the time of God's favor (69:13–15). He trusts God and counts on His mercy and love, yet his struggle is severe. He hopes for a quick resolution, and he continues to detail his circumstances in his prayer (69:16–21).

David's persecutors are absolutely merciless, and in verse 22 he begins to pray more for retribution against them than deliverance for himself. Essentially, he wants them to experience the same things he is feeling: weakness, isolation, and despair. Even worse, he wants God to judge them harsher by blotting them out of His book of life (69:22–29).

Critical Observation

The book of life is mentioned from time to time throughout scripture. It appears to be an image that represents a record of those whom God has declared righteous. New Testament references to this book suggest that those whose names are listed can anticipate eternal life with God (see Philippians 4:3; Revelation 3:5; 13:8).

David is fully convinced that God hears those who are in need, and he is surely included in that category. Therefore he is able to glorify God in spite of his suffering. He could have offered sacrifices, yet he realizes God is more pleased with his heartfelt expressions of praise and thanksgiving. God will deliver David and all of His people (69:30–36).

The addition of verses 34–36 expands the usage of the psalm. It is not just one person's struggle to endure the taunts of his or her enemies but also a challenge for the entire nation to raise their voices to God.

PSALM 70

Although similar in theme to the previous psalm, Psalm 70 is more closely tied to Psalm 40. It appears to be a reworking of 40:13–17.

In verses 1–3, David again prays for God's hasty deliverance from a crowd of hostile enemies. They are mocking him while he is unable to retaliate, so David asks God to let them experience shame and confusion.

If David's deliverance is witnessed by others, they can then see for themselves that God is faithful and trustworthy (70:4). As a result, David's salvation might inspire the praise of many who believe in God.

David continues to be at the mercy of his enemies, but he has put his trust in a merciful God. He anticipates God's response soon—hopefully without further delay (70:5).

PSALM 71

Psalm 71 was written by someone who had the benefit, or perhaps the liability, of age. The psalmist looks back over his life and attests to his ongoing faith in God throughout the years. No introduction is provided. However, the next psalm is attributed to Solomon, which suggests to some scholars that this one may have been written from David's perspective as an older man. Psalms 71 and 72 close out Book II of the biblical book Psalms.

There is much to be said about an older person who continues to recognize his or her need for God. In verses 1–3, the psalmist expresses complete dependence on God. Surely the aggression of one's enemies seems even worse during old age (71:4), but God remains the psalmist's rock and refuge.

One advantage of the psalmist's age is his ability to look back over his life and see repeated proof of God's faithfulness. God had been involved in his life since birth, so he has no reason to think God will abandon him now (71:5–6).

Some people assume his problems are a sign that something is amiss in his spiritual life (71:7). Others simply want to attack while he is weak and it seems God has deserted him (71:11). But the psalmist doesn't overly concern himself with what others say or do. He may have been older and weaker, but his God is as strong as ever (71:8–13).

Speaking with the wisdom of age, the psalmist continues to place his hope in God. He had not yet discovered the full extent of God's righteousness and salvation, but he had seen more than enough to proclaim God's goodness to others (71:14–16).

Thinking back to his childhood and to his current world as a gray-haired man, he can attest to God's power throughout his lifetime (71:17–18). With that knowledge, he is more eager than ever to have God near him. In his lifetime he has seen his share of problems, but he is confident that God will again restore him. Meanwhile, he will continue to acknowledge God's righteousness, praise His faithfulness, tell others of His steadfastness, and sing and shout with joy (71:19–24).

PSALM 72

Psalm 72 is one of two psalms attributed to Solomon, the other being Psalm 127. As with many of the superscriptions throughout Psalms, there is much debate as to whether the designated writer is actually the author. Many argue that rather than being written *by* Solomon, Psalm 72 may have been written *for* Solomon. John Calvin even suggests that this psalm is David's dying declaration, recorded by Solomon for posterity.

The content of Psalm 72 makes it an appropriate prayer or tribute for any king, and it is likely that it was used during various coronation ceremonies. The opening verses repeatedly emphasize a desire for justice and righteousness. Israel's king is in a position to help the poor and downtrodden as judge, provider, and protector (72:1–4, 12–14).

Verses 5–7 vary according to translation. Conceivably, the assurance of blessing and life beyond the sun and moon could apply to God. However, the poetic language may be intended to refer to the human king. In that case, the intent of the verses would be that the righteous reign of a good king continues to influence many generations to come.

The boundaries of Israel were never larger than during the reign of Solomon. The psalmist anticipates the king's widespread influence that includes the Euphrates, Tarshish (modern Spain), Sheba (the Arabian Peninsula), and Seba (northern Egypt). The specific sites are not named to detail the outer boundaries of the kingdom but rather to suggest that it will have no limits. The king's enemies will be submissive, and many kings from around the world will bring him tribute (72:8–11).

The psalmist then reiterates the concern of the king for the weak and oppressed in verses 12–14, followed by a wish for his long life and prosperity. He also calls on the people to support their king with prayers and blessings. The king's influence will extend to many nations (72:15–17).

The next verses apply to the entire second book of Psalms, not just Psalm 72. A doxology concludes each of the five sections (72:18–19).

Demystifying Psalms

The notation in verse 20 most likely referred at one time to a more limited collection of psalms that were all ascribed to David. The psalms of David do not end here, but they begin to be scarcer. Book III of Psalms begins with a long series of poems attributed to Asaph.

Take It Home

Book II within Psalms comes to an end at just about the midpoint of the biblical book. Based on what you've read so far, what recurring themes have you detected? Has any of the content surprised (or confused) you? What do you think about David's and others' frankness in their appeals to God?

PSALMS: BOOK III

PSALMS 73–89

Setting Up the Section

Book III of Psalms contains seventeen psalms, eleven of which are attributed to Asaph. However, several of the psalms contain references to events in Israel's history that would have been later than Asaph's lifetime, so there is good reason to believe that some of these psalms were penned by his descendants.

PSALM 73

According to their superscriptions, Psalms 73–83 are all credited to Asaph, one of the three men David had assigned to head Israel's choirs. The other two leaders are Heman and Ethan (Jeduthun [see 1 Chronicles 15:16–19]), who each are credited with one psalm in Book III of Psalms (Psalms 88 and 89).

Psalm 73 demonstrates the difference one's acknowledgment of God can make in his or her spiritual outlook. The psalmist is surprisingly honest in describing his envy of prosperous people. The fact that they are also arrogant and wicked only intensifies his confusion (73:3).

According to verses 4–9, the psalmist had paid close attention to such people. Based on his observations, they are healthy, strong, and worry-free. They have little in common with the average person, so they tend to be proud, insensitive, and self-centered. They have a sense of entitlement that surpasses earthly bounds and leads them to lay claim to heaven as well. Since it appears that the proud and selfish people aren't held accountable for their actions, others become enamored and even tempted to join their ranks (73:10–11).

From the psalmist's initial perspective in verse 12, such people seem to become ever wealthier and perpetually carefree. This distresses him. His thoughts even take a dark turn in verse 13, as he wonders if his commitment to righteousness and innocence has been for nothing. And with such a perspective, his sufferings make no sense (73:14).

Then, at exactly the midpoint of his psalm, the psalmist has an epiphany. He goes to the temple and realizes he is only seeing half the story. He is glad that he hasn't spoken his thoughts out loud (73:15-17). When he is able to see things from God's viewpoint, he realizes where the wealthy, arrogant people are headed. They are not on solid ground; they are traveling a road to ruin and destruction. Those who terrify others will be faced with terrors of their own (73:18-20).

After regaining his spiritual sight, the psalmist is contrite before God. According to verse 22, he feels like a "brute beast" (NIV)—senseless and ignorant. He has wasted time being bitter and hurt. He realizes that God has always been there for him and will continue to lead him. Nothing in heaven or earth can compare to that reality (73:21-26).

The psalmist closes in verses 27-28 with the comforting promise that God remains a refuge for all who remain near to Him. But in contrast, those who defy God will surely be destroyed.

PSALM 74

The temple in Jerusalem fell to the Babylonians in 586 BC, and the people of Judah were carried off in successive waves. Some of the psalms, such as Psalm 74, were written while they were in exile.

The loss of both God's temple and their beloved city was hard on the people of Jerusalem, even though they realized the judgment of God was well deserved. In this case, the psalmist never claims innocence but wonders how long God's anger will continue. The Israelites are still God's sheep, whom He had delivered in times past. God had indeed used the Babylonian army to impose His judgment on Judah, but the psalmist realizes that Judah's enemies are still enemies of God as well.

The Babylonians offended and insulted God. In verse 4, the psalmist points out their blatant disregard for God's dwelling place and His sanctuary. Their violent actions are bad enough, but their arrogance toward God is far worse (74:4-8), so the silence of God is mystifying. When Egypt had opposed God's people, God had responded with many miraculous signs to free His people. This time, however, there are no signs, and God's prophets appear to be absent (74:9).

Critical Observation

We know that prophets continued to minister throughout the exile. For example, Ezekiel went to Babylon (Ezekiel 1:1-3) and Jeremiah went to Egypt (Jeremiah 43:6-7). Conceivably the psalmist was with the remnant of people left in the Jerusalem area, who may have had no working prophet among them. Or his comment in Psalm 74:9 may mean that he isn't receiving the answers he is seeking.

Sadly, the silence of God is offset by the jeering of Israel's enemies (74:10). In verse 11, the psalmist boldly suggests that God is sitting with His hands in His lap, and he urges the Lord to retaliate. The psalmist certainly does not doubt the power of God, who is Israel's only source of salvation (74:12–13). The *Leviathan* mentioned in verse 14 represents the forces of chaos, which are no match for the power of the Lord. Creation itself is under God's control, including seasons and heavenly bodies. God can create springs of water where none exist and stop mighty rivers in their tracks (74:15–17).

Therefore, the psalmist has confidence that God will protect His people, even in their terrible situation. Adding to his confidence is the fact that God had established a covenant with Israel. For now, their enemies have the upper hand and demonstrate a continual uproar, but their clamor will not last forever. God will surely silence them as He protects and delivers Israel, His dove (74:18–23).

PSALM 75

Psalm 75 is an expression of confidence in God during a time when Israel is surrounded by arrogant and powerful nations. Verse 1 opens with the psalmist's thanksgiving for God's presence. The connection between the nearness of God's name and people telling of His deeds can be understood in two ways. Perhaps it means that those who worship the name of God naturally begin to talk about the great things He has done. Or it may be the other way around: As people recall the wonderful deeds of God, they can't help but give thanks that He remains so near.

In verses 2–3, the psalmist abruptly shifts to God's voice, and God speaks as a judge. God's judgment may shake the earth and its people, yet He continues to be a stabilizing force.

Verses 4–6 portray arrogant people as unruly animals with outstretched necks and raised horns, resisting any kind of control. God warns such people to humble themselves. No power on earth can overrule God's judgment, so it is the essence of wisdom to yield to God while there is still time.

When God's judgment is pronounced, it is like a potent wine the guilty are forced to drink, replacing their self-confidence and arrogance with an intoxicating stupor. The psalmist wants no part of such judgment and commits himself to praise God for as long as he lives (75:9). It appears that he returns to God's voice in verse 10. Almost certainly it is God who intends to lift up the righteous while cutting off the horns of the wicked—their source of power and pride.

PSALM 76

A victorious song celebrating the power of God, Psalm 76 focuses on what God has done for Judah. The psalmist writes of God's deliverance from Israel's enemies after an aggressive action toward Jerusalem. (Both Salem and Zion are references to Jerusalem [76:2].) Some scholars attempt to pinpoint the exact battle the psalmist refers to, and their opinions vary. Others believe his intent is more general—that God had delivered His people from any number of warring nations (76:3).

Demystifying Psalms

After God's people left Egypt, they soon became known as the nation of Israel, or the Israelites. After Solomon's reign, when the kingdom was divided, a distinction began to be made between Israel (the northern tribes) and Judah (the southern kingdom). But after both Israel and Judah had been defeated and their people exiled, the distinction was not as necessary. In many cases, as in verse 1, the two names are used interchangeably.

The description of God in verse 4 is magnificent. He is the essence of light and majesty. His rebuke of the wicked is a severe and perhaps final display of His wrath (76:5–6). For those who oppose God, His judgment is terrifying, producing silence across the land. But others will delight in the judgment of God because it means that at last they are free of those who regularly afflict them (76:7–9).

Verse 10 can be translated a couple of different ways. One option is to understand that God's wrath against people brings Him praise. In that case, the praise comes from those whom He delivers as well as from any who realize they might have been included in His judgment, yet were spared. A second option is to interpret the verse to read that the wrath of people brings praise to God. In that sense, when people stand defiantly against a sovereign Lord, God is always triumphant. Consequently, His sure and certain victories bring Him praise.

With such an understanding of God, it becomes incumbent on people to devote themselves to Him. Instead of fearful defiance, God wants people to submit to Him, honor their vows, and offer gifts to the sovereign Lord (76:11–12).

PSALM 77

Sometimes prayers begin with a focus on God and eventually work their way into the needs and desires of the individuals. Other times prayer starts with what is on the mind of the pray-er, and only after unloading one's concerns is the person able to shift to spiritual matters. Psalm 77 is in the latter category.

To the psalmist's credit, he has turned to God in his misery and unease. He is spiritually and emotionally fragile—in distress, unsettled, and faint of heart (77:1–3). But prayer doesn't seem to help at first. In the past he had been able to rejoice at nighttime and sing of the deliverance of God; now, because of his personal troubles, he is simply unable to sleep (77:4–6).

In verse 5, the thoughts of how God had helped him in the past, contrasted with God's seeming distance in the present, have the psalmist in a quandary. God doesn't appear to be responsive now. Would He ever respond again? The psalmist acknowledges God's unfailing love, so the thought that it might have failed is quite disconcerting (77:6–9).

Still, the psalmist can't stop thinking about God's power that had been displayed time after time to deliver previous generations of His people. There is simply too much evidence of God's involvement in Israel's history for the psalmist to give up hope at this point (77:11–12).

God is still holy, all-powerful, and a worker of miracles. No person, no force, no so-called god is greater. With renewed enthusiasm, the psalmist begins to recall one of God's greatest deliverances, the exodus of the Hebrew people from Egypt. To begin with, God's involvement was evident in the fact that the Israelites had made it safely away from Egypt and into the well-protected confines of the promised land. But more than that, God's presence had been dramatically displayed through the miraculous parting of the Red Sea, thunder and lightning atop Mount Sinai, earthquakes, and other means. Beyond a doubt, God had been with His people. Therefore, any doubts about God are unfounded. He is still a God of power and love who will deliver His people (77:13–20).

PSALM 78

Several of the psalms recall God's deliverance of His people from Egypt as evidence of His strength, love, and care for Israel. However, few are as extensive as Psalm 78.

The purpose of recalling God's previous faithfulness is to inspire and assure future generations. The stories are to be passed along. In one sense the teachings of God are parables and "hidden lessons" (78:2 NLT), yet not in any kind of mystical or secretive sense. They are clearly understandable (78:2–8). Jesus' parables are similar, as Matthew will later point out (Matthew 13:35) by quoting verse 2 of this psalm.

Hearing the facts about God's previous miracles is one thing; responding properly is another. Generations of Israelites had been stubborn and rebellious because they forgot the wonders of God (Psalm 78:8–12). Verse 7 points out the goal for future generations: to not forget and to place faith in God and keep His commands.

In the psalmist's recap of the Exodus, he points out the great contrast between God's faithfulness and the people's lack of faith. According to the image in verse 13, God had made the water of the Red Sea firm like a wall. When people complained of thirst in the wilderness, God had split rocks to create a source of flowing water (78:15–16). Such miracles that demonstrate God's unique power were performed purely for the benefit of His people.

Yet the Israelites were not long impressed with abundant water. They soon complained about the lack of food. Their utter disregard for the things God had done for them, and their instinct to immediately gripe about what they didn't have, made God angry. Still, God did not desert them. He provided food on a regular basis (78:23–25), as well as occasional feasts of quail (78:26–29). The manna was the "bread of angels" (78:25 NIV)—food dropped from heaven to feed thousands of people every day.

But the people continued to sin and rebel (78:17–18). God sent fire as a warning (Numbers 11:1–3; Psalm 78:21–22). Still, they didn't learn. Some of those who disregarded God's provision and continued to crave other food were stricken with a plague and died (Numbers 11:33–34; Psalm 78:30–31). God was attempting to lead them to a land flowing with milk and honey, yet the generation of those who began the journey died in futility and terror because they refused to acknowledge God's wondrous provision of food and water along the way (78:32–33).

The only thing that seemed to capture their attention was God's anger. When a group of people died as a result of their sinful actions and attitudes, the survivors eagerly turned to God again. But their repentance was short-lived. They would continue to say the right words, but they were not sincere. Again and again they provoked God, but in His mercy He had not ultimately destroyed them (78:34–41).

The Israelites *should* have learned from God's dealings with the Egyptians. They had seen the series of plagues fall on Egypt (78:42–51)—displays of God's anger, wrath, and hostility. And then He led His people like a shepherd leads sheep, through a path that took them right through a dried-up Red Sea to the promised land. Upon their arrival, He went before them to drive out the hostile nations and allow the Israelites to settle (78:52–55).

In spite of everything God had done for them, the people were no better in the promised land than they had been in the wilderness. During the era of the judges, the Israelites were quick to forsake God and turn to idols. By the time of Samuel, God had allowed the ark of the covenant to be lost, and many Israelites were killed in battle (78:56–64).

Demystifying Psalms

Ephraim was a large, prominent, and well-protected tribe in the northern kingdom. Judah was a much smaller tribe to the south. Yet it was from Judah that God chose David to rise up, confront, and defeat the many enemies of Israel. It seems that the people of Ephraim had an opportunity to prove themselves but had failed to do so (78:9–11, 67–68), although the specific occasion is not known.

If it seemed that God was sleeping as the Philistines ran roughshod over Israel, it wasn't long before He awoke to deliver His people yet again. In something of a surprise, the tribe of Judah rose to prominence with the exploits of David, who not only proved to be a great military figure but a spiritual leader as well. It was David who had established Jerusalem (Zion) and had brought the ark there (78:65–69).

In the observation of the psalmist, David had never stopped being a shepherd. God had simply moved him from tending his family's sheep to shepherding the Israelites. In contrast to so many kings who would come after him, David led his people with integrity and skill (78:70–72). The reign of David was a high point in the history of Israel being passed on for future generations to learn and repeat.

PSALM 79

Psalm 79 is one of the poems written during Israel's exile, recalling the tragic destruction of Jerusalem and the current helpless situation of the people. It was a perplexing state of affairs. Clearly, the fall of Judah and the exile had been God's judgment on His people, and He had used the Babylonians to carry it out. But now, from the psalmist's standpoint, a bigger problem is the attitude heathen nations show toward God.

Jerusalem was God's city, and the desecration of the temple was a particular insult. The Israelites had deserved punishment, and they had suffered for what they had done. But as verses 1–4 show, it seems that God's reputation is at stake. The mocking and scorn they continue to receive is also a derision of their God.

The question in verse 5 ("How long?") is a common query of the psalmists. The people had suffered personal pain and loss. Now their suffering is intensified as foreign nations laugh at the perceived impotence of their God. The psalmist requests mercy for Israel but judgment for the other nations that arrogantly assume that they are strong and in control (79:6–8). The sins of the fathers in verse 8 include generations of widespread idolatry and apostasy, with little concern for the things of God. But the people exiled in Babylon were contrite and repentant, so the psalmist feels emboldened to ask God to take action against Israel's enemies (79:9–11).

The Israelites are prisoners in the sense that they are imprisoned in another country. They are condemned to die away from the freedoms and blessings they had taken for granted. The psalmist's prayer is not simply for their release and return but also for God's retribution. *Seven* (79:12) is a number of completeness, in essence a request that God's action against the nations be total destruction.

The Israelites had strayed and had been reprimanded for it, but the psalmist still believes that they are God's people, the sheep of His pasture (79:13). And as he looks to the future, he envisions not a continuation of suffering and exile but many successive generations all offering their praise to God.

PSALM 80

Psalm 79 concludes with the concept of God as a Shepherd and the people as sheep, and Psalm 80 begins with similar imagery. Going further into the psalm, it becomes clear that the people *need* a shepherd—someone far more powerful than their enemies. In this case, the heavenly Shepherd is on a throne among angels, and His power is beyond question. So in his prayer for deliverance, the psalmist asks God to show His mighty power (80:1–2).

The three tribes mentioned in verse 2 suggest that the psalm is referring to the northern kingdom. When the nation divided after the reign of Solomon, his son Rehoboam was left with only the tribe of Judah. Geographically, portions of Benjamin were adjacent to Jerusalem—clearly as far south as Judah, but still considered at that point a northern tribe. If indeed the psalmist writes of the northern tribes here, then the aggressors would have been the Assyrians.

God is angry with His people, and as a consequence they have become a laughingstock for their enemies. Such mocking is difficult to endure. Tears had become both the food and drink of the Israelites (80:4–6). The psalmist's request for restoration is repeated throughout the psalm, in verses 3, 7, and 19.

The psalmist compares Israel to a vine that God had uprooted in Egypt and grafted into the promised land (80:8–10). At first its influence had been only positive, providing grapes and valuable shade to a large area. In verse 11, the sea is most likely the Mediterranean, and the river probably the Euphrates.

Eventually, however, God had withdrawn His protection. Without the security of walls, the vine is exposed to both passersby who take the grapes and wild animals that feed on it (80:12–13). In time the vine is cut down and burned (80:16). But the God who had grafted the vine to begin with is still more than capable of reviving it (80:14–15).

Demystifying Psalms

The terminology in this psalm may sound oddly familiar to those who have read the New Testament. The references to God's son (80:15) and son of man (80:17) are both commonly applied to Jesus. In the Old Testament world, however, "the son of God" was often a reference to the nation's king. And in this case, the reference might have been to Israel. (The word translated *son* can also mean "branch," and in the context of what the psalmist had written about the vine, this option would make sense.) Another possibility is that the son of man is a reference to Benjamin. This figure is also addressed as "the man at your right hand" (80:17 NIV), and the literal interpretation of *Benjamin* is "son of the right hand."

It is unclear exactly whom the psalmist refers to as the son of God, the son of man, and the man at God's right hand (80:15–17). What *is* clear, however, is the psalmist's desire for God's protection over that figure as well as the entire nation. In verse 19, the writer once again appeals for God's deliverance and restoration. And this time, as he says in verse 18, the people will stay committed and no longer turn away from God.

PSALM 81

The Day of Atonement was the most solemn and somber observance in the Hebrew year. But it was soon followed by the Feast of Tabernacles (Numbers 29:12–38; Deuteronomy 16:13–17), a weeklong joyful celebration of harvest and God's blessings. Psalm 81 is frequently thought to be a song used during the Feast. Some people prefer to associate the psalm with Passover because it mentions Israel's ordeal in Egypt and the wilderness, but the enthusiastic tone of the psalm makes it appropriate for a more festive celebration.

God had instructed people to be joyful at the Feast of Tabernacles (Deuteronomy 16:14), so the psalmist's opening instruction is to sing for joy and shout aloud. Harvest was a time when it was impossible to overlook what God was doing for His people. The jubilant mood is heightened with instrumental music to accompany the singing (Psalm 81:2). The ram's horn mentioned in verse 3 was probably used less as a musical instrument than to provide a ceremonial signal (Exodus 19:13, 16, 19).

Critical Observation

The Jewish year was established on a lunar cycle. The first day of the seventh month occurred with the new moon (Psalm 81:3), acknowledged by the ram's horn trumpet blast (Leviticus 23:24). This eventually became the Jewish New Year, because it wrapped up the harvest season and began a rainy, planting season. The Feast of Tabernacles did not begin until the full moon on the fifteenth of the month (Psalm 81:3), and the horn was sounded again.

Joseph, mentioned in verse 5, is a term for the northern kingdom (as opposed to Judah)—not a personal reference to the Old Testament patriarch. The reference to the language they don't understand is to the tongues of the various nations that Israel encounters.

The verses that follow (81:6–16) shift to a first-person address from God to the people. (This section would probably have been spoken by a designated Levite.) God had set His people free and had rescued them both from the Egyptians and the elements as they trekked through the wilderness. Meribah was the place where God had instructed Moses to strike the rock to provide water for the people (Exodus 17:1–7; Psalm 81:7). God had also provided ample food (81:10) and would have continued to do so, except the people had disobeyed His clear instructions to keep away from the gods of the alien nations (81:8–9, 11–12).

God had allowed the Israelites to go their own way, and they had suffered for it. Yet He is eager for the situation to improve. He promises immediate victory over their enemies if the people will listen and obey (81:13–14).

At this harvest celebration, the people would have certainly responded to the closing verses of being fed with the finest wheat (81:15–16) rather than finding themselves cringing before God. The honey from the rock mentioned in verse 16 is, in this case, a product of bees that had made their nests among the rocks. In many instances, however, when the Bible speaks of honey, it is a reference to a sweet concoction made from the fruit of the date palm.

PSALM 82

With the opening verse of Psalm 82, the reader is immediately faced with a question: Who are the gods the psalmist writes about? To the nations surrounding Israel, such a reference would make them think of their own pantheon of gods, much like the Greek deities thought to operate from atop Mount Olympus. Even the kings of many secular nations were often referred to as gods. The Israelites might have conceivably thought of angels among the great assembly of God.

In Israel, judges and kings are supposed to represent the Lord and model His concern and protection for people who might be taken advantage of. Yet those human rulers are included among those taking advantage of the poor, weak, and otherwise helpless (82:2–3). The description of such people in verse 5 is accurate, but truly bleak.

This psalm serves as a reminder of a ruler's job description. Rather than adding to the woes of the weak and poor, Israel's leaders are supposed to defend and rescue such people. But in order to save them from wicked people, those in authority first must stop being wicked themselves.

In the end, the only judge who matters is God. The human rulers may have a high position for a while, but they will meet the same end as everyone else. The more the psalmist thinks about the difference between God's rule and human leadership, the more he desires God's authority (82:6–8).

PSALM 83

David writes a number of psalms imploring God to intervene when he is being attacked by numerous personal enemies. This psalm is similar to those of David's, but here the threat is to the nation of Judah as a whole; the enemies are not individual people, but foreign nations.

The psalmist appeals to God to take action, and as he provides more details, the situation is indeed critical. Israel's enemies have formed a coalition with the goal of completely obliterating the nation (83:1-4). The list of enemies in verses 5-8 includes several nations that have regularly initiated conflict (Edomites, Moabites, Ammonites, Philistines, and Assyrians), along with some less familiar names. If the psalmist writes of a specific historic event, it is not recorded elsewhere in scripture. It may be that he lists a number of nations that have oppressed and corrupted Israel, intending for them to be representative of *all* of Israel's enemies.

In order to understand what the psalmist is asking of God in verses 9-12, some readers may need a history lesson to identify the names he recalls. Sisera and Jabin were the oppressors of Israel under the judgeship of Deborah and Barak (Judges 4-5). The four men named in verse 11 were defeated by Gideon (Judges 7-8). All the listed opponents of Israel had been strong and threatening, and Israel's victories had been clear signs of God's power and protection.

The psalmist asks God to respond the same way with Israel's new batch of enemies. The power of God has not diminished, so the psalmist wants to see his nation's enemies blown away like tumbleweeds. God's pursuit could be like fire spreading through a thicket or a deadly storm rolling in, resulting in both terror and shame (83:13-16). But the goal is not simply the removal of enemies; the desired result is that people will witness the power of God and turn to Him.

The list of nations represents much power in the ancient world. But the psalmist's closing reminder is that God alone is the Most High over all the powers on earth. And since those who oppose Him die in shame and confusion, perhaps others will acknowledge God and change their wicked ways (83:17-18).

PSALM 84

After someone has experienced a rich and rewarding relationship with God, it changes the person's perspective on life. Psalm 84 is an expression of longing by the psalmist to be closer to God and *remain* close. The opening verses appear to focus on the temple building with its courts, yet by the end of the psalm it becomes clear that it is the presence of God Himself that the writer desires.

Worshipers tend to feel closer to God at the temple. A person's approach to God is heightened through priestly intercession, and praise and worship take on a more public, communal feel. The psalmist is even jealous of the birds that nest in and around the temple, living among the priests (84:1-4).

But the writer appears to be one of many pilgrims who journeys only occasionally to Jerusalem (84:5). The Valley of Baca mentioned in verse 6 is not a known geographic location. *Baca* can refer to balsam trees or weeping, and the psalmist's phrase may be metaphorical, like David's "valley of the shadow of death" (23:4). A long journey to Jerusalem could be strenuous and even dangerous, but the psalmist thinks only about the positive aspects of the trip and the ultimate destination (84:6-7).

Verses 8-9 include a prayer for the king. The psalmist also tries to express the degree of his love for God's temple. He declares it a thousand times better than being anywhere else, and he would rather be a doorkeeper there than to live and thrive elsewhere (84:10).

Being in the presence of God at His temple is akin to standing in the brightness of the sun, yet being shielded and protected at the same time. For those who can stand before Him blameless, God will grant blessing and deny nothing good (84:11). Trust in God, however, is essential in receiving what He has to offer (84:12).

PSALM 85

Psalm 85 is another of the songs where the author acknowledges experiencing the wrath of God. Many such psalms have to do with the period of exile of the Israelites. Some people believe this particular psalm speaks of the situation that the people faced shortly afterward, when they returned to their homeland from Babylon, although no strong proof exists.

The psalmist takes hope as he looks to the past and reviews how God has previously shown His anger and yet forgiven the people and relented (85:1-3). The psalm contains no outright confession of wrongdoing, although the psalmist implies as much in verses 4-6 by asking God to suspend His anger and once again restore the nation.

God's love is unfailing, and His salvation is always available (85:7). He offers guidance that results in peace for those who listen and obey. But the pursuit of folly prevents people from benefiting from God's wisdom (85:8-9).

The psalmist emphasizes the gifts of God by describing them in pairs: love and faithfulness, righteousness and peace, faithfulness and righteousness. Even more than pairs, they appear to be married together in verses 9-11. Despite the current troubles of his nation, the psalmist maintains confidence that God will still provide good things for His people. The Lord's righteousness will prevail (85:12-13).

PSALM 86

Of all the psalms in Book III of the biblical book of Psalms (Psalms 73-89), this is the only one attributed to David. While many of the previous psalms are appeals to God on a national level, Psalm 86 is the prayer of an individual concerning his personal troubles.

Verse 1 provides David's general state of mind. He is poor and needy, but the specifics of his situation aren't revealed until later. First he wants to appeal to God for mercy and protection. David's trust is in God and he is quick to seek help, but his current situation has robbed him of joy (86:2-4). He is counting on God's love and forgiveness, fully expecting an answer (86:5-7).

David next acknowledges God's uniqueness. No other entity is like God in character or in accomplishments. God's "wondrous deeds" (86:10 NASB) single Him out from all other potential contenders. Consequently, David expects that all the nations will eventually worship and glorify God (86:8–9).

David desires instruction from God. He wants to know truth and to cultivate an undivided heart. God has loved him and delivered him, and he wants to praise and glorify the Lord as a result (86:11–13).

Only then does David get to the crux of the matter: He is being personally attacked by numerous unrighteous people who want his life. But his specific complaint doesn't matter; he has already entrusted himself to God, so the nature of the problem is inconsequential. God can handle it (86:13–14).

Demystifying Psalms

David's observation in verse 15 may have been based on his recollection of the law, specifically Exodus 34:6. If so, his recitation stops at a point that maintains a positive focus on his situation. As he prays for his enemies, he could have easily included the next phrase of the Exodus quote: the observation that God will punish the guilty (Exodus 34:7).

In addition, David acknowledges God's great grace and compassion. Since God has been slow to become angry with David in the past, perhaps the psalmist can understand why God doesn't immediately condemn others who are behaving sinfully. Therefore, rather than ask for his enemies' quick demise, David asks God to do something good for him that they will see—and perhaps shame them into repentance (86:16–17). In the meantime, David counts on God's strength, deliverance, help, and comfort.

PSALM 87

Psalm 87 is a distinctive and intriguing psalm that focuses on Zion as God's city and dwelling place. The date of the psalm is unclear—whether before, during, or after the exile of Israel.

Zion is certainly special because of the presence of God there. The earth is the Lord's (24:1), but of all the locations on earth, God has designated one particular mountaintop as a headquarters, of sorts. Even among the geography of Jacob (Israel), Zion is prominent in the eyes of God (87:1–2).

Psalm 87 stands out because of its inclusion of nations who are persistent enemies of Israel. The Babylonians and Philistines have been aggressive foes. *Rahab* is a name for the upper Nile region of Egypt (originating in mythological references). *Cush* is the area that is now southern Egypt, northern Ethiopia, and Sudan. And *Tyre* is the representative city of Phoenicia. These nations have created havoc and suffering for Israel. In other psalms, they are the nations the psalmists might ask God to destroy. Here, however, they are being granted citizenship into God's city and given privileges associated with birthright (87:4–6). The psalmist makes it clear in verse 4, however, that the reason these peoples are invited into the rolls of the city of God is because they acknowledge the Lord.

The fountains mentioned in verse 7 typify the blessings of God. Therefore, the music of the nations will acknowledge that God is the source of all good things.

PSALM 88

David is credited with several gloomy and dismal psalms, but Psalm 88 (by a different psalmist) is as grim as any that David ever wrote. It is similar to David's Psalm 22, which Jesus quotes while hanging on the cross.

The psalmist is clearly a person of faith, which makes his situation all the more excruciating. He steadfastly clings to his belief in God, but he can hardly come up with a single positive event in his life. The precise nature of his affliction is unknown, although it appears to be life threatening. In fact, he has already begun to associate himself with those already dead (88:3–5). And dead people, in the thinking of Old Testament believers, are no longer under God's care.

His suffering appears to be a consequence of God's anger. The psalmist is overcome with personal misery that is further complicated when his closest friends abandon him in his pain. It feels like being trapped in a deep and dark pit with no escape (88:6–8).

Still, day after day the afflicted psalmist cries out to God. His is not just an emotional plea; he uses reason as well. He is eager, almost desperate, to experience the wonders of God and to respond with praise. If he is pushed any further, to the point of death, he will regret being no longer able to worship (88:9–12).

The psalmist will not give up on God. His cry in verse 13 echoes those in verses 1 and 9. He continues to pray each morning, even as he keeps wondering why God seems so distant. His problems began during his youth, and he is still seeking relief. Yet despite all his efforts, nothing has resolved the problem.

The final verse is perhaps the bleakest of all. His despair from the ongoing terrors he has suffered is too much for his friends. His companions have deserted him, and his closest companion is darkness (88:18). Still, he will continue to cry out to God day and night, awaiting the Lord's intervention in his life (88:1).

Demystifying Psalms

Levi had three sons—Merari, Gershon, and Kohath (1 Chronicles 6:16)—who oversaw divisions of tabernacle musicians. In turn, Levi's three sons had descendants who assumed the same roles (1 Chronicles 25:1, 6) and who appear in the superscriptions of the psalms. Jeduthun (Ethan) was from Merari's family. Asaph was a descendant of Gershon. Heman, the leader mentioned in connection with Psalm 88, was from the family of Kohath. Both Heman and Ethan (the designated author of Psalm 89) are noted for their wisdom in 1 Kings 4:31.

PSALM 89

This final entry in Book III of the biblical book of Psalms is another that scholars find difficult to date or to link to a historic event. It begins as a bold and confident expression of praise to God, but it takes a sudden shift at verse 38 and concludes as a lament.

In verses 1–2, the psalmist begins with acknowledgement of God's great love and faithfulness, characteristics that are evident both in heaven and on earth and will be noticed by all generations of people. At verses 3–4, he introduces the covenant God had established with David—a theme the psalmist will soon return to.

God is to be praised for many reasons. His work in creation is evident throughout the heavens (89:5), the earth (89:11), and the seas (89:9). The mountains (Tabor and Hermon) sing for joy in response (89:12). No other being can compare to the Lord (89:6–8). His works are apparent everywhere. He had destroyed Egypt (Rahab)—just one example of His great power (89:10, 13). His character is unquestionable; He is surrounded by righteousness, justice, love, and faithfulness (89:14), and His qualities influence and inspire humanity (89:15–18).

In verses 17–18, the psalmist uses a couple of metaphors for Israel's king. The human ruler serves as both a *horn* (a symbol of power) and a *shield* (a symbol of protection). Then the psalmist reviews the covenant that had been established between God and David.

David receives the support and blessings of God. He is victorious in all his battles. He calls God *Father*, and the Lord bestows on him the entitlements of a firstborn son. No one will be more successful as king. As a result, God promises to establish David's line forever. As it turns out, David's descendants aren't as faithful as they should be, and some blatantly disregard God's commands. They will receive God's punishment for their disobedience, but even so, God will not break His covenant with David. Israel can count on God's promises to endure forever (89:19–37), or so the psalmist thinks.

The reality of life, however, does not seem to fit the promises God has made, and the psalmist begins to bemoan his nation's situation. The current king (anointed one) has not proven faithful to God, and therefore God has become angry and rejected him (89:38). God's relationship with this king is antithetical to His relationship with David, as described in verses 40–45. This king experiences not only defeat in battle but also the scorn of his enemies. The nation has been plundered. Its former splendor has disappeared, and the king is impotent to do anything about it. From all appearances, it looks as if God has gone back on His covenant (89:39).

And yet the psalmist continues to seek answers. He is tired of hearing the insults and mocking of others directed toward his king. He knows life is short, and he wants to again experience the love of God. He knows God has made promises to David that are still in effect, but he just can't understand his nation's state of despair. He ends the psalm on that unsettled note.

The positive message of verse 52 is not part of the psalm. This final verse is a doxology inserted as a conclusion for Book III. Following the lament that ends Psalm 89, it is a welcome addition.

PSALMS: BOOK IV

PSALMS 90–106

Setting Up the Section

This section contains the compilation of psalms comprising Book IV of the biblical book of Psalms. In this portion of Psalms, the introductory superscriptions are less specific than previous ones, and several psalms lack introductions altogether. Only three of the seventeen psalms in this section identify the writer, so there is more mystery and speculation as to authors and dates.

PSALM 90

This psalm is attributed to Moses, which makes it several centuries older than the other psalms. It begins in verses 1–2 with an acknowledgment of the eternal God—the Creator of the world and everlasting refuge for humanity. He is the source of everything people need. "From everlasting to everlasting" (90:2 NIV) is an expression to emphasize God's eternity.

But in contrast to the always-existing God is the impermanence of humanity. Human lives are transitory. The longest recorded life is Methuselah's—a 969-year span (Genesis 5:27). But to God, a thousand years go by like a single day (or a short segment of one night) for a human being. In the context of eternity, a human life is akin to grass that sprouts new in the morning but has withered away by day's end. In a short time, people return to dust (Psalm 90:3–6).

Critical Observation

For the Israelites, a "watch in the night" (90:4) was about four hours. The night was divided into three watches: (1) sunset until 10:00 PM; (2) 10:00 PM until 2:00 AM; and (3) 2:00 AM until sunrise. In the New Testament, references to watches in the night may not conform to this schedule because the Romans scheduled four watches of three hours each.

The holiness of God quickly becomes evident to sinful humans, so the shortness of their lives is spent in struggle. When people sin and offend God, they may experience God's wrath. Some people spend the entire span of their lives feeling that God is angry at them, and they try to keep their secret sins hidden, to no avail (90:7–9).

The lifespan of seventy or eighty years referred to in verse 10 is respectable. A study of Egyptian mummies has suggested that an Egyptian from the same approximate time period had an average life expectancy of forty to fifty years. However, if a person's years are filled with nothing but trouble and sorrow, then long life is nothing to cherish (90:10).

Sin will always be offensive to God, and people will continue to sin. But rather than attempting to hide sin and provoke God's anger, Moses entreats God both for instruction that will lead to accumulated wisdom (90:11–12) and for divine compassion (90:13). If human life is but a day in the time frame of God, then let the morning begin with God's unfailing love that results in lasting joy and gladness (90:14).

Verse 15 may refer to a specific traumatic time for the nation. The exact nature of the trouble mentioned is not known, although under Moses' rule, Israel offended God numerous times and suffered affliction as a result. So Moses' prayer is for God to replace their trouble with gladness. The people may have been unfaithful to God, yet God has not failed to show His favor to Israel. As the people remain aware of His actions on their behalf and teach their children about the splendor of God, life will take on new meaning as God blesses their work (90:16–17).

PSALM 91

In the opening verse of Psalm 91, the psalmist uses two of the most laudable names for God: *Most High* and *Almighty*. In doing so, the psalmist begins a reasoned argument for why people can feel secure even during times of trouble. Rather than use first-person to speak only of his own experiences, he uses third-person to indicate that the comforting protection of God is available to anyone willing to seek God's guidance.

Many psalmists write of God as shelter, refuge, and fortress. In verse 2, the psalmist uses those same images but then goes into more specific examples of God's protective presence. In verses 3–6, enemies are presented symbolically: bird hunters who have set traps, widespread plague and pestilence, night terrors, and incoming arrows. These are not theoretical dangers; indeed, such threats have the capability of killing tens of thousands (91:7).

That is why taking refuge in God is so important; it's what makes the difference between security and susceptibility to danger. God covers His people like a mother bird covers her chicks with her feathers (91:4). While in His protection, righteous people observe the demise of the wicked (91:8). Verse 9 is crucial to the understanding of the promises in this psalm. No ultimate harm will befall someone *if* he or she takes refuge in the mighty God.

According to verses 11–12, the Lord commissions angels to care for His people. However, this is the Old Testament's sole mention of angels in a guardian capacity. Again, in verse 13, the psalmist uses well-known dangers (great lions and deadly serpents) to symbolize human attackers.

God loves people, and some choose to return His love, prompting God's rescue and protection. When they call on God, He answers. When trouble strikes, He delivers them. And as a result, such people tend to experience longer, more satisfying lives (91:14–16).

Demystifying Psalms

It should be noted that the rewards in this psalm are *generally* true, but not in every case. A relationship with God is no guarantee of a long life, although those who adhere to His instructions will avoid much of the pain and struggles others are likely to face. In fact, a portion of this psalm is quoted in the New Testament by Satan himself. When tempting Jesus, Satan tries to convince Him to act irresponsibly and then count on the promise of angels rushing to His assistance. Jesus wisely replies that people should not test God in such a manner (Matthew 4:5–7).

PSALM 92

After the return from exile, the worship ceremonies of the Israelites included a weekly schedule of psalms sung to accompany the morning offerings. Psalm 92 is the song used each Sabbath morning. This psalm continues with some themes found in Psalms 90 and 91.

Praising God is not merely an obligation but a privilege—and not a privilege to be taken for granted. In verses 1–3, the psalmist reminds the people that it is good to praise God and to make music for Him. The poetic expression of the writer can be confusing to modern ears. The point of verse 2 is not to detach the love of God from His faithfulness and to set aside different times to acknowledge each one. Rather, God's love and faithfulness are intertwined, and people should proclaim them all the time (morning and night).

The psalmist has insight into the eternity of God and is inspired by God's actions (92:4). Those who don't have that perspective, he realizes, mistakenly think they are succeeding in life when in actuality they are wasting a woefully short lifetime (92:5–8). According to verse 9, if they continue to live for themselves and become enemies of God, they will surely perish and be destined for failure.

Speaking from personal experience, the psalmist attests to the positive results of God's presence in his life. Verses 10–11 sound as if they may have been written by a king. The word *horn* is a metaphor for power. *Oil* symbolizes joy and blessing. The writer's different senses (sight, hearing) detect the faithfulness of God all around him.

While evildoers spring up like weeds and quickly disappear (92:7), righteous people are deeply rooted and productive like palm or cedar trees. They continue to prosper even in old age, still praising God as they have throughout their long and happy lives (92:12–15).

PSALM 93

In one sense, Israel was a monarchy like the surrounding nations, under the rule of a king. But in reality, it was a theocracy—a nation subject to the rule of God. Some of the psalms, such as this one, were written to acknowledge God's rule over not just the nation but the entire world. Such writings are frequently called *enthronement* psalms, and they include Psalms 47, 93, and 95–99.

Regardless of the various forms of human government, the truth of the matter is found in verse 1: The Lord reigns. Human kings can be identified by their clothing; God's royal clothing is His majesty. He needs no weapon other than His own strength.

His kingdom (the world) is unshakable. His right to rule is established from eternity—it has always existed and always will (93:1–2).

The pounding waves of the sea form one of many voices of nature that rise up to God. The sea offers no threat to Him, and He is mightier than the strongest forces that human beings can envision (93:3–4). (Sometimes seas symbolize the nations of the earth, which may also be the case in this instance.)

Critical Observation

The oceans were frequently perceived as turbulent, chaotic, uncontrollable expanses. The followers of Baal believed that their god had risen to power by overpowering the god of the sea.

Human kings can issue orders on a whim and misuse power, but God doesn't. The Lord has established statutes to be followed, but they have proven to be beneficial to His people and will endure. The holiness that sets God above all other beings is both attractive and enduring. His rule will never end (93:5).

PSALM 94

Few things in life are as disturbing as seeing people commit intentional offenses against others, knowing that their actions are wrong, and then laugh because they continue to get away with their cruel behavior. The writer of Psalm 94 had such an experience, and his psalm is a plea for God to take vengeance on unrepentant evildoers.

The people the psalmist describes are not just wicked—according to verse 3 they gloat about what they are doing. The psalmist desires God's justice in the matter, and he details several of their many offenses. They are proud and boastful. They oppress God's people. In the case of the weak and helpless, their oppression has even led to death (94:4–6). They are convinced God either doesn't see or doesn't care, which implies that they know full well that their actions are wrong and that they are getting away with it (94:7).

Yet the psalmist realizes that God *is* aware of the situation. The One who created eyes and ears can surely see and hear what is going on in the lives of His creation. More than that, God knows every thought that passes through the human mind, no matter how futile those thoughts may be. Through the psalm, the writer issues a warning to the wicked people, exhorting them to become wise and avoid the punishing discipline of God (94:8–11).

God's discipline can be a wonderful gift that turns people from potential trouble and allows them to share everything God has to offer. Continued wickedness becomes a pit that consumes those who never change their behavior, but righteous people need not fear judgment. God will not allow faithful people to suffer forever at the hands of evildoers (94:12–15).

As troubling as it is to witness the evil around him, the psalmist finds help from God, who provides consolation for his anxiety and helps him maintain spiritual footing. Without God's intervention, he feels that his enemies might have been too much of a problem, possibly forcing him to his grave (94:16–19).

Retribution against the wicked people has not yet taken place, but the psalmist is certain it will occur. God will have nothing to do with a corrupt throne—those who create misery rather than administer justice. They band together for even greater power, but they are still no match for God. He is the fortress, the rock, and the refuge of the psalmist and other righteous people. God will destroy the wicked—the only adequate payment for all they have done (94:20–23).

PSALM 95

Psalm 95 is another *enthronement* psalm, as is Psalm 93, which glorifies God as far superior to all other gods. The psalm is intended for a group setting when the Israelites gather to worship. Not surprisingly, it opens in verse 1 with praise to God, the rock of salvation. God is the reliable, immovable support of the Israelites. He can be counted on to deliver them. The appropriate response, then, is praise, thanksgiving, music, and song.

For anyone with a monotheistic upbringing, verses 3–6 may sound like obvious statements: God rules the heights and depths, lands and seas of the entire world. However, this concept would have been perplexing for many of the nations surrounding Israel, who had gods of the mountains, gods of the seas, and so forth. Those polytheistic beliefs had frequently infiltrated into the thinking of the Israelites. So to make things perfectly clear, the psalmist states in verse 3 that God is not only the great God but also a great King above all gods. He is the creator, sustainer, and owner of the entire earth.

And yet that almighty God has established a personal relationship with humanity. The Israelites are under His care and provision (95:7). The psalmist calls the people to bow before God and worship Him.

However, an outward show of worship is not enough. The people are also to recall and take warning from the stories of their ancestors who had defied God along the way from Egypt to the promised land. The account of what happened at Meribah ("quarreling") and Massah ("testing") is found in Exodus 17:1–7. Those people had seen sign after sign that God was with them and leading them, yet they continued to complain and resist. As a result, an entire generation of people missed out on the peace and security that God offered them.

Psalm 95 ends on that stark note with verses 8–11, yet it is an appropriate ending. If indeed the Lord is the great King above all gods, He is due both outward worship and praise that wells up from a grateful heart. Hard hearts and stubborn wills will have severe consequences.

PSALM 96

God's rule over the earth has been a recurring theme in the previous three psalms, and it will continue in Psalm 96 and several that follow. In verse 1, the psalmist calls the people to sing a new song to the Lord. The occasion for a new song may well have been a new action of God to benefit His people, perhaps a recent act of salvation (deliverance) as mentioned in verse 2. Whatever the occasion, the psalmist exhorts the people to sing praise to God and to make sure other nations hear of all His glorious works among His people (96:3).

But the people shouldn't need a specific occasion to initiate their praise to God. According to verse 4, He is worthy of praise simply because of who He is. Anyone who puts trust in any other god should truly fear Israel's God, because in reality, all other gods are mere idols. The Lord is the authentic Creator who exhibits splendor, majesty, strength, and glory (96:5–6). Therefore, the nations should give God the glory that He is due.

The thrice-repeated phrase "ascribe to the LORD" in verses 7–8 echoes the three commands to sing to the Lord in the psalm's opening verses. The fact that the Lord reigns is cause for deepest reverence and trembling as well as exultant rejoicing (96:9–13). God will indeed judge the earth, and those devoted to His righteousness and truth have nothing to fear. Nature itself—heavens, seas, fields, and trees—will celebrate the justice of God.

The psalmist is dealing with his present time, yet he is looking forward to the coming of the Lord (96:13). The cause for celebration will only increase when the Lord arrives to enforce His justice, righteousness, and truth.

PSALM 97

In verse 1, the acknowledgement that the Lord reigns is a common reminder of the writers throughout this section of Psalms (93:1; 96:10; 99:1). Yet the Israelites may not have absorbed the full significance of that truth. They knew that God reigned over *them*, but the psalmists acknowledge God's rule over all other nations as well—in this case, expressed as "the distant shores" (NIV).

The psalmist's description of God gives evidence of His unchallenged authority. With a foundation of righteousness and justice, the Lord is surrounded by thick, dark clouds. He is also encircled with fire that destroys those who attempt to oppose Him. His presence is accompanied by lightning that strikes fear in all who see it. All nations witness His glory. Even the mountains and heavens are said to yield to the power and righteousness of God (97:2–6).

Critical Observation

The clouds that covered God would have shielded any observers from seeing His full glory. Even Moses, who was as close to God as anyone, was told that no one could see God and live (Exodus 33:20). In addition, dark clouds are signs of an impending storm and may have symbolized approaching judgment.

Anyone who gets a clear picture of God will be shamed to have ever worshiped anyone or anything else. Throughout their history, the Israelites were susceptible to the idolatry practiced by neighboring nations. In verse 7 the psalmist points out, with no small bit of sarcasm, that if other gods really exist, they will submit to and worship the true God.

The judgment of God will be a joyous time for His people (Zion and Judah) who remain faithful (97:8). For those who hate evil, the Lord is a guardian. Judgment will fall on the wicked, effectively freeing those who have been victimized by evil actions. The result, then, should be rejoicing and praise from the righteous followers of the Lord (97:9–12).

PSALM 98

Psalm 98 and Psalm 96 are quite similar, as they both celebrate the work of the Lord. The psalms may have been written in response to a particular act of deliverance, although they were probably used by groups of worshipers in expectation of God's *ongoing* involvement with His people.

The acts of God attract attention. The Israelites acknowledge His deliverance and attribute it to His faithful and loyal love. As the other nations look on and observe how God protects and provides for His people, they can't question His power or His righteousness (98:1–3).

Consequently, all the earth should respond with jubilant singing accompanied by harps, trumpets, and shouts of joy (98:4–6). If a human king was present among them, a great celebration would be expected. How much more, then, should they celebrate the presence of the Lord, the one true King?

Critical Observation

In most cases when a psalm refers to a *trumpet*, the word indicates an instrument made from a ram's horn. But verse 6 refers to the trumpets used at the temple—the only such mention in the book of Psalms. The official trumpets were long and straight, and made of hammered silver. They were used to assemble the community and to celebrate special feasts and festivals (Numbers 10:1–10).

People and nature alike are to respond with joy to the work of God. According to verse 1, He has already done incredible things, but His work is not finished. The whole world can look forward to the day when He will come as judge, bringing righteousness and justice. In anticipation of that day, joy and singing are quite appropriate (98:7–9).

PSALM 99

Following the theme of the series of preceding psalms, the writer again makes the observation that the Lord reigns (99:1; see also 93:1; 96:10; 97:1). Such knowledge makes nations tremble and the earth shake.

Demystifying Psalms

The observation in verse 1 that God is enthroned between the cherubim means more than angels attend to Him. When God provided instructions for building the ark of the covenant, He designed a covering (lid) on which two angels were sculpted, one at each end facing each other (Exodus 25:17–22). God agreed to meet with the high priest between the two cherubim (Exodus 25:22). With God's primary dwelling perceived to be heaven, the ark eventually came to be known as His footstool (1 Chronicles 28:2; Psalm 99:5). And in time, references to God's footstool eventually broadened to include the temple (Psalm 132:7) and even the city of Jerusalem (Lamentations 2:1).

God's reputation among His own people (Zion) causes other nations to exalt Him. As His holiness becomes apparent, people respond in praise (99:2–3).

When human kings become mighty, they sometimes lose touch with reality, becoming self-absorbed and using their power for their own pleasures or advancement. But the mighty, heavenly King has an undying commitment to justice and equity. A review of all He has done for Israel (Jacob) reveals His persistent righteousness. Therefore the psalmist calls for the people to worship their holy God at the temple, His footstool (99:4–5).

Throughout Israel's history, God had appointed individuals to oversee spiritual leadership and to intercede with Him on behalf of the people. Three such outstanding and well-respected leaders were Moses, Aaron, and Samuel—all of whom served during challenging and difficult times (99:6).

All of Israel had witnessed God's leadership as they followed Him in a pillar of cloud, and He had provided them with clear instructions for how to live (99:7). But the Israelites had frequently disobeyed God's statutes and decrees. When they did, they found themselves in trouble and called out to God, who never failed to respond. In His justice, God punished them. Yet in His mercy, He always forgave them and does not hold past sins against them (99:8).

The psalmist acknowledges God's holiness with a repeated exhortation for the people to exalt God and worship Him (99:5, 9). The footstool of God mentioned in verse 5 is later defined in verse 9 as God's holy mountain. Wherever one encounters the holiness of God, it is a location appropriate for worship.

PSALM 100

Psalm 100 concludes a series of psalms (93–100) that were all written to inspire people to praise God as Lord over all the earth. In verse 1, God's rule is the inspiration to shout for joy—or as the King James Version translates it, to "make a joyful noise." In verse 2, the psalmist challenges all the earth to participate in glad worship and songs of joy.

People have good reason to praise God. To begin with, He *is* God—the one and only sovereign Lord—a fact to be acknowledged. In addition, He is the Creator. Created humanity should identify with their Creator (100:3). Beyond that, God initiated a loving relationship with His people. They are not just created beings left to fend for themselves; they remain in God's care as the sheep of His pasture. These are all observations that should motivate people to be joyful.

Joy should be shared with others in communal worship. In verse 4, the gates and courts are references to the temple. Worshipers have to go through one of several gates in order to get to the inner courts. All along the way to worship, then, people are to express praise and thanksgiving to God. Praise and thanksgiving are often linked, and for good reason. Praise is grateful acknowledgment of who God is, and thanksgiving is appreciation for what He has done.

God is perfect in every way. The psalmist concludes this song in verse 5 by citing three strong reasons to praise and thank Him: His goodness, His enduring love, and His continual faithfulness.

PSALM 101

Psalm 101 is attributed to David, the first one so designated since Psalm 86. It is a royal psalm in which the king commits to be faithful in both his personal life and his rule over his house.

The Lord is a God of love and justice, and for that reason David opens his psalm with praise. But almost immediately, in verse 2, he responds to the justice of God. He wants to devote himself, both privately and publicly, to model a blameless life. And once his heart is blameless, he is determined not to get involved with things that might corrupt it (101:3).

Critical Observation

The word frequently translated *vile* (101:3) has the same root in Hebrew as the name *Belial*—a name regularly connected with evil (2 Corinthians 6:15). In many cases the phrase "sons of Belial" is translated simply as "wicked men."

David also intends to stay away from people who are involved with evil. Those with perverse hearts have no place around someone with a blameless heart (101:2–4). As king, David can do something about such people. He has the power to silence slanderers and humble the proud, and in verse 5 he commits to do so. Liars and deceivers will be banned from his presence (101:7).

Verse 6 makes clear that there are other faithful people in the kingdom, and the king will seek them out as his ministers and peers. Yet he will continue daily to address the problem of wickedness in his nation. Most likely this will be done in his role as judge, hearing cases brought before him. He will rule in favor of upright and honest people, regularly and relentlessly silencing evildoers (101:8).

In essence, David wants to rule much as God does, by recognizing and rewarding faithful people while confronting the regrettable problem of widespread evil.

PSALM 102

The introduction to Psalm 102 is like no other. It neither identifies the author nor provides a clue as to its usage or historical setting. Instead, it simply announces the travail of an individual pouring out his sorrows to God. Although normally classified as an individual lament, some people think the psalm could have been used in group assemblies because the reason for the author's troubles appears to be a national catastrophe that would have affected others as well. And some speculate that because the state of the nation was so closely tied to the king, one of the kings of the exile might have penned this lament.

The psalmist wastes no time expressing his distress and raising a plea for God to listen and respond. Days are going by with no substance and no purpose (102:3), and he fears that his life will soon end having had little effect (102:23). Meanwhile, his condition is appalling. Physically, he hurts all over. He has no appetite and has lost weight. He groans aloud. Emotionally, it feels like his heart has withered (102:4–5).

In his agony, he suffers alone. In verse 6, he shares the solitude of an owl in a desert wasteland. At night he feels vulnerable and exposed, unable to sleep. During the day he hears the insults of his (Israel's) enemies, using him as an example of how far someone can fall. He sits in ashes as he mourns and cries continually. To make things worse, he is convinced that God has brought about his desperate situation. God had been angry, resulting in the psalmist's being cast aside. The writer feels near death, like withered grass or the shadows of evening (102:7–11).

It isn't until readers get to verses 13–16 that they discover the source of the psalmist's dismay: The holy city has been destroyed. But he has not given up on God. He reminds himself that God is eternal—enthroned forever and always worthy of receiving honor (102:12). In addition, God has always been, and will always be, compassionate. Therefore, the psalmist has confidence that God will again show favor to Jerusalem (Zion). The city will be rebuilt and renewed to reflect God's glory. Many of the same enemies that are currently taunting the psalmist (and Israel) will eventually have a change of heart. Nations and kings will be humbled and show respect to God.

Considering himself to be among the destitute, the psalmist anticipates God's response to his prayer. He is so sure of it, in fact, that he wants it on the record that God will indeed hear His people and release them from their woeful situation (102:17–20). If God is to rebuild Zion (102:16), it is only a matter of time until people will again assemble there to worship and praise Him (102:21–22).

Even though the psalmist has confident hope in soon witnessing God's intervention in Israel's situation, for the time being he will continue to suffer (102:23–24). He asks the eternal God to allow him to live a while longer. People come and go, and the heavens and the earth will pass away also. But God remains unchanged, and those who choose to live in His presence will continue to experience His faithfulness (102:25–28).

Demystifying Psalms

The psalmist yearns for a more lasting relationship with God. It is interesting, then, that the author of Hebrews quotes Psalm 102:25–27 in connection with Jesus as the eternal Creator (Hebrews 1:10–12). Those who place their trust in Christ can experience what the psalmist so strongly desires—life forevermore in relationship with a loving Lord.

PSALM 103

Psalm 102 ends with the writer asking God for help and steadfastly hoping for a better future. Psalm 103 celebrates the work of God as He forgives and acts on behalf of His people. The two psalms weren't necessarily written at the same time, but the people who compiled the Psalms might have placed them together since 103 appears to complement 102.

Psalm 103 is attributed to David, who opens the song with personal praise. ("O my soul," the phrase found in verses 1, 2, and 22, was used as someone today might say, "Note to self.") The verbs used in verses 3-5 to describe acts of God are revealing: David has been forgiven, healed, redeemed, crowned, satisfied, and renewed. He has experienced the love, compassion, blessing, and infusion of strength that only God can provide.

After acknowledging God's work in his personal life, David writes of God's work among the nation of Israel. The people had experienced their share of oppression, and God had been with them all along. God had revealed to Moses His expectations for worship and for living, and He had provided other helpful guidelines. The people had seen His mighty deeds beginning in Egypt as they grew into a nation, and ever since (103:6-7).

David realizes that the Lord is a forgiving God. The iniquities of the people had at times resulted in His wrath, but it had been clear that God is slow to become angry and shows mercy to His people (103:7-10). God's wrath tends to get people's attention when nothing else does, but the psalmist points out that God's anger is just as evident as His compassion, grace, and love.

God receives no satisfaction from punishing human sin. Verses 11-12 are often quoted as a reminder that God's anger is not lasting because of His forgiveness. He desires for people to forsake their iniquities and turn to Him. When they do, He gladly removes sin as far as the east is from the west (103:12). Nothing is greater than the love of God.

It is difficult to comprehend such a degree of love, and the closest people can come is to consider the love they feel for their children. God, as the great Creator, is well aware of the weaknesses and impermanence of humanity—His children. People quickly come and go, but the love of God remains everlasting with those who know His commands and obey them. And ideally, as people model reverence to God and obedience to His laws, their children will notice and will continue the righteousness they have been shown (103:13-18).

Regardless of human response to the Lord, God's rule is total and unquestionable. He is praised and obeyed by the mighty angels of heaven. Creation itself speaks its praise. How much more, then, should people respond to the love and mercy of such a mighty God (103:20-22)?

PSALM 104

The greatness of God described in Psalm 103 is also affirmed in Psalm 104, although this psalm has no superscription to identify the author, and there is no reason to presume the same person wrote both. The previous psalm focuses more on God's relationship with humanity, while this one dwells on the evidence of His sovereignty in the realm of creation. It is difficult not to recall the creation story of Genesis 1 while reading through Psalm 104.

Beginning with a description of God Himself, the psalmist writes in verses 1-2 of the Lord's clothing, which includes splendor, majesty, and light. Then moving right away to the *works* of God, the writer envisions the creation of the heavens as if God were setting up a tent. It's as if heaven is an upstairs level of earth where God can dwell, built on beams that have been laid across the oceans as a foundation. God moves as if in a chariot borne on the winds (104:2-4). Wind and fire are often included in descriptions of God's presence.

In conjunction with creating the heavens, God established the earth (104:5). He separated the land from the waters, and the waters that had covered mountains receded (104:6–9). With the abundance of water throughout the lands, life of all kinds was sustained; springs in the ravines watered wild donkeys and other field animals, and trees were nourished, allowing birds to nest and sing beside the streams (104:10–13).

Grass and plants sprang up as well, providing food. God's people received not just basic nourishments of bread and oil but also wine. Whether in the mountain heights, the pine and cedar forests, or the rocky crags, God's creation is evident. He provides for all His creation wherever they are (104:14–18).

God also designed the cycles of day and night, and the rotating seasons. The lions and animals seek their food from God just as people do. Verses 19–23 are the psalmist's portrayal of nocturnal beasts hunting during the night and retiring at dawn, just as human beings are setting out for their day's work.

The assumption must be made that God has created certain creatures that human beings don't even know about. The earth is full of His creatures, and the sea contains too many creatures to count. Even the animals that are large and intimidating to people are small to God. The fearful leviathan, for example, is described as playing in the sea (104:24–26).

Critical Observation

The leviathan was a symbol of power in Canaan, although exactly what it was is uncertain. Its connection with the sea allows for numerous possibilities. In some cases the word seems synonymous with crocodiles. But in local mythology, the leviathan was represented by many heads, suggesting that it was more imposing than any known animal. Sperm whales have been sighted in the Mediterranean, fueling speculation of that possibility.

God's provision sustains the entire animal kingdom. His presence comforts; His absence terrifies. He supplies life and determines life spans, when it is time to return to the dust. And as impressive as His creation is, God is far greater (104:27–32).

Those who fail to connect with God in light of all He has done have no place in His world, and the psalmist prays that they will simply vanish from earth. He, on the other hand, commits to sing praise as long as he lives, rejoicing in all that God has done and attempting to please Him with worship (104:33–35).

PSALM 105

In Psalm 105 the writer praises God through a review of Israel's history, spanning the call of Abraham to the arrival of the Israelites in the promised land. No author is designated, although the first fifteen verses duplicate the content of 1 Chronicles 16:8–22, a passage that is associated with both David and Asaph.

In the opening verses, the psalmist challenges people to get involved with their relationships with God: to give thanks, call on God's name, tell other nations what He has done, sing, offer praise, recall His actions, take joy in Him, and continually turn to Him for strength and assurance (105:1-4).

The Lord is a God of wonders, miracles, and judgments. To prove his point, the psalmist recalls a series of stories from Israel's past. Addressing the people as both descendants of Abraham and sons of Jacob, he begins a concise, but systematic, review (105:5-6).

God hasn't simply interacted with Abraham for a bit; He has established an eternal covenant with the patriarch. God's promises to Abraham are passed on, in turn, to Isaac, Jacob (Israel), and Joseph. They all look ahead to the fulfillment of the promise of the land they are to inherit (105:8-11).

Verses 12-22 describe the period when Israel was only a family, prior to becoming a nation. According to verse 12, they were few in number, but God still watched over them. In the Genesis account of the story of Joseph (Genesis 37), it appears that Joseph's brothers had been in control when they sold their little brother into slavery. In retrospect, as the psalmist points out in verses 16-17, it became clear that God was sending Joseph ahead of the rest of the family to Egypt. What began as one person's imprisonment and anticipated life sentence turns out to be God's plan to honor His promise to Abraham to build a nation of his descendants.

Verses 23-36 review Israel's time in Egypt, during which a family of around seventy grew into a nation so sizable that it created military concerns for the Egyptian Empire. God's people became too numerous for their foes (Psalm 105:24). Four hundred years after Joseph, God's chosen leaders were Moses and Aaron (105:26). But it was the power of God displayed through the plagues that eventually secured the release of His people.

Then came the Exodus, described in verses 37-41. In verse 37, the silver and gold that Israel possessed was the result of gifts the Egyptians gave the people to induce them to hurry and leave, although God was behind the generous giving of Egypt (Exodus 12:33-36). All during Israel's time in the wilderness, God provided food, water, and a clear sign of His presence through a cloud and fire (Psalm 105:39).

This particular review highlights only the positive aspects of the journey; the psalmist mentions nothing of Israel's rebellion. His point is to show how God had followed through with what He promised Abraham. Israel inherited a wonderful land that other nations had worked hard to cultivate. Ideally, the Israelites should then have worshiped and obeyed God in the new land. It didn't turn out that way, but perhaps the people who used Psalm 105 in their worship would get the point and not make the same mistakes.

PSALM 106

Psalm 105 is a description of what God had done for His people throughout their history. As such, it is an overwhelmingly optimistic song. In contrast, Psalm 106 deals with many of the same events but looks at the actions and reactions of the people. Consequently, it is not nearly as positive.

Both psalms open with a command to give thanks to God, and the first five verses of Psalm 106 recall the faithfulness of God and the need to respond to His mighty acts. But verse 6 begins a confession of sin that continues throughout the psalm. God remained faithful to His people throughout their history, but they repeatedly disobey and rebel.

Verses 6–13 describe the Red Sea experience. The people panicked and wanted to turn back, but God miraculously led them through the sea and then drowned the Egyptian army behind them. In response they believed God and praised Him, but they quickly forgot what He had done for them (106:13).

The attitude of the Israelites went from bad to worse as they moved on into the wilderness (106:14–33). They tested God and questioned the leadership of Moses and Aaron. When Moses was absent for a few days, they had Aaron create a golden calf. When they finally got to the promised land, they lacked the faith to enter. They rebelled against God in order to follow the gods of other nations. Their grumbling was so persistent and unrelenting that they provoked foolish words from Moses that kept him from entering the promised land. In each of those instances, God responded with a disciplinary action, but to no lasting effect. The people felt sorry for a little while, but in a short matter of time they reverted to their whining and griping.

Demystifying Psalms

Psalm 106 lists a number of inglorious actions of the Israelites and the consequences they experienced because of their sin. Some of the original stories may be unfamiliar. If so, they are found in the passages listed below.

Crossing the Red Sea	Psalm 106:7–13	Exodus 13:17–14:31
Demands for food	Psalm 106:14–15	Numbers 11:4–34
Envy of Moses and Aaron	Psalm 106:16–18	Numbers 16
The golden calf	Psalm 106:19–23	Exodus 32
Despising the promised land	Psalm 106:24–27	Numbers 13–14
Idolatry, adultery, and Phinehas	Psalm 106:28–31	Numbers 25
Waters of Meribah/Moses' rash words	Psalm 106:32–33	Numbers 20:2–13

The people finally mustered enough faith to enter the promised land, but soon thereafter they again began to rebel against God. Verses 34–46 tell the sad story. They did not evict the inhabitants as God had instructed. Instead, they mingled with the Canaanites and soon began to worship their various gods, which sometimes included atrocious acts (106:37–38).

In response, God allowed Israel to be overpowered again and again, but the people would not make a permanent commitment to Him. Each time they cried out, He lovingly forgave them and sent help. But their faith never lasted long (106:40–46).

Apparently Israel has found itself in a similar situation in the present time because the psalmist asks God to "gather us back from among the nations" (106:47 NLT). After seeing their temple and the city of Jerusalem destroyed, Israel's exile in Babylon was certainly pitiable.

Verse 48 is an added doxology to conclude Book IV in the biblical book of Psalms. Each of the five books ends with such a note of praise.

Take It Home

Several of the psalms in this section describe the perfections and mighty acts of God. Sometimes such a perspective of God inspires confession and repentance. Other times the psalmist's intent is purely praise and thanksgiving. Do you acknowledge the good gifts of God on a regular basis, or do you tend to wait until you're in a situation when you miss them and only then begin to think about better times? What are some areas in your own life that might benefit from your intent concentration on who God is and what He has done?

PSALMS: BOOK V

PSALMS 107–134

Setting Up the Section

This section begins the last of the five books contained within the biblical book of Psalms. It is likely the final book compiled chronologically, so along with some additional psalms of David there are other songs that contain references to events later in Israel's history. This first half of the final book contains the shortest psalm, the longest psalm, and the series of fifteen psalms known as the Songs of Ascents.

PSALM 107

As Psalm 107 opens, verses 1–3 are a call to worship. The reference in verse 3 to people gathering suggests that the psalm was written during or after the exile. If so, the foe in verse 2 would have been the Assyrians and Babylonians.

The next section, verses 4–32, dwells on God's salvation (deliverance) of His people. Again and again, the psalmist describes people who find themselves in desperate situations. Then they cry out to God and He delivers them (107:6, 13, 19, 28). In response, the psalmist encourages the people to give thanks to the Lord, whose love is repeatedly described as unfailing (107:8, 15, 21, 31).

The situations described by the psalmist are varied: people wandering in desert wastelands needing food and water (107:4–5), shackled prisoners who have rebelled against God and find themselves subjected to hard labor (107:10–12), some who have rebelled and suffered physical near-death experiences as a result (107:17–18), and sailors who face frightening and turbulent storms at sea, battling waves the size of mountains (107:23–27). In each case, God is gracious and merciful as He forgives and delivers those who ask.

Clearly, these four cases are representative of God's ability and willingness to help anyone in any situation. In return, people should give much consideration to God's unfailing love and offer Him their thanks.

In addition to the regular and willing deliverance of God that should be received with thanksgiving, the closing section of Psalm 107 provides reasons to offer praise to the Lord. In God's sovereignty, He has power to change human situations. Rivers dry up and become deserts, or deserts are suddenly infused with water and become springs that sustain vineyards and human civilization (107:33–38).

Such examples are more than theoretical considerations for the Israelites who have experienced droughts—usually following times when they had forgotten the Lord. God had always forgiven them and restored life to their land. And yet the people eventually go too far in their rejection of God. He allows them to "wander in a trackless waste" (107:40 NIV). Many die, and the rest suffer (107:39). But again, God's discipline is temporary. He once more delivers His people, increasing the families of the upright and silencing the wicked. The psalmist's concluding challenge in verse 43 is for people to exhibit wisdom and give much thought to the tremendous love of God.

PSALM 108

If we think of the psalms as songs, then Psalm 108 is a medley of Psalms 57 and 60. Verses 1–5 of Psalm 108 echo Psalm 57:7–11. Verses 6–13 are a repetition of Psalm 60:5–12. The two previous psalms are credited to David, as is Psalm 108. Combined as they are here, the psalm is a song of victory to celebrate God's incomparable love and faithfulness as displayed in His deliverance of Israel from their enemies.

The first portion of the psalm, verses 1–5, expresses praise to God. David rejoices in having a steadfast heart, attributed to God's power and glory. His praise is followed by a prayer for continued triumph over the nation's enemies (108:6–13). God is sovereign over both Israel (Shechem, Succoth, Gilead, Manasseh, Ephraim, and Judah) and the enemies of Israel (Moab, Edom, and Philistia). Realizing that human power is worthless, David gives all credit to God (108:12–13).

PSALM 109

Attributed to David, Psalm 109 is sometimes placed in the category of *imprecatory* psalms (those that call for harm to come to the enemies of God and His people). Not all scholars agree, however, that such a category should exist. Several psalms contain sections of imprecations yet still are categorized as praise, lament, or so forth.

David wastes no time laying out his case before God. His enemies have been busy speaking lies and deceit, spouting hatred toward him. David has attempted to initiate friendship, but to no avail. He has given his opponents no cause to attack him, yet they do. Throughout it all, he continues to be a man of prayer (109:1–5).

The plural *men* and references to *they* in verses 1–5 are replaced in verses 6–19 with the singular *he*. Some scholars feel that verses 6–19 are the psalmist's recounting of his enemies' words toward him. More probably, David switches to singular because his many enemies have a ringleader who incites them, and it is that individual who warrants the most attention. Or perhaps criticism of David is so widespread that addressing one person effectively speaks to *all* his critics.

Demystifying Psalms

Psalm 109:6 can be interpreted different ways. The NIV translates the Hebrew as: "Appoint an evil man to oppose him; let an accuser stand at his right hand." But another equally valid translation is: "Appoint the evil one to oppose him; let Satan stand at his right hand." David clearly desires for his most outspoken critic to be confronted by a powerful accuser of his own.

David wishes the worst on the person who has caused him so much suffering and grief, and he uses strong words to express his feelings (109:7–15). But David also includes why he is so intent on seeing this person suffer. He explains his reasoning in verses 16–20. This person is an evil man who takes advantage of the weak and helpless. He never blesses people but is always quick to curse. Cursing others is his nature—not just an outer shell like clothing but steeped into his flesh and bones. So David prays that the man's heartless mentality be strapped around him forever, like a belt.

In contrast, David pours out his own condition to God. He is poor, needy, and heartsick. He has fasted until he became physically weak, and he is still an object of ridicule to his many accusers (109:21–25). Yet he continues to count on God to deliver him and leave his enemies in shame and disgrace. God will help the needy, and David is determined to continue to praise and honor Him (109:26–31).

This psalm, specifically verse 8, is cited in Acts 1:20 when the disciples choose a replacement for Judas.

PSALM 110

The third of a short series of Davidic psalms, Psalm 110 opens with a statement that immediately raises questions. The Lord God is the speaker, so who then does David have in mind as "*my* Lord" in verse 1? Clues in the rest of the psalm reveal that the figure is both king and priest, so that narrows the options.

Some people try to assign a late date to the psalm to match its contents with Jewish life during the Maccabean era, when the nation's priests sometimes held political power as well. However, Jesus acknowledges David as the author, confirming a much earlier date, and He also applies the psalm to Himself in Matthew 22:41–45. This psalm is quoted several times in the New Testament as proof that Jesus is the Messiah (Mark 12:35–37; Acts 2:34–35; Hebrews 1:13; 5:6; 7:17, 21).

Critical Observation

Some people question the messianic classification of this psalm. They argue that if David had received a revelation about Jesus, then his prophetic insight in this psalm predates other similar revelations of the prophets. Some prefer to believe that David possibly wrote the psalm to commemorate Solomon's coronation. By referring to his son as "my Lord," David would have acknowledged the transfer of power. Later generations would have applied the messianic references.

After a battle, the losing king would sometimes bow before the victor, and the winning king would ceremonially place his foot on the other's neck. The image in verse 1 of making an enemy one's footstool is probably derived from this ancient custom.

The Lord God invites this other lord to sit at His right hand (a position of great honor), and He promises to give him total victory over his enemies (110:1). In verse 2, extending the scepter is a way of promising an ever-increasing kingdom. The figure being addressed will have many supporters—willing volunteers to go with him into battle. Their comparison to dawn and dew in verse 3 implies freshness, youth, strength, and significant numbers.

More than a mighty warrior, this lord is also a priest in the order of Melchizedek (110:4). From the time of the Exodus onward, priests had to come from the tribe of Levi. But Melchizedek predates the Mosaic Law. He was the king/priest to whom Abraham paid tribute after a battle (Genesis 14:17–20). The Messiah will be both priest and king, holding a position higher than those who serve in the Aaronic priesthood. His priesthood will be forever (Psalm 110:4).

David, a warrior, describes God's Messiah in military terms. He will overcome all opposition and rule supreme, judging the nations. The reference to drinking from a brook in verse 7 suggests that he will be refreshed and will not fade during the rigorous demands of battle. Lifting up his head indicates victory and power.

PSALM 111

Scholars have long linked Psalms 111 and 112. Both are in the format of an acrostic poem, and the content is quite similar. It is possible that the same person wrote both psalms, probably after the exile. The two psalms are written in praise to God and with the intent of imparting wisdom among the worshiping community.

Verses 1–3 of Psalm 111 set the tone for extolling God. The setting is public, as verse 1 indicates. The reasons for praising God are many: His great works, His glorious and majestic deeds, and His enduring righteousness (111:2–3).

After these generalities, the psalmist gets more specific in verses 4–9. The Lord is a God of grace and compassion. He initiates a covenant with His people. He provides them with food, and He gives them victory over their enemies. He is powerful, faithful, and trustworthy. He has redeemed them. All such actions reflect the love of a God who is both holy and awesome (111:9). Popular usage may have diminished the intended definition of the word *awesome*. The meaning here is "awe-inspiring." When someone begins to comprehend the holiness of God, the result is a deep, fearful reverence.

Fear and awe are good things in this case, as the psalmist points out in verse 10. Such a response to God is wise. A reverential, submissive attitude initiates a better understanding of God and prompts praise from those who know Him.

PSALM 112

Continuing the theme of the previous song, Psalm 112 picks up where Psalm 111 leaves off. Those who fear God discover the joy of following Him, and therefore are eager to praise Him (112:1). The previous psalm focuses more on the work of God among His people, while this one enumerates some of the blessings that might be anticipated by those who acknowledge the sovereignty and holiness of God.

To begin with, a righteous upbringing is beneficial to children, helping them to thrive. And in the thinking of the time, the way in which an upright person would be remembered forever was through his line of descendants (112:6). Prosperity is also tied into righteousness. Verse 3 promises wealth and riches in the homes of godly people.

Everyone experiences dark times, but the darkness doesn't last for those who remain gracious and compassionate (112:4). Generosity and justice certainly benefit those who receive such gifts, but those who administer them are rewarded as well (112:5). God provides such people with stability and security. When bad news comes, they need not fear. Enemies may attack, but they will not prevail. As righteous people give to the poor to supply what they don't have, God supplies those righteous people with honor and power (symbolized by the horn in verse 9).

The psalmist ends this otherwise positive and uplifting psalm with a caveat for those who do not pursue righteousness. Wicked people will witness God's goodness to others and be vexed. Their longings will remain unfulfilled. Rather than praising God, they will grind their teeth and waste away (112:10).

PSALM 113

The power, glory, and majesty of God are not reserved for the segment of humanity that considers itself powerful, glorious, and majestic. Just the opposite. Psalm 113 is a reminder of both the greatness of God and His love for those who have nothing to offer Him except their praise.

Indeed, the first two verses of the psalm open with repeated calls to praise the Lord. Praise is due God at all times and at all places (113:2–3). The reason God deserves the praise of humanity is because no one, no thing, no power is greater. Israel knew of many nations and many gods, but God was exalted over them all (113:4). The events of earth may appear overwhelming or traumatic to human beings, but God has to step down from His throne on high to see what is taking place.

When the Lord sees poor and needy people among the dust and ashes, He lifts them up. Israel's history contains no shortage of stories of barren women—a condition of utter humiliation and subsequent sorrow in their culture—who eventually conceive and rejoice at the powerful intervention of God. Abraham's wife, Sarah, is perhaps the best-known case in point (Genesis 18:9-15; 21:1-7). Other familiar examples include Rebekah (Genesis 25:21-22), Rachel (Genesis 30:1, 22-24), and Hannah (1 Samuel 1:9-20). These are all examples of barren women who, in the psalmist's words in Psalm 113:9, settle into homes and become happy mothers of children.

In contrast with the high enthroned and mighty God, *all* humanity is poor, needy, and barren. So when people begin to comprehend that the great God of the universe has chosen to be actively involved in their lives, they should heed the psalmist's repeated exhortation to praise the Lord.

PSALM 114

The story of the Exodus was told and retold in Jewish songs and ceremonies. Numerous psalms refer to God's miraculous deliverance and protection of His people during that time. But Psalm 114 is one of the most unique, stylized portrayals on record of Israel's journey from Egypt to the promised land.

The psalmist is apparently reviewing Israel's past from a point beyond the reign of Solomon. His distinction between Judah and Israel in verse 2 suggests that he is writing during the period of the divided kingdom. But when the people first came out of Egypt, they were still the house of Jacob (114:1).

God performed many miracles during the Exodus. Only a few are mentioned in this short psalm, but they are creatively portrayed. In verse 3, two bodies of water are described as seeing God and fleeing before Him. The crossing of the Red Sea (Exodus 13:17-14:31) is well-known. Less familiar, but equally miraculous, is the sudden drying up of the Jordan River at flood stage while the people cross into the promised land (Joshua 3). In addition, God's presence was frequently associated with earthquakes—times when the mountains skipped like rams (Psalm 114:4).

It is as if the psalmist is interviewing various elements of creation to see what they think about the miracles God had performed (114:5-6). If rivers, seas, and mountains respond to the work of God, the implication is that people should notice and acknowledge the mighty deeds of the Lord as well. Comprehension of God's involvement among humanity results in reverential trembling (114:7).

Verse 8 concludes the psalm with one final miracle of God during the Exodus. A hard rock stood in the midst of an arid wilderness, and yet God turned that solid rock into flowing streams of water. With a mere sampling of the mighty works God had performed for His people, the psalmist makes his point and thus ends his song.

PSALM 115

Idolatry was a recurring temptation for the Israelites. They were surrounded by other nations with their various gods. And many times when some disaster or difficulty befell Israel, those nations would question the presence of Israel's God (115:2).

In the opening verse, the psalmist makes it clear that God deserves glory because of His love and faithfulness. He is an unseen God who rules from heaven, yet He is in complete control (115:3). This would have been a foreign concept to the polytheistic nations around Israel.

Critical Observation

The idols of this time period and location were usually carved of wood and then overlaid with thin sheets of gold or silver. They have been discovered in assorted shapes and sizes, including some that were life-sized. The carvings weren't believed to be actual gods, but the foreign deities were thought to use the idols to make known their desires. Some cultures took great care of their idols, going to the point of dressing and washing them each day, and even "feeding" them with sacrifices of food.

Almost all the surrounding nations worshiped visual, tactile idols that reminded them of their gods. They made them as lifelike as possible. The psalmist's description in verses 5–7 is detailed, with mention of idols with mouths, eyes, ears, noses, hands, feet, and throats. Yet as he makes clear in verse 4, the idols are carved by humans—totally inanimate and impotent.

On a more poignant note, the psalmist observes in verse 8 that those who put their trust in idols become like those idols—helpless and ineffective. In contrast, those who trust in Israel's powerful God are empowered, and those who put their faith in the compassionate God receive help (115:9–11).

Israel's God is unseen, but He is living and active. He has proven to be ever present with His people and will continue to respond to their needs (115:12–13). The psalmist includes a prayer that God will bless both those who are listening and their families. The maker of heaven and earth is the only One qualified to help them (115:14–15).

God is not only the Creator of heaven but also its owner. In His grace, He created the earth and then provided it as a dwelling for humanity. The dead no longer have voices with which to express appreciation, so in verses 16–18 the psalmist challenges people to offer their praise while they are able.

PSALM 116

There are many reasons to love God. The reason cited in this case is God's protection during a difficult time in the psalmist's life. The writer cried out for the mercy of God, and the Lord responded (116:1).

Whenever someone discovers that God answers, the wise and reasonable response is to continue to call on Him, as the psalmist commits to do in verse 2. He does not fully explain his situation, but it sounds quite severe. Overcome by problems made worse by emotional turmoil, he is afraid of dying (116:3). Yet it is at that low point of his life that he discovers God's grace, righteousness, and compassion. He doesn't attempt to feign strength or pretend that everything is all right. He depends on God to deliver him (116:4–6).

He has made a good choice. Who but God could have changed the psalmist's tears, stumbling, and nearness to death into a walk in the land of the living (116:8–9)? Apparently everyone else had lacked the faith that God would deliver him, creating great dismay. But the psalmist had believed, and God had restored him to health and safety (116:10–11).

Consequently, the psalmist is eager to repay the Lord for His goodness. He has been delivered, so he will worship God publicly and intently (116:12–14). The cup of salvation mentioned in verse 13 may have been a drink offering (Numbers 28:7, 10, 14, 31) to accompany the thank offering he later cites in verse 17. Even though he has been spared from death this time, he knows that God is well aware of the deaths of His faithful followers (116:15–16). After his recovery, the psalmist intends to gladly continue to fulfill his vows to God, setting a good example for everyone.

PSALM 117

There isn't much to say about Psalm 117, simply because the psalmist doesn't write much. At only two verses, it is both the shortest psalm and the shortest chapter in scripture.

The first verse exhorts everyone to praise the Lord—not only all peoples but also all nations. This psalm is another reminder that God's great love extends far beyond the Jewish states of Israel and Judah. The apostle Paul quotes this verse among a list of scripture references to make that very point in Romans 15:11.

In verse 2 the psalmist associates God's great love with His enduring faithfulness, which is a common pairing in the psalms. And he concludes with the phrase so frequently repeated in this section of Psalms: Praise the Lord (or Hallelujah).

PSALM 118

Psalm 118 is one of the more celebratory songs in the entire collection of Psalms, but the *reason* for the celebration is debated. It may be written by one of Israel's kings who rejoiced because God's people prevailed after a particularly difficult battle. Or the expression of thankful celebration may have been written after the Israelites returned from exile, with the psalm used to commemorate rebuilding the walls and temple at Jerusalem.

Critical Observation

Jewish traditions evolved to use particular psalms for specific festivals and events. Based on the knowledge of such traditions, it is possible that the hymn Jesus and His disciples sing as they leave the Last Supper for Gethsemane (Matthew 26:30) is Psalm 118.

The opening in verse 1 is a popular one in Psalms (106:1; 107:1), and verses 1–4 may have been written in a call-and-response format to get all the worshipers involved. Then, beginning with verse 5, the psalmist goes into a specific account of his situation. The point of view may have been that of the king at the time or one of the priests or Levites leading the worship. Regardless of the original author, the content of the psalm is applicable for worshipers of all generations.

In verses 5–7, the author describes a commonly expressed problem: being surrounded by enemies and experiencing anguish. But he had cried out to God and the Lord had freed him. He is victorious and no longer afraid, but he has not had a pleasant experience. His enemies have been numerous and they swarm like bees around him (118:10–12). But calling on the name of the Lord results in a quick response. Therefore, as the psalmist makes clear in verses 8–9, seeking refuge in God is far preferable to placing one's trust in people—even princes who have soldiers and wealth at their disposal.

God is never at a loss for strength. The symbol of His power, His right hand, is always there for support (118:15–16). It's never too late to call on Him for help. The psalmist feels as if he is about to fall (118:13), yet God delivers him. As a result, shouts of rejoicing are heard throughout the land (118:14–15).

In verse 18, the psalmist interprets his difficult times as God's chastening, yet he is thrilled to be alive and still able to testify to God's work in his life. God has delivered him, so he will go to the temple and give thanks (118:19–21).

Verse 22 may sound familiar because Jesus will later interpret it as a reference to Himself (Matthew 21:42). The original rejected stone, however, is probably the king of the time, looked down on by other leaders who thought themselves more powerful, yet who ultimately triumphed over them. Another possibility is that the stone is the nation of Israel, small and seemingly insignificant, yet continuing to persevere with the love and help of God.

Verse 24 is another frequently quoted verse, usually used to encourage rejoicing on any given day. Originally, however, it referred to a specific day of deliverance and victory.

The next section contains a prayer for God's continued protection (118:25), the recognition of those who value the name of the Lord (118:26), a public expression of the difference God's presence makes in life (118:27), and a commitment to exalt and thank God (118:28). When Jesus rides into Jerusalem on Palm Sunday, the crowds quote from verses 25–26, and they meet Him with boughs in hand (118:27; Mark 11:8–11).

Psalm 118 ends in verse 29 as it began in verse 1, with a call to give thanks to God for His goodness and everlasting love.

PSALM 119

Psalm 119 is the longest of the psalms (by far), and it is also a distinctive work of art. It stands out from other psalms in that it focuses primarily on the Word of God, rather than the works of God or the character of God. The psalmist constructs his observations as an acrostic poem, comprised of twenty-two stanzas of eight verses each. Other psalms are also written as acrostics (Psalms 111 and 112). But in this case, each of the first eight verses begins with the first Hebrew letter, the next eight verses start with the second Hebrew letter, and so on through the alphabet.

Almost every one of the 176 verses of Psalm 119 contains a reference to the Word of God. The psalmist uses eight different Hebrew terms for variety. The terms are used approximately the same number of times throughout the psalm (ranging from nineteen times to twenty-five times apiece). English translations vary, however, and the assortment of interpreted words include *word, law, decree, command(ment), statute, precept, promise, saying, judgment, testimony, way, path,* and perhaps others.

Verses 1–3 serve as an introduction: Those who keep God's laws are blessed. The psalmist immediately expresses a desire to be in that category of people (119:4–8). He wants a pure life. With God's Word as his internal guide, he can then recount God's laws to others. God's statutes are a source of joy for him as well as the subject of his meditations (119:9–16).

The psalmist is well aware of the influence of evil people. He mentions them several times in this psalm, first in verse 21. Rather than allowing their influence to affect him, he prays for God's enlightenment and protection (119:17–24). Even though he is weary with sorrow (119:25, 28), he chooses to cling to God's promises and continue to obey God's Word (119:25–32).

His understanding of God's Word results in delight. Ignorance or disobedience, on the other hand, leads to selfish gain, worthless pursuits, and disgrace (119:33–40). The laws of God also provide great confidence. The psalmist is prepared to stand before kings to declare the truth God has revealed to him (119:41–48).

Those who steadfastly follow God are subject to mocking, and perhaps even suffering at the hands of others. Yet the psalmist's comfort remains in God's laws. He feels indignation toward his tormentors, yet at night he focuses his thoughts on God and regains perspective on his life (119:49–64).

The psalmist writes from experience. He had previously gone astray and knew what it was like to be out of favor with God. It had ultimately become a positive experience for him, because after he returned to the Lord he realized what was really important. Afterward he wouldn't have traded his commitment to God's laws for silver and gold (119:65–72). He also acknowledges God as his Creator and wants to spend his life telling others about the Lord, offering them truth and hope (119:73–80).

Still, he admits to experiencing periods when he didn't feel the comfort and presence of God. His spiritual condition began to get dry and brittle like "a wineskin in the smoke" (119:83 NIV). But during such times he remained patient and persevering, faithfully looking and longing for the promises of God to return (119:81–88).

In spite of persistent attempts by his enemies to destroy him (119:95), the psalmist has nothing but good things to say about God's faithfulness. God had established the world, and He continues to sustain it by His Word. God's laws not only give the writer hope but also make him wiser than his opponents (119:98). With such wisdom, he is able to stay away from paths of evil (119:89–104).

The world can be a dark and imposing place, but according to verse 105 (a favorite of many people), God's Word provides a lamp to one's feet and a light to one's path. Thanks to God's precepts, the psalmist has so far evaded the traps that have been set for him. His determined commitment to the light of God's Word allows him to rebuke the evildoers who keep trying to trip him up (119:105–120).

Sometimes people who devote much time and effort to studying scripture develop a kind of spiritual arrogance, but that is not the case for the psalmist. He realizes he will always have more to learn about God, and he remains a humble servant to God (119:122, 124–125). He detests the arrogance of the evildoers, and he will have nothing to do with that attitude, leaving it to God to deal with the problem (119:121–128). In fact, he is so captivated by the Word of God that he weeps when he sees others disobey it (119:129–136).

The psalmist isn't committing to some set of randomly assembled rules. The Lord is a righteous God, and the laws He provides reflect His righteousness (119:137–138). According to verse 140, the writer has thoroughly tested God's promises and has seen them work, even in the worst of circumstances. Not only are they functional and effective—they are a delight (119:143–144). But the psalmist has no run-of-the-mill commitment. In seeking God's truth, he calls out with all his heart (119:145). He is up before dawn and awake through the night to meditate on God's promises. Wicked people are nearby, but as long as God is nearer with His commands, the psalmist knows he will persevere (119:145–152).

Appealing to God for deliverance, the psalmist continues to profess his great love for God's law. He realizes that the wicked people who pursue him have no hope for deliverance, which gives him a greater appreciation for God's compassion toward him (119:153–160). He is being persecuted by powerful people who have no cause to do so, yet what really gets to him is the power of God's Word. Each new insight is like discovering valuable treasure (119:161–162). The reference to "seven times a day" in verse 164 is a way of saying "all the time," because seven is a number that indicates completeness or perfection. His focus on God provides a sense of peace even in trying times (119:165–168).

The psalm's closing stanza, verses 169–176, looks to the future. The psalmist intends to keep crying out to God, asking for help, praising Him, and singing. He wants God to continue providing understanding, deliverance, teaching, help, and delight. In return for continued life, he will offer continued praise. And yet after all the writer has said about his devotion to God, he concludes with a confession that he has strayed (119:176). In the context of everything else he has written, this is probably not so much an admission of falling away as an expression of desire to be closer to his heavenly Shepherd.

Demystifying Psalms

Psalms 120–134 are identified as Songs of Degrees, or Songs of Ascents, a title that is not totally clear. The Jewish Mishna associates the fifteen psalms with the fifteen steps that led to the temple, where the Levites who led the music would sing the songs. More common is the belief that this group of songs was sung by people making pilgrimages to Jerusalem. Three such journeys for community-wide religious festivals were expected each year (Deuteronomy 16:16–17). (The pilgrims had to ascend to the high altitude of their capital city.) The psalms were likely not written for such a purpose but were later grouped together for special use. This seems clear from the fact that four are attributed to David and one to Solomon, while the remaining ten are anonymous.

PSALM 120

The first of the Songs of Ascents isn't one of the more positive ones. The unnamed psalmist opens with complaints of distress and being the target of lies and deceit, so he had called on God and God had heard him (120:1–2).

The question in verse 3 is directed to the wicked people and is not so much a query as a preface to the warning in verse 4. God's judgment is coming, and the wicked will be punished. The "broom tree" (NIV) mentioned in verse 4 is reference to a desert plant with a trunk of very hard wood that was a popular source of charcoal.

The psalmist writes that being surrounded by such negative people is like being in faraway places noted for their hostility (120:5). Meshech was far north, in Asia Minor. Kedar was in northern Arabia.

Verses 6-7 conclude with the writer's longing for peace. The wording suggests that he could have been a king. Most people might speak of conflict, disputes, arguments, or such. But in this case the alternative to peace is war.

PSALM 121

The protection of God is the theme of Psalm 121. Pilgrimages could be dangerous journeys with both geographical challenges and criminal elements to contend with. As the psalmist looks upward toward Jerusalem, his destination, he acknowledges that his help comes from God, who had created those mountains (121:1-2). Verses 3-4 offer additional assurance: God's protection is effective around the clock, because He does not sleep. (Gods of other nations were thought to need sleep, a frequent excuse for their being out of touch with people.)

Critical Observation

Psalms that are designated for public religious ceremonies might use different voices. Psalm 121 is a good example. One speaker probably began with verses 1 and 2. (Note the first-person *I*.) But verses 3-8 then shift to the second person: *you*. It is likely they were spoken by different people.

God's protection is like shade in the hot and sometimes hostile climate of the Middle East. It was also thought at the time that too much exposure to the moon could cause problems as well. (English words such as *moonstruck* and *lunatic* are examples of such a belief.) But God's protection works day and night (121:5-6). In addition, verses 7-8 affirm that God will watch the pilgrim for the round-trip—coming *and* going.

PSALM 122

Psalm 122 is the first of the Songs of Ascents attributed to David. He had conquered Jerusalem, taken it from the Jebusites, and established it as the capital city of Israel (2 Samuel 5:6-10). It is not surprising, then, that he takes great pleasure to stand in the gates of the city and consider how it had become a place to offer praise to God (Psalm 122:1-4). During a pilgrimage when hundreds of nonresidents gathered to worship and celebrate, the mood would have been festive and the city would appear to be compact (122:3).

Those in attendance had heeded the statute given Israel to go to Jerusalem three times a year for special occasions of worship (Deuteronomy 16:16-17; Psalm 122:4). Jerusalem was a place for both spiritual pursuits and political justice. Verse 5 highlights the thrones of judgment that were there.

Jerusalem means "city of peace," an appropriate title in the days of David and Solomon.

But those people who sang this psalm in the period following the exile of Israel would soon realize how turbulent the recent history of Jerusalem had been. The call to pray for the peace of Jerusalem (122:6) probably has more significance in later years.

After the psalmist calls for others to pray for the peace of Jerusalem, in verses 8–9 he offers his personal prayer for the city. The ongoing security and prosperity of Jerusalem will benefit all the pilgrims who continue to make the journey, seeking to restore their relationship with God there.

PSALM 123

It is not uncommon for those who are devoted to God to suffer ridicule or contempt from those who are not believers. Such is the case described in Psalm 123. As the psalm closes in verse 4, the writer finally identifies the problem. The source of the ridicule is not known, but the description is of one entire group of people being harassed by another large group.

In such cases, it is difficult to ignore the verbal jeers, yet the psalmist has been able to divert his attention and place his eyes on the Lord (123:1). With no thought of personal revenge or frontier justice, he leaves the matter in God's hands. He compares his status to that of a slave or handmaiden, looking to the master (or mistress) of the house for mercy.

According to verse 3, the people need mercy from God because their enemies have treated them with great contempt. In this case, no request is made for the persecutors to be silenced, but the people need strength from God during this difficult time.

PSALM 124

Psalm 124 is attributed to David, although there is more question about his authorship of this psalm than many others bearing his name. The theme appears to fit Israel's history after the exile rather than before. If so, the reference to David in the superscription would indicate a subsequent king in the line of David.

Regardless of the author, the placement of Psalm 124 fits nicely following Psalm 123. The awareness of God's involvement with His people is the only thing that consoles them. They have been attacked by angry men, who are described as a flood intent on swallowing Israel alive (124:1–5). But rather than being swept away by the rage of their enemies, the Israelites weathered the storm because of God's deliverance.

Critical Observation

The images used by the psalmist of exposure to raging waters and wild animals would have been appropriate descriptions of Israel's captivity. The escape from the flood and release from the fowler's snare suggest their eventual release. If that were the case, then David could not have authored the psalm.

Using examples from the animal kingdom, the psalmist offers praise to God. Verse 6 summons the image of a vicious animal baring its fangs, but the terrible teeth have done no damage. Verse 7 expresses the joy a bird must feel to be momentarily trapped in a hunter's snare but then escape to its freedom. And in this case, the snare is broken to be a threat no more.

The Israelites believed God had created the heavens and the earth. Therefore, He is more than able to deliver them from human powers and the problems they might present (124:8).

PSALM 125

Psalm 125 is yet another of the Songs of Ascents that celebrates the security that only God can offer. The psalmist differentiates between those who trust in the Lord and those who don't. The former group is compared to Mount Zion on which Jerusalem was built, protected all around by surrounding mountains. Similarly, God surrounds His people to prevent them from being shaken by their circumstances (125:1–2).

The *scepter* in verse 3 indicates foreign power. If God had not limited the foreign domination of Israel, in time even the righteous people might have become corrupted by the pervasive wickedness.

The psalmist doesn't take God's protection for granted. He prays that God will do good for those who are upright in their hearts (125:4). They need God's help to overcome the temptations that surround them. There is always danger that some will turn away, and those who do will come to the same end as the evildoers (125:5). The writer then closes with a short but emphatic prayer for peace upon Israel.

PSALM 126

The author of Psalm 124 compares God's people to a bird that has been released from a fowler's snare—an escape from captivity to freedom (124:7). The writer of Psalm 126 describes a more realistic account of that event. Imagine seeing (or hearing of) the destruction of God's temple and the cherished city of Jerusalem, and then being carried away to a foreign land (Babylon) for seventy years. Think of the sorrow and helplessness the people must have felt. But then, after the Persians defeat the Babylonians, imagine getting word that it is okay to return home.

It was like being sick and suddenly getting well again. Spontaneous laughter was heard instead of the wailing and the unsettling questions about whether or not God knew or cared about their situation. Joyful songs quickly replaced the sad songs of captivity. (See Psalm 137, for example.) Israel was certainly overjoyed at God's deliverance, but more than that, the other nations could clearly see that Israel's God was at work (126:1–3).

The release from captivity was just a start, however. In verse 4 the psalmist prays for a restoration of Israel's fortunes. He thinks of the wilderness of the Negev with its seasonal streams. In hot weather they either reduce to a trickle or dry up completely, but when the rainy season arrives they fill up again. The psalmist wants Israel to once again overflow with God's blessing.

The closing image in verses 5–6 may sound confusing for those who thoughtlessly proclaim, "You reap what you sow." The principle still holds true here, but with a slight twist. The sowing is done with tears and sorrow, *but it is done*. Perhaps the psalmist is describing the people's return to Jerusalem after seventy years to start over again with planting and building. No doubt many tears were shed when they saw the destruction that had been done to their homeland. However, as time passed between sowing and reaping, the attitude of the people gradually improved. The harvesting is accompanied by songs of joy. The seeds may have been sown with salty tears, but they will eventually produce an abundance of grain that will be reaped and stored amid much rejoicing.

PSALM 127

Any pilgrimage to Jerusalem held a sense of excitement and expectation for the travelers. For those who lived in agrarian communities or small towns, the regular visits to a large city were no doubt highly anticipated. Psalm 127, however, is an on-the-road reminder of the appropriate priorities in life.

A day-to-day life that doesn't rely on God is in vain. The pilgrims have left their various houses, and the psalmist wants them to realize the importance of allowing God to be the foundation in each home. Then, as the pilgrims begin to get glimpses of Jerusalem in the distance, the psalm reminds them that only God's watchfulness will effectively protect the city. Without God's presence, the watchmen are just wasting their time (127:1).

God is the provider for His people. Those who don't acknowledge that fact can lose a lot of sleep attempting to do things that God would willingly do *for* them. They get up early and stay up late, always fretting about little things. But trust in God allows people to sleep well (127:2).

Verses 3–5 follow the same line of thinking: People should acknowledge their children as blessings of God, not merely products of their own biological design. In the ancient culture, sons were especially valued. As male children grew, they provided help on the farms, protection against danger, and representation of the family. The more sons that parents produced, the more they felt that God had blessed them (127:5).

Whether the topic is domestic life, national security, or family trees, God should be acknowledged as the source of all success and contentment.

Critical Observation

Psalm 127 is attributed to Solomon. The content certainly appears to reflect the message of Ecclesiastes, that all pursuits in life are meaningless apart from a basic underlying relationship with God.

PSALM 128

In the thinking of ancient Israel, prosperity and happiness were signs of God's favor. As pilgrims made their way to Jerusalem for their festivals and worship ceremonies, they tended to dwell more consciously on the blessings of God, so Psalm 128 was especially appropriate during those times.

According to verse 1, it is the fear of the Lord that prompts His blessing because it motivates people to obey and persevere. God rewards their labor with plentiful harvests, prosperity, and fertility (128:2–4). Grapes (vines) and olives are key crops that symbolize both God's bounty and long life.

It is, of course, a blessing to arrive safely in Jerusalem for times of celebration. But in verses 5–6, the psalmist looks beyond those special times, asking for God's blessing all the days of their lives. And with God's blessing, those days are more likely to stretch out into long lives, enabling faithful followers to see several generations of descendants before they died.

The psalmist also prays for the prosperity of Jerusalem. The people would have understood that as long as Jerusalem remained well protected and under the rule of a righteous king, the entire nation had no need to fear. This thought is emphasized in the final phrase as the writer asks God for peace upon Israel.

PSALM 129

After a series of positive and celebratory psalms (124–128), Psalm 129 is quite a contrast. The psalmist reflects on how Israel has suffered in the past. Although the nation has a long history of outside oppression, it has never been ultimately defeated (129:1–2).

The imagery in verse 3 is harsh, with the nation personified as someone who has long furrows from foreign plows dug down his back. This is perhaps a reference to the recent Babylonian takeover of Jerusalem. But even as bad as that experience had been, God had eventually freed His people from their bondage (129:4).

The offenses of the wicked are not forgotten, however. The psalmist has no tolerance for those who oppress God's people (and thereby resist God). He wishes them nothing but shame and failure. They may have plowed the back of Israel, but Israel has roots (129:3). Evildoers are like grass seeds that have blown onto a rooftop, growing with no source of nutrition or fertilization, destined to quickly wither and die (129:6–7).

It was customary in those days for passersby to greet strangers by wishing them God's blessing. In the case of Israel's enemies, however, the psalmist will not extend that wish (129:8). Because they are unable to harvest even enough to fill a person's arms (129:7), it should be clear that God's blessing is *not* upon them.

PSALM 130

Psalm 130 is one of the seven psalms in the *penitential* classification (along with Psalms 6, 32, 38, 51, 102, and 143). The psalmist expresses remorse for the sins he has committed and anticipation that God will forgive him and redeem him.

Verses 1–2 reveal the writer's mental state. He is crying out from his emotional depths, asking God to hear and be merciful. He realizes that God is not a heavenly recorder of wrongs—no one would ever be able to please Him. God chose to forgive the sins of His people, which is an astounding fact. The response, then, should be reverential fear of God—not cowering in panic or horror but willfully submitting to Him in worship and obedience (130:4).

While awaiting full restoration to a faithful relationship with God, the psalmist remains hopeful and watchful. Like a night watchman longing for daylight, he waits. The new day will bring both light and the regular morning offerings to God, so the writer yearns for his spiritual darkness to come to an end.

Verses 7–8 expand the scope of his prayer. No longer limited to his own situation, the psalmist challenges *all* of Israel to place their hope in God, seeking complete forgiveness and redemption.

PSALM 131

Although Psalm 131 is ascribed to David, it is not surprising that it is included among the Songs of Ascents. Psalm 131 would have been particularly appropriate for pilgrims approaching Jerusalem to worship. It is a song of contentment and complete hope placed in God.

David begins by declaring that his heart is humbled and his eyes are not haughty. The latter part of verse 1 is a commitment not to seek grandiose adventures that draw attention to himself. If his hope is in God, as he is advising Israel in verse 3, then God should get credit for all the victories and achievements of his life and career.

Instead of seeking glory, David strives to quiet himself. (His *soul* is his very being.) He compares himself in verse 2 to a young child who takes great comfort in the nearness of his mother. Specifying a weaned child may suggest that in the same way a young child outgrows a dependence on something as desirable as mother's milk, David has gotten past the need to distinguish himself as a warrior and empire builder. His inner being has become stilled and content. All his hope—now and forevermore—is in God (131:3).

PSALM 132

This psalm is a request for God to favor the king, a descendant of David. It may have been written considerably earlier than many of the other psalms in this section. It may have originally commemorated the dedication of the temple (2 Chronicles 6:41–42; Psalm 132:8–10), or it possibly was used during coronations. (The use of the psalm after the exile would probably have raised questions as to how the restructuring of the government during Jerusalem's rebuilding would mesh with the promises God had made to David.) In its position among the Songs of Ascents, the psalm would have been a historical reminder of how special the place was to which the pilgrims were traveling.

David had many great achievements, but the one thing he was unable to fulfill was his desire to build a house for God (132:1–5). (The details are provided in 2 Samuel 7, although the oath, or vow, mentioned by the psalmist in 132:2 is not to be found.) God denies David's request and instead gives the task to Solomon, a man of peace. But David does much of the groundwork and collecting of materials.

Demystifying Psalms

Ephrathah, mentioned in verse 6, is a more ancient name for Bethlehem that eventually came to refer to an area *around* Bethlehem. The additional mention of the fields of Jaar points to the more specific location of Kiriath Jearim, the place where the ark of the covenant was housed for twenty years after it was returned by the Philistines (1 Samuel 6:21–7:2).

Part of David's preparation involved moving the ark of the covenant from Kiriath Jearim to Jerusalem. The location of the ark soon came to be known as God's dwelling place and His footstool (132:7–8). The temple was eventually built and priests were assigned to care for all aspects of community worship (132:9).

The first half of Psalm 132 deals with David's commitment to God; the second half addresses God's promise to David. One key element is that God said one of David's descendants would sit on the throne forever (132:11–12).

God also confirms David's choice of Jerusalem (Mount Zion) for His dwelling (132:13–14). Verses 15–16 relate God's promise to bless the city at all levels—the poor, the priests, and all the godly people (the saints).

Another promise of God closes the psalm in verses 17–18. With His previous covenant with David in mind, God promises to make a horn grow. The image is borrowed from the animal kingdom, where horns are symbols of power, so in this case it refers to the king, or the anointed one. God's king will rule in glory; his enemies will experience only shame and defeat.

In the original Hebrew, the word for *grow* is related to the word *branch*, which is a title often used for the prophesied Messiah. So the closing of the psalm hints of the ruler yet to come, who will be the ultimate fulfillment of God's promise to David.

PSALM 133

When Israel's priests are ordained, they are anointed with oil made from a special formula. It is sacred, not to be used for any other purpose (Exodus 30:30–33). The high priest, as in Aaron's case (Psalm 133:2), is dressed in his official priestly uniform, including a breastplate on which the names of the twelve tribes are found (Exodus 28:21, 29; Leviticus 8:1–13).

This would have been the image in David's mind as he wrote Psalm 133. The first time this special ceremony had been performed, the oil was poured on Aaron's head to consecrate him for service. David feels the same sense of wonder when he thinks of the unity of his people coming together to honor and serve their Lord (Psalm 133:1). Perhaps this psalm was written in response to the uniting of the kingdom after David had struggled for several years to bring together those who supported him with others who would rather have had a second king from Saul's family.

The thought of oil flowing down Aaron's beard is reinforced by the image of dew on Mount Hermon. At an altitude of more than 9,000 feet, Mount Hermon was often the only splash of green on an otherwise dry and brown landscape. The refreshing difference that unity made for the people of Israel was no less striking than the effect that water had on an arid land. These thoughts would have been especially appropriate for pilgrims making their way to Jerusalem to worship with their brothers.

PSALM 134

In this last of the series of Songs of Ascents, the servants of the Lord are acknowledged in verse 1. These servants are the priests who minister in the temple, both day and night (1 Chronicles 9:33; 23:28–31). In this case, perhaps the evening ceremonies are wrapping up and the participants, as they leave, are encouraging the priests who remained behind on the night shift. Verse 2 reflects the image in Psalm 28:2 of priests lifting their hands toward the sanctuary (the Most Holy Place that contains the ark of the covenant and signifies God's presence).

The closing verse of the psalm, and therefore the concluding thought of the series of Songs of Ascents, is a prayer for God's blessing. It may have been the prayer of the pilgrims directed to the priests. Or perhaps Psalm 134 was used as a dialog, where the community would recite the first two verses and a designated priest would respond with the blessing in verse 3.

Take It Home

As a group, the Songs of Ascents covers a wide variety of thoughts and emotions, all appropriate for people journeying toward Jerusalem to worship. As they sang the same songs along the same route year after year, the songs surely took on special significance. Can you think of songs that do the same thing for you—that highlight certain places or seasons when you feel especially close to God?

PSALMS: BOOK V, CONTINUED

PSALMS 135–150

Setting Up the Section

This section finishes up Book V, and therefore the biblical book of Psalms as well. Of the sixteen psalms that remain, half of them comprise a series attributed to David. The remaining ones are anonymous.

PSALM 135

Although not designated as one of the Songs of Ascents, Psalm 135 appears to have been used for special occasions in the temple worship ceremonies. It begins and ends with the familiar cry to praise the Lord, and the psalm contains many specific reasons to do so. The first challenge to praise God goes out to the temple servants—the priests and Levites.

God is deserving of praise from His people. To begin with, He is good (135:3). In addition, He has reached out to people. He chose Jacob (Israel) and all Jacob's descendants (the Israelites) to be His treasured possession (135:4).

The people of the surrounding nations cannot make the same claims about their gods. God is sovereign and able to do whatever He wishes (135:5–7), yet He chooses to create, sustain, and bless His people.

Verses 6–7 are reminders that God's power is seen in all of nature—earth, skies, and seas. Clouds, wind, rain, and lightning are all part of His wonderful design. Rain was a particularly appreciated blessing of God in the climate and geography of the Middle East.

But God is not limited to working through nature. He is a God of miracles that defy the laws of nature. In verses 8–9, the psalmist recalls the plagues sent upon Egypt—perhaps the best known of God's miracles. But Egypt's Pharaoh was only one of many leaders who caused problems for Israel. As God continued to lead the Israelites toward the promised land, there were other kings who tried to stop them. Each time, God delivered His people (135:10–12).

Demystifying Psalms

The Israelites had encountered Og and Sihon (135:11) in the wilderness on the way from Egypt to Canaan (Numbers 21:21–35). And when they finally entered the promised land, they were immediately confronted with a series of other powerful forces they had to defeat before they could settle in the land (Joshua 6–12). But God was with them all along the way and gave them the land as an inheritance, just as He had promised Abraham.

Those events had taken place long ago, yet God is still a reliable source of protection and compassion (135:13–14). Other nations had tried to overthrow Israel, and Israel had even turned to the gods of those nations from time to time, but God had never forsaken His fickle people. The psalmist points out the impotence of idols in verses 15–17. They may be designed to *look* like people or gods, yet they remain handmade lumps of wood and metal unable to speak, see, hear, or breathe. The tragic effect of idol worship is that the people who worship idols become like the idols—spiritually impotent with no hope of real life or positive change (135:18).

So the psalmist again calls all who will listen to praise the Lord—both those who are responsible for spiritual leadership and the laypeople who are assembled to worship (135:19–21).

PSALM 136

It seems pretty clear from the structure of Psalm 136 that it was used for public worship, with a designated Levite reciting the first portion of each statement as a temple choir, or perhaps the worshipers in attendance, responded with, "His love endures forever." The format of the psalm makes it unique, but its content is similar to that of Psalm 135. Both psalms begin with the affirmation that God is good (135:3; 136:1) and then detail ways to indicate that He is also great.

God is good (136:1). He is God of gods and Lord of lords (136:2–3). With these initial observations, the accompanying triple command to give thanks in the first three verses is an emphatic opening.

Verses 4–9 provide a short synopsis of the creation story using language similar to that found in Genesis 1. In verse 4, the list of great wonders of God begins with His creation of heaven and earth, sun and moon.

From Creation, the psalmist moves to the Exodus in verses 10–15. God had done what the people assumed was impossible at the time: freed them from the power of the mighty Egyptians. The plagues are summarized with only the last, most effective one (136:10). Israel had been powerless, so they had to depend solely on God's power and sovereignty (136:12). When Pharaoh changed his mind and gave pursuit, God remained in complete control even though deliverance included having His people walk through the midst of a divided Red Sea, pursued by the Egyptian army that ended up drowning (136:13–15).

After escape came the challenge of the wilderness wanderings. Again, the people made it harder than it should have been, yet God's love endured. God dispensed with the opposing kings both in the desert and after the Israelites crossed the Jordan into the promised land. (For information on Sihon and Og, see comments on Psalm 135.)

Verses 23–26 summarize the ongoing work of God. He never forgot His people when they were suffering. He had always delivered them from their enemies. He provided food and necessities, and His provision went beyond Israel. God had been Creator of the world, and His gifts were available to every living thing (136:25).

There are many reasons to give thanks to God. But at the top of the list, as the psalmist reminds his listeners twenty-six times during this song, God should be thanked because His love endures forever.

PSALM 137

Psalm 137 begins as a mournful recollection of Israel's time spent in Babylon, and it ends with a brutal imprecation against those responsible for the destruction of Jerusalem. The request of Israel's captors in verse 3 adds insult to injury. The Israelites were in great distress over the fall of their city and temple. They experienced the end of life as they had known it. They were powerless in a foreign land, and then the people there started asking to hear some of their native music, which heightened their despair. So they hung up their harps and opted for silence (137:1–3).

Critical Observation

The prophet Jeremiah had encouraged the Israelites to make the most of a bad situation—to settle down in Babylon, increase in number, and pray for the people there. He told them their stay would be limited and that God would then return them to their homeland (Jeremiah 29:4–14). Clearly it wasn't a terrible place to be because the people were dwelling beside rivers with poplar trees (Psalm 137:1–2). Still, the losses they had incurred were painful to them.

Verses 4–6 attest to the people's great love for Jerusalem. They were far away from home, but they weren't about to forget what it had meant to them. They had taken much for granted in the final years of the monarchy, and they had suffered the consequences.

But memories of Jerusalem—the setting of their temple, worship, feasts, celebrations, and more—had become their greatest source of joy. They even called down curses on themselves if they dared to forget their home city.

Finally, in verses 7-9, the Israelites wish the worst possible retribution upon the people who had been responsible for the terrible treatment of Jerusalem. The Edomites had been longstanding enemies of Israel and Judah, and they had taken cruel pleasure in seeing the Babylonians invade and conquer Jerusalem. The Israelites wish the same end to come to Edom—an end that is, in fact, later prophesied (Isaiah 63:1-6; Lamentations 4:21).

Worse than the Edomites, however, are the Babylonians. Even after the Medes and Persians conquered the Babylonian Empire, Babylon remained a symbol for everything opposed to God. The wish of Israel was that Babylon would become the victim of the same atrocities that they had inflicted on others.

Psalm 137:8-9 contains the most severe of the imprecations in Psalms. It is interesting to note, however, that while Israel was a rocky country, Babylon was not. The desire for infants to be dashed against rocks may well have been a general cry for God's justice rather than a specific, literal request.

PSALM 138

Psalm 138 begins a series of the final eight psalms of David that have been recorded. In this song, David offers his praise to God for a number of reasons, and his praise is unrestrained.

The gods he mentions in verse 1 may be foreign kings (men with a seriously inflated sense of importance), or they may be the actual worshiped deities. Either way, David is comfortable worshiping the Lord in front of these other gods. And as with other psalms attributed to David, his use of the term *temple* in verse 2 is presumed to mean the temporary housing he established for the ark of the covenant before it eventually took its more familiar position in the Most Holy Place of Solomon's temple (2 Samuel 6:17).

David gives God credit for making him "bold and stouthearted" (Psalm 138:3 NIV). He had called out to God, and God had answered him, resulting in his praise for God's love and faithfulness. He knows that God's name and God's Word are above all things (138:2).

David's prayer is that *all* kings will hear the words of God and respond with praise, acknowledging His glory (138:4-5). Much will depend on their individual attitudes. God is highly exalted, yet He is always willing to respond to the lowly—those who humble themselves and seek His help. Those who attempt to exalt themselves in pride, however, miss out on God's compassionate help and support (138:6).

David is among those who had humbled themselves. He had frequently found himself threatened, and God had always delivered him (138:7). In verse 8, David first states his belief that God will accomplish His will. Then he affirms his faith that God's love will endure forever. And finally, even in light of the confident faith he had expressed, he asks God yet again to continue to work in his life.

PSALM 139

Psalm 139 is an amazing expression of God's loving familiarity of David, and David's unrelenting devotion in return. David's description of God's awareness of his life might be off-putting for many people. God is watching when the psalmist wakes up, goes to bed, sits down, and gets up. He knows every word David says and thinks (139:1–4).

How does David feel about the close scrutiny of God? It depends on how one interprets his comments. When he writes in verse 5 of being hemmed in, both in front and behind, and of having the hand of God upon him, does he feel restricted? Protected? In verses 7–12, is he describing futile attempts to carve out a little personal time and space for himself? Or is he speculating about the unlimited ability of God to watch over him wherever he might find himself—heights or depths, day or night, one side of the sea or the other? Either way, his musings have shown him that the omnipresence of God is both too lofty and too wonderful for him to absorb (139:6).

Demystifying Psalms

Throughout Psalm 139, David's use of the term *wonderful* (139:6, 14) is not what modern English speakers might assume. David uses this word in the sense of *wondrous* or *miraculous*—beyond human comprehension.

David acknowledges God's involvement in his life from conception (139:13–16). The word *for*, that opens verse 13, connects this thought with the previous sections. Since God creates a person's inmost being and knits him or her within the mother's womb, doesn't it only make sense that He would also have an acute awareness of everything that person does as an adult? David surmises that God had his life span and accomplishments in mind before David was born.

Such deep thinking fascinates David. Verses 17–18 describe his thoughts as precious, vast, and innumerable. Every morning brings new wonder that God is still available and accessible to him.

Even though God knows David intimately, there is still much about God that David does not understand. He expresses confusion over why God allows wicked people to continue in their bloodthirsty pursuits, apparently unimpeded (139:19–22). They have no regard for God and even less for righteous people, so David declares any enemy of God an enemy of his. Yet as David was wont to do, he leaves vengeance up to God (139:19).

Finally, verses 23–24 offer one of the most fascinating challenges of scripture. David had certainly committed some grievous sins against God on occasion. But at this point in his life, he is able to ask God to examine both his actions and his thoughts to attempt to detect anything offensive or improper. Few people get to a point in their spiritual lives where they will consider making such an invitation.

PSALM 140

Much of David's life was spent on the run from people who wanted to see him dead. Psalm 140 recounts one such time when he cried out to God for help. David's adversaries are both evil and violent (140:1–2). In verse 3 he compares them to snakes, with sharp tongues like serpents and poison like vipers. They are cunning and devious, setting snares and traps (140:5).

David prays for both rescue and protection (140:1, 4). He feels threatened and vulnerable, yet he is confident that God is strong and merciful (140:6–7).

In verses 8–11, David's prayer takes an imprecatory turn as he asks God to allow his wicked adversaries to suffer. However, David's desire is essentially an eye-for-an-eye request for justice. His persecutors had troubled others with their words, so David asks that their lips cause *them* trouble. They have stalked innocent victims and set traps like hunters, so David wants them to become the prey, hunted down by some kind of divine disaster. The ultimate result, he hopes, will be a permanent end to their slander and violence.

On a more positive note, David concludes in verses 12–13 with an affirmation of God's justice and His care for the poor and needy. Righteous and upright people ultimately have nothing to fear.

PSALM 141

One of the insidious consequences of wickedness is that people are prone to instinctively return evil for evil. In Psalm 141, however, David prays that God will prevent him from responding in such a way to people who provoke him. In the opening verses, he compares his prayer to the worship ceremony that took place in the tabernacle, including the smoke of incense rising to God as a prayer and the lifting of his hands as might be done during an evening sacrifice.

David is aware of the actions and intentions of wicked people. They have gotten away with their evil behavior and are enjoying fine foods and an elegant lifestyle as a result. It is tempting to want to join them in their opulence, yet he wants nothing to do with them. He asks God to guard both his lips and his heart (141:3–4).

Verse 5 makes clear that David is by no means opposed to discipline or rebuke. He welcomes constructive criticism from righteous people, even if it is frank and harsh. He considers such help refreshing, like oil on his head. David has no tolerance for the words of the wicked, however. He wishes them to be thrown down from cliffs, realizing in their final moments that he has used only well-spoken words in his dealings with them. Verse 7 is not clear in its intent, but it seems to be a desire for the bones of the wicked to be dispersed like clods of dirt in a farmer's field, indicating the lack of a proper burial.

Much clearer is David's next declaration of trust in God (141:8). God, as always, is his refuge. He will keep his eyes on God and trust Him for deliverance from death. He knows the snares of the wicked are still out there (141:9–10). With God in control, however, David will be able to travel in safety while the evildoers become entangled in their own traps.

PSALM 142

The fifth of the eight psalms of David in this section, Psalm 142 has common themes with others in the set. This is the only one of the series, however, that provides a clue in its introduction as to David's situation. As David writes this psalm (as well as Psalm 57), he appears to be thinking about the time when King Saul unexpectedly went into the cave where he was hiding (1 Samuel 24).

When strong and powerful enemies threatened David, he turned to God for help. Not only did God hear David's cry, but He also responded with mercy and protection. God was a consistent guide and supporter even when David grew weak and found himself in danger (142:1–3).

To this day, people speak of a right-hand man, meaning much the same that David does in verse 4. The position to one's right is where a bodyguard, advocate, or loyal friend would have stood. David points out that he has no one there. He is alone.

With no other source of support, David turns to God as his sole refuge. Even in his desperation, he is counting on God to deliver him. Without God, David's enemies are too strong for him. But after God's intervention, David fully expects to gather with other righteous people in the land of the living to praise the name of God and thank Him for His goodness (142:5–7).

PSALM 143

This prayer of David is classified among the *penitential* psalms, the final one of this category in the book of Psalms (along with 6, 32, 38, 51, 102, and 130). Although similar in content to many of David's other psalms, this one contains the acknowledgment that he is among the unrighteous people worthy of judgment, and he asks to be spared (143:1–2).

Critical Observation

The author's content within the psalm is only part of the reason the song might be classified as penitential. Another criterion is how the psalm is later used by the early Christian church.

As was his habit, David turns to God when his enemies begin to threaten him. His situation is certainly unenviable. Verse 3 describes how his pursuers crush his spirit and create a deathlike darkness. He is fainthearted and dismayed, but he takes comfort in recalling better days (143:4–5). He knows of God's faithfulness in the past, and he continues to count on it. He thirsts for God, realizing his need is like parched land needing water for any life to continue (143:6).

David's condition leads to his request for God to answer *quickly* in verse 7. Those who go down to the pit, who are mentioned in verse 7, are people who die. The darkness in David's life is severe. He needs light, so he asks God for relief by the morning. His trust remains in God, and he is eager for God to act (143:8).

David doesn't just ask for deliverance from his enemies. He is also eager for God to teach him and provide a solid foundation for his life (143:9–10). When God delivers David, it will reflect His righteousness and power.

According to verses 2 and 12, David considers himself God's servant throughout this whole ordeal. From beginning to end of this psalm, he remains humble. The psalm doesn't reveal if his prayer is answered, but David's willingness to allow God to handle the situation is a likely indication that it is.

PSALM 144

Another psalm attributed to David, Psalm 144 combines the psalmist's praise for God with a request for deliverance. Verses 1–2 begin immediately to list reasons God should be praised. Ever the military man, David notices the strong and powerful aspects of God. The Lord is a rock, fortress, stronghold, shield, and refuge. He can be counted on for training and skill in battle, delivering His people, and subduing enemy nations. Yet David doesn't miss the point that the Lord is also a loving God.

Verses 3–4 touch on the almighty God's concern for weak and temporal humanity—the same themes as David's Psalm 8, where they are a bit more fully developed. David then asks to witness the strength of his mighty God in the form of rescue from his enemies. David's foes are liars and deceivers (144:7–8, 11), so he wants God to scatter them with lightning and power (144:5–6). In return, David will play and sing a new song to acknowledge God's victory (144:9–10).

David is looking to the future, to a time when Israel's enemies will no longer be an influence and God will rule supreme. Children will be strong and productive. The country will be prosperous. The city will be safe. And above all, God's blessing will be felt by the people, who will be loyal to Him in return (144:12–15).

PSALM 145

Psalm 145 is a psalm of praise—the only one in the entire book of Psalms so designated in its introduction. It makes a satisfying finale for the series of eight psalms attributed to David, who asks for nothing for himself, but rather keeps his focus on God throughout this song. It is also a fitting transition into the final five songs in the Psalter. From this point onward, much emphasis will be placed on the importance of praising God. And while the psalmist is communicating his many reasons to praise the Lord, he structures this song as an alphabetic acrostic.

First and foremost in verses 1–2 is David's commitment to praise God—every day, for ever and ever. Next he describes why God deserves praise. To begin with, the greatness of God is incomprehensible (145:3). His mighty actions and splendor are topics of teaching and conversation between generations (145:4–5).

David makes sure to include himself among the worshipers. In verses 5–6 he uses both third-person and first-person references: "*They* will speak. . .and *I* will meditate." "*They* will tell. . .and *I* will proclaim." In doing so, he notes God's splendor, His wonderful (awe-inspiring) works, His goodness, and His righteousness.

Verses 8-9 continue the list. God is gracious, compassionate, slow to anger, and rich in love. His goodness and compassion are evident from everything He has created. People who identify and appreciate the work of God will not only praise Him for His works but will also tell other people. God's kingdom is enduring and everlasting (145:10-13).

People in need will especially be glad for the gifts of God. He is loving, He honors His promises, He uplifts the fallen, He provides food, and He is the source that can satisfy all desires (145:13-16).

For all these reasons and more, David concludes this psalm in verses 17-21 with his final expression of praise to God, inviting every living thing to join him. Those who call on God will discover that He is near. Those who love God will be protected. But those who reject Him to continue to live in wickedness will eventually be destroyed.

PSALM 146

When people need help, they have a choice. They can depend on other people or they can turn to God. This psalm offers praise to God because He is always dependable.

Critical Observation

Psalms 146-150 focus on praising God. Each of these songs that close out the Psalter both begin and end with the phrase, "Praise the LORD" (or "Hallelujah").

According to verses 3-4, putting one's trust in people eventually leads to disappointment. All people, even those with power and influence, are mortal. Their ability to help is limited in both time and degree. Situations will arise where their power is insufficient. And their influence ends with death.

So the psalmist offers praise to God, who is not limited in any way (146:1-2). God is the Creator of all things, and He remains faithful (146:5-6). The people who need help most can always count on Him: the oppressed, the hungry, the prisoners, the blind, those who are bowed down, the alien, the fatherless, and the widows (146:7-9).

God's love and help extend to all who are righteous, the psalmist declares in verse 8. Those who are wicked, however, will find themselves frustrated. God should be praised regularly because His reign will last forever (146:9-10).

PSALM 147

This psalm of praise is in regard to God's faithfulness to Israel after their exile. Immediately after the opening call to praise, the psalmist begins to recount the events after the people's release from captivity. Verses 2-3 recall the gathering of the exiles and the building (actually, the rebuilding) of Jerusalem. The people were brokenhearted to see what had been done to the city and how much repair needed to be done, but God was there to heal their wounded spirits.

The psalmist reminds everyone that the same God who helped them is the One who had created, numbered, and named the stars. The rain He provides supplies life-supporting water for both domestic and wild animals. His understanding and His power are unlimited. And while His power will be used to subdue the wicked, it will always provide support for the humble (147:4–9).

People tend to be impressed by strong animals and athletic feats, but God delights in those who fear Him and respond to His unfailing love (147:10–11). The psalmist challenges His people to praise the Lord because God will strengthen Jerusalem and bless those within the city with peace and prosperity (147:12–14). God's care for the earth can be seen in the seasons—some with frost, ice, and hail, and others with warm breezes and flowing water (147:15–18). But the people of Israel have an additional reason to praise God that no one else has. Verses 19–20 conclude with the reminder that God has revealed His Word to the Israelites. No other nation knows His laws and has the same privilege of responding and relating to the great God of creation and redemption.

PSALM 148

Psalm 148 is a call for everyone and everything to praise God. Verses 1–6 exhort those in the heavens to praise Him: angels and heavenly hosts, sun, moon, stars, clouds and waters above the skies. All have been created and established by God, and He deserves their praise.

Verses 7–12 bring the praise more down to earth as the psalmist beckons the great creatures of the sea, the elements (lightning, hail, snow, clouds, and winds), mountains, trees, wild and domestic animals, human rulers (kings and princes), and *all* people—young and old, male and female. Of everything the psalmist lists, nothing is worthy of praise except the name of the Lord. People have limited knowledge of heaven and earth, but God's splendor is unbounded (148:13).

The horn mentioned in verse 14 is a symbol for power that frequently represents the king. But sometimes, and this may be one such case, the horn is symbolic of the glory God has provided for His people. God's people are close to His heart, and for that reason (among many others) He should be praised.

PSALM 149

Psalm 149 is a call for the entire community of Israel to offer praise to God. As God continues to act on behalf of His people, the appropriate response is to sing a new song of praise to Him (149:1).

The people should praise God for their salvation (149:4). According to verses 2–5, their praise should take various enthusiastic forms: dancing, tambourine and harp music, songs during the night, and an overall attitude of gladness and rejoicing.

In addition, the people should praise God because He has empowered them to be victorious. They have not sat idly waiting for God to remove their problems; they have taken up swords to protect their nation. The victory will always be God's, but His people are involved and faithfully committed to Him, which entails occasional struggles and conflicts with other nations.

Critical Observation

The double-edged sword mentioned in verse 6 was a relatively new invention at this time. Earlier mentions of a sword in scripture, such as the time period of Joshua and the judges, frequently refer to a curved instrument with the outside edge sharpened. By this time, though, the sword had evolved into a straight weapon with both sides of the blade sharpened and able to inflict blows.

With God providing victory and safety for His people, they should always be prepared to praise Him.

PSALM 150

Psalm 1 appears to be positioned intentionally to introduce the book of Psalms. Similarly, this concluding psalm may have been written to close the book with a final emphasis on the importance of praise. Each book within the biblical book of Psalms ends with a short doxology. In this case, the final psalm serves as the doxology for Book V.

The Israelites perceive that God has a temple in heaven as well as the one they are familiar with in Jerusalem, and verse 1 calls for God to be praised in both locations. God is to be praised for the feats He had performed for Israel in His power and for His greatness that surpasses all others.

The long series of instruments listed in verses 3–5 includes strings, wind instruments, and percussion. When united, the result will be an enthusiastic accompaniment to praise, along with dancing (150:4). God, the Creator of all things, should be praised by everything that has breath (150:6). The psalm (and the book of Psalms) concludes with one final "Praise the LORD."

Take It Home

Many of the psalms in this section reflect life in Israel after the Babylonian invasion and the captivity of God's people. A few of the psalms focus on the negative aspects of the experience. Some look back to review the blessings the people had before they were conquered. Several dwell almost exclusively on praise for a new beginning. When things have gone badly in your life, do you tend to dwell on the past, or are you quick to attempt to learn from your mistakes and move on in faith and praise to God?

PROVERBS

INTRODUCTION TO PROVERBS

As the preface to the book states, Proverbs is about wisdom. On one level, wisdom is a skill of living, a practical knowledge. Wise people know how to say the right thing at the right time and to do the right thing at the right time. They live in a way that maximizes blessing for themselves and others in the world that God created.

But at a deeper level, wisdom is more profound than an ability to navigate life well. Indeed, it begins with a proper attitude toward God characterized by "fear." This is not the type of fear that makes someone run away, but it is more than respect. It is the awe that a person should feel when in the presence of the sovereign Creator of the universe.

Proverbs is a book about wisdom, and it intends to make its reader wise.

AUTHOR

The book of Proverbs is associated with Solomon, Israel's wisest king. His writings—or his teachings put into writing by a scribe—form most of the book. It was revealed in 1 Kings 4:32 that Solomon spoke three thousand proverbs, and it is good to have the book of Proverbs to see what he was teaching. A few additional short sections come from other contributors: anonymous writers (22:17–24:22), Agur (chapter 30), and Lemuel (chapter 31).

PURPOSE

The purpose of the book of Proverbs is stated in 1:2–3: to provide wisdom that, when applied, will lead to a godly life. Solomon seemed especially eager for his son to learn and apply the principles in this book, but they are general enough (and simple enough) for everyone to benefit from.

THEMES

The theme that runs throughout Proverbs is the value of wisdom, particularly in contrast to folly in its various forms. Wisdom should permeate one's life in personal attitudes and behaviors, family relationships, business dealings, worship, and every other aspect of the human experience. The fact that such teachings are associated with the wealthiest king in Israel's history gives them added weight.

CONTRIBUTION TO THE BIBLE

Proverbs belongs to the collection of Old Testament books called Wisdom Literature, which comprises the books of Job, Psalms, Proverbs, Ecclesiastes, and Song of Songs (also known as Song of Solomon). These books are all concerned with ordinary life and how to live it well.

The book of Proverbs has two major parts. In chapters 1–9, the reader encounters speeches. Mostly, they are the speeches of a father to a son (see 1:8–19), but occasionally a figure named Wisdom speaks to all the young men (1:20–33).

The second part of the book is filled with proverbs, short observations, warnings, and encouragements that are typically very practical.

A proverb is a very important literary device that played a prominent role in Israel and also the Middle East. A proverb is a short saying that combines knowledge with action. It is a truth that is applied to real life.

Look at Proverbs 13:3: *Whoever guards his mouth preserves his life; he who opens wide his lips comes to ruin.* (ESV)

There is a truth being put into real life. A person who speaks without thinking, and thus speaks things that are hurtful or harmful, will in the end hurt himself. A person who takes responsibility for his thoughts, guards his heart, and thus watches what he says, will not suffer the fate of the careless.

This proverb deals with the issue of a person's heart (there is the lofty principle)—what we are thinking about and what we are focusing on—and offers a practical application of how to guard the heart

OUTLINE

PROVERBS 1:1–9:18

FATHERLY WISDOM

Setting Up the Section

The book of Proverbs is not just a grouping of pithy sayings but rather the application of the knowledge of God to real life. This is true wisdom. When we acquire such wisdom, we have more than just good advice; we have the key that unlocks the door to instruction, moral discernment, guidance, and spiritual insight.

The book of Proverbs does not begin with a long set of instructions as to how we are to live our lives. It begins by telling us the great value of wisdom and that the first step in gaining wisdom is to fear God.

📖 1:1–7

TOWARD A PURSUIT OF WISDOM

Verse 1 establishes the credibility of the proverbs in this book by identifying them with Solomon, the wisest man (except for Jesus Christ) who ever lived. When Solomon took the throne, God gave him "a wise and discerning heart, so that there will never have been anyone like you, nor will there ever be" (1 Kings 3:12 NIV).

Verses 2–6 outline several purposes of the book of Proverbs, all having to do with wisdom and understanding. The Hebrew word translated *knowledge* in verse 7 is a synonym for *wisdom*. This type of knowledge is not just possessing information; it is the ability to apply that information in real life. Many people are what could be called *practical* fools. A practical fool might mentally acknowledge the presence of God, but God plays no part in the way this person lives his or her life.

Critical Observation

The NLT Study Bible defines "fear of the Lord" this way:

Fear implies respect, awe, and (at times) knee-knocking terror. It also acknowledges that everything, including knowledge and wisdom, comes from total dependence on God. The fear of the Lord leads people toward humility and away from pride (3:7; 15:33). With such an attitude, readers of Proverbs are more apt to listen to God than to their own independent judgment. (*New Living Translation Study Bible*. Carol Stream, IL: Tyndale House, 2008, page 1030)

📖 1:8–19

FROM GENERATION TO GENERATION

According to verse 8, wisdom begins when a child listens to his father and mother. The word *listen* in this text carries the idea of listening with the intent to obey. The implication here is that the parents are themselves wise and godly people.

The articles in verse 9 (variously translated as crown, pendant, garland, etc.) are signs of success and blessing.

The greatest threat any young person faces is that of being deceived into falling with a group of people who do not love what God loves (1:10–12). The enticement of sin is to acquire things that God has not given (1:13–14).

The warning in verse 15 is clear: The goal is not to get as close to a sinful lifestyle and see how much of your Christian virtues you can keep. The goal is to stay off the path altogether.

It is foolish to try to trap a bird by setting a trap while the bird is watching (1:17). It is just as foolish to try to profit illegally (1:18). If you follow this path, you will self-destruct (1:19).

📖 1:20–33

THE CALL OF WISDOM

Wisdom is personified as a woman in Proverbs (1:20). Wisdom is not waiting for people to come to her. Instead, she is going into the streets to meet people (1:21). God does not wait in some passive manner for His people to come to Him; He goes to them.

The simple ones mentioned in verse 22 are immature or ignorant, and they are perfectly content in this situation. The scoffers, or mockers, hear the wisdom of God but make fun of it.

They have a condescending spirit toward the truth. The fools reject the very notion that God exists. They do not simply avoid wisdom as the simple do, or make fun of it as the scoffers; they oppose it and reject it outright.

Yet to these three groups wisdom continues to speak with a strong message of mercy: If you seek wisdom, wisdom will not run from you (1:23).

Verses 24–25 are transition verses, telling what is going to happen because the simple, scoffers, and fools do not listen: disaster. Wisdom has four responses to the calamity that comes upon those who have rejected her. She laughs, mocks, refuses to answer, and hides (1:26–28).

Take It Home

The responses outlined in verses 26–28 might seem callous. Is God really so hardened that when human folly leads to disaster He will not respond? The reality is that before God responds this way, He reaches out over and over again. This response is not the first response of God but the last.

Yet it is a merciful response. Only when we see the fullness of the folly of our ways will we be able to walk away from our folly. God's consequences are the means and the tools God uses to break us of our foolishness.

Those who have chosen folly do not do so out of ignorance; they have made a conscious decision to do things their own way rather than doing things God's way (1:29–31). They will experience the pain and misery that comes from doing things their own way, while the wise will enjoy security and freedom from fear (1:32–33).

📄 2:1–22

THE PURSUIT OF WISDOM

In chapter 2, the father again speaks. He lays out three conditions for true knowledge, using *if* statements. One must receive wise advice with respect and with the intention of taking it to heart (2:1–2). One must not only accept wise guidance when it is offered but seek it out (2:3). In fact, one must value wisdom so much as to make the pursuit of wisdom a high priority (2:4). Then he or she will gain the fear of the Lord (2:5). (See the Critical Observation at 1:7 for a definition.)

The father is not talking about just listening to his own words with this gusto but rather to the wisdom of God. The Lord loves to give wisdom to people, and He does so with generosity (2:6).

Take It Home

The role of teaching in the home is not simply teaching a trade, or even all our personal ideas about life. The role of the parent is to point children to the wisdom of God.

There is a moral dimension to gaining wisdom; those who are upright will find that God will go before them, protecting them in this world (2:7–8).

Verse 9 begins with the word *then*, which shows that this is a result of what has just been said. If a person seeks wisdom from God, many things will happen. He will understand what is right—how the holiness of God is meant to express itself in time and space. He will be a person who is fair, good, and noble. He will know what path to take and what decisions to make (2:9).

Knowledge will become pleasant to the seeker (2:10). He will develop such a taste for it that he will pursue it more and more. The wisdom and discretion he gains will protect him from the folly that comes when one does not operate as a wise person in this world (2:11).

Verses 12–19 outline two specific forms of protection. First, a wise person will be protected from falling in with a bad crowd (2:12–15). Only wisdom will keep a person from falling into this path. Second, a wise person will be protected from sexually immoral people (2:16–19). This protection does not come from living an ascetic lifestyle. The true solution comes from fearing the Lord and living for God's glory and seeking after wisdom as a way of life.

Demystifying Proverbs

The book of Proverbs identifies two main categories of temptation. The first is that of being tempted to run with a crowd of people who pursue sin. The second is to be pulled into an immoral relationship with a woman. Wisdom protects against both, as 2:12–19 promises.

In verse 20, the end result is that the wise person will walk in a manner that pleases God. Those who do walk in this manner will have the promised blessing that all Israelites seek (2:21). But those who do not walk in this way will have the pain and misery that comes from folly (2:20).

📖 3:1–35

TRUSTING IN THE LORD

Since a young person does not have as much experience, he should heed the wisdom of his parents (3:1). The fruit of this obedience is a life that escapes the pain associated with foolishness (3:2).

What one has around the neck—close to the throat—influences one's words, and words reflect character. The heart refers to the core of what motivates all that one does. Thus, the whole person is to be influenced by love and faithfulness (3:3).

Such a person will be respected by both God and people (3:4). Those who are at odds with God and others will have difficult lives. Those who are in favor with God and others have true success.

Verse 5 is not setting the mind in opposition to the heart but rather teaching that humanistic reasoning will not lead to wisdom. Only when a person's heart is fixed on God can a person begin to think properly. Walking according to God's will puts someone in the position to have God lead the way and open the doors to the life that He desires (3:6).

Trusting in one's own wisdom is nothing more than pride, and this, in the eyes of God, is pure evil (3:7). A life lived in this way is a life in which the body feels the weight of sin. A life that is in accordance with wisdom is one that finds peace and refreshment with God (3:8).

Demystifying Proverbs

Living against the will of God invites physical trials into that life. A life lived in the will of God has rescue from the consequences of sin. This does not mean that a person living for the glory of God in the wisdom of God will never get sick. Every human being lives life on this side of heaven in a fallen body. What the promise in 3:7–8 refers to is the reality that walking in the wisdom of God means the person will be spared from adding to the depravity of godless living. The will of God is a true healing balm—which is what the Hebrew literally says—for the body. Wisdom has both a spiritual and physical benefit for the one who follows it.

The focal point in verses 9–10 is not the offering as much as it is the heart behind the offering. We give to God because we acknowledge Him as our provider. This giving from a heart of trust does have an apparent blessing associated with it— God will continue to abundantly provide. This principle is meant to establish a basic assumption, not an automatic response.

Verses 11–12 are also cited in Hebrews 12:5–6. The child of God should not despise God's discipline. God's discipline is the way that God corrects and makes the child better.

Verses 13–18 constitute a song of praise, book-ended with the promise of blessing, or joy. Wisdom is a better investment than silver or gold (3:14–15) because it never fails to increase in value for the one who possesses it. Wisdom is depicted as a woman holding blessings in her hands and as the tree of life (3:16–18).

Critical Observation

The tree of life in verse 18 first appears in Genesis 2:9. Separation from the tree of life was a consequence of the fall (Genesis 3:24). By using this image, God is making an important point: The life that is coming to the one who partakes of wisdom is not just a good physical life; it is an eternal spiritual life.

The earth is a place where the very wisdom of God became the logic and the order by which the world was created (3:19–20). Those who abandon wisdom run against the very structure by which the world was made.

Even when problems come to the wise, they know how to handle them. This is what wisdom brings to people—not escape from the sin of the world, but the ability to handle problems as they come (3:21–26).

The irreducible heart of wisdom is true and genuine love for others. The wise are called to live in true kindness and love toward others (3:27–30).

Those living in this way have no need to envy those who pursue easy prosperity by violence and crime (3:31). Such people miss out on God's friendship, blessing, grace, and honor (3:32–35). To envy the wicked is to envy those who are on a path to destruction.

MORE FATHERLY WISDOM

The home is the primary place of education, especially moral education (4:1–4). The affectionate and pleading tone of these verses shows that parents who love their children make the best teachers.

The short discourse in praise of wisdom in verses 5–9 maintains the personification of wisdom as a woman who rewards those who embrace her.

Critical Observation

In some Bible versions, the Hebrew of verse 7 has been translated, "Wisdom is supreme." The better translation, "The beginning of wisdom is 'Get wisdom,' " is difficult in that it is both redundant and uses an imperative phrase as a predicate. But this can be a deliberate anacoluthon (violation of syntax) meant to drive home the idea that the first step in the pursuit of wisdom is to determine to obtain her. Wisdom is the greatest possession anyone can have, and the young man should make winning her the primary goal of his life.

The appeal in verses 10–19 has the normal structure of a paternal exhortation: an opening appeal to listen (4:10–13) followed by an exhortation in a specific area (4:14–19). In this case, the exhortation warns the reader to avoid one of the two tempters, the criminal. But the relative length of the appeal to listen implies that the family bond is a major concern of this text. If the young man should go wrong, he not only hurts himself but also his parents.

The passage also presents in vivid colors the depravity of the wicked. They live for crime. It is their food, drink, and sleep (4:16–17). They do not commit crimes in order to live but live to commit crimes. Even so, their punishment will be appropriate. Their greatest satisfaction is in making others fall, but they, too, shall fall and not know how or why.

In the closing appeal in verses 20–27, the father does not concern himself with specific moral issues. Instead, his focus is to encourage the son to stay true to wisdom. The imagery of body parts floods this text. The eyes are to stay fixed on right teaching (4:21, 25), and the feet are to stay on the right path (4:26–27). The mouth and lips must shun using crooked words (4:24). Above all, the heart must be guarded by sound doctrine (4:21, 23). If the son listens to his father, the whole body will be healthy (4:22).

Demystifying Proverbs

When Proverbs refers to the *heart*, it is not referring to the physical organ but to the mind, the whole personality of the individual. It is the wellspring of life in that the capacity to live in this world in peace comes ultimately from within and not from circumstances. The corrupt heart brings one down to the grave, but wisdom protects the heart from being brought down to the abyss. Thus, if the heart is protected from folly, then life, joy, and peace become available.

The fourth exhortation, in verses 25–27, closes with a return to the image of the path. The warning to move neither to the right nor to the left (4:27) is also found in Deuteronomy 5:32; 17:11; 28:14; and Joshua 23:6. The idea is that one should not be distracted from the way of wisdom. The way of wisdom should not be ignored, added to, or subtracted from. Wisdom provides the way of life, and everything around it is the way of destruction.

📖 5:1–23

MORAL FIDELITY

In verse 1, the father again appeals to the young man to pay attention to his teaching. Morality is always an issue of the heart. If one's heart remains pure, then one can maintain a life of integrity (5:2). Current history is littered with those who have failed to live with integrity and have lost their voice in the world.

In verse 3, the immoral woman uses flattery to draw the young man in. Her lips are filled with words that appeal to the pride of the man and pull him into an inappropriate relationship with her. Verses 4–6 describe the bitter outcome of this relationship: torment, disappointment, emotional suffering, and even death. In other words, there is no upside to this relationship; all it does is harm people. To join this woman on her path to destruction is to join with death (5:6).

Demystifying Proverbs

The writer of Proverbs is not exaggerating when he says that consorting with an immoral woman can lead to death. In ancient Israel, sexual sin was punishable by death (see Leviticus 20:10).

In verse 7, the father warns his sons not to stray from his warning. A contemporary image is that of a man guiding his sons through a minefield. The goal is not to get as close to danger as possible but rather to stay far away (5:8). Then the sons will not have to worry about their reputations, losing their money in fast living, or sexually transmitted diseases (5:9–11). The use of the plural in this passage has led many to believe that this woman could be a prostitute or someone who is involved with a whole immoral system that will draw this young man in and destroy him.

Even when the sons are older, they will still feel the impact of an immoral relationship. They will regret the day until they are old (5:12–14).

In contrast to the dire consequences of sexual immorality, the father now extols the joys of sex within marriage in verses 16–17. He makes the point that one's body is meant to be shared with a spouse and no one else. Men and women who hold to this view will have the blessing of a great life of intimacy together (5:18). God-pleasing sexuality is intended to be joyous and satisfying. In such a relationship there is no need to look elsewhere (5:19–20).

The Lord knows not only what everyone does but also everyone's thoughts. A secret rendezvous is no secret; God will know (5:21). Those who abandon God's plan for marriage will suffer the pain that is associated with this lifestyle (5:22). There is no moral neutral ground—to consider this immoral action is a step toward death. Such a person will die for lack of discipline. In short, the man will sow the seeds of his own destruction if he follows this path.

LIFE SKILLS

At face value, verses 1–5 seem to say that one should not cosign a loan. The heart of this text, however, is that no one should get into legal entanglements and debts that are out of their control.

The ants are models of diligence. They have a work ethic that drives them to work hard and prepare for winter (6:6–8). In contrast, laziness leads to certain poverty and ruin (6:9–11). The lazy person places rest and sleep as the non-negotiable in life. Sleep is meant to give the body energy for work; it was never intended to be a way of life. Laziness will siphon off resources until the slothful have nothing left.

The people referred to in verses 12–14 can best be described as hucksters. A huckster is someone who pretends to be a friend; they tell people all the things they want to hear. But they do this to get something in return. A huckster takes advantage of people. This person will use every deceit in the book to get his or her way. This lifestyle is one that God will not bless. Because they sow destruction in the lives of others, they will reap destruction (6:15).

Verses 16–19 enumerate things that God hates, in a clear, numerical manner for easy memorization. The first five things mentioned in this list are body parts. These body parts are set in a sequence that moves from the head to the feet (6:17–18). These five items concern general moral characteristics: pride, dishonesty, and a violent or manipulative character. The last two are types of people that specifically belong to a court or governmental system (6:19).

The final section of Proverbs 6 contains another warning about sexual immorality. The exhortation begins in verse 20 with the now-familiar appeal for the son to heed his father's words. The father's teachings function as a guide, guardian, and companion (6:22). They are meant to accompany the son wherever he goes. The father's teaching is to shed light on the moral decisions of life and to help the young man recognize when a woman seeks to pull him into her web of sin through seductive words (6:23–24).

Such a woman is alluring and even beautiful to the young man (6:25). Yet she is deadly. To embrace her is to embrace destruction and death. A prostitute can impoverish a man, and the consequences of messing around with a married woman are even worse: The outraged husband will bring all his fury down upon the adulterer (6:26, 29). A person can't play with fire and not get burned (6:27–28).

In verses 30–31, the writer makes a comparison between adultery and theft. Even a thief who steals out of hunger must repay his victim seven times over. How much more will adultery bring down a harsh verdict on an adulterer—for this is the worst of all of actions. The marriage bed is to be held in high honor, and those who violate this will be punished to the worst degree. The young man must understand this, for it will serve him well as he enters the world where this kind of behavior goes on.

7:1-27

BEWARE OF THE ADULTERESS

As this section opens, the father urges the son to keep his commands (7:1-3). This is said with the same force that is often used of God's commands. In other words, what is about to be said has to be heeded and treated with the utmost respect.

In verse 4, *sister* is a term of endearment for a girlfriend or wife. The young man is to love wisdom rather than the immoral woman. He is to love what God loves and not offer his heart to immorality (7:4-5).

In order to make his point in the most powerful manner, the father tells of an occasion when he actually observed a young man being seduced by an adulteress. When the father looked out his window, he saw a young man walking toward the house of an immoral woman at twilight. It is not clear whether he was intentionally going there or just passing by. The woman's loud, seductive, and inappropriate behavior shows that she is the type of woman that he should run away from (7:6-13).

The woman has either paid her vows or needs to do so (7:14). If she has paid her vows, her sins are atoned for, and she apparently feels free to start accumulating a load of sin again. Or perhaps she is suggesting exchanging her favors for the animal she needs to sacrifice. Her husband is gone with all the money (7:19-20), so she is turning to prostitution to pay her vow. This might be a deceptive ploy to get the man to agree with her. Because of the serious nature of vows, he might seek to help her with this promise.

Demystifying Proverbs

Deuteronomy 23:17-18 warns against using money earned by prostitution for paying vows. Apparently this was one of the ways that people sought to raise the money to pay their vows.

Now, having dealt with the young man's moral qualms, she devotes the rest of her seduction to a promise of a night of passion (7:15-18). In his acquiescence, the young man is both passive, like the ox going to slaughter, and dim-witted, like a deer or bird going into a trap (7:21-23). He is about to pay the full price for this sin—his life.

When the son comes across a woman like this, he is to run from her as far and as fast as he can. Her heart and her house are the way of death; there is no upside to following her (7:24-27).

8:1-36

A SECOND MESSAGE FROM WISDOM

In verses 1-3, wisdom calls for an audience at the places where people need her message: from the heights by the road, at crossroads, and at entrances to the city. Her message is not just for the elite but is brought for all people to hear.

While claiming that her gifts are for everyone, wisdom especially offers understanding to the foolish and simple (8:4-5). Nonetheless, her words are profitable for everyone because they are right, honest, and wholesome, without anything twisted or perverse (8:6-8). The wise as well as the foolish will benefit from wisdom's instruction because God's wisdom is worth more than all the riches in the world (8:9-11).

Critical Observation

The placement of wisdom's second message here in chapter 8 is significant. The previous chapter highlights the dangers of ignoring wisdom. Now, to make sure that we get the point, wisdom calls out for everyone to listen to her message.

Even though wisdom is accessible to everyone, it is still the most deep and profound reality in the world. This is first seen by the way it deals with the world. Observe that wisdom claims to possess prudence, knowledge, and discretion (8:12). The word *prudence* carries the idea of sensible behavior (1:4; 8:5). The word *discretion* refers to careful behavior that arises from clear and wise thinking. Wisdom teaches how to live a balanced and careful life as opposed to a reckless life that leads to suffering the pain of folly.

This prudence is attained by fearing the Lord. According to verse 13, those who fear the Lord will hate what God hates and love what God loves. Wisdom also gives direction to life as well as strength to endure whatever the world brings (8:14).

Take It Home

The prudence that comes from fearing the Lord implies one strong and important point: If a person fears the Lord, then evil behavior, pride, and wicked speech are all rejected (8:13). Those who practice such foolish behavior, however intelligent they may be by earthly measures, are fools because they have rejected the wisdom of God.

The reach of wisdom is not just for independent followers of God. Wisdom is also meant to be used by the leaders of the world. Wisdom is essential for those who have been given the responsibility to lead in government (8:15–16).

God has not made His wisdom inaccessible; His wisdom is available to all those who seek it (8:17). When wisdom arrives, she will bestow blessings and treasures on those who love and seek her (8:18–21). But improper motives with the pursuit of wisdom do not mix. In other words, we cannot try to pursue wisdom for the sake of gain. Rather, the pursuit of wisdom is the pursuit of the things that God loves for the purpose of the glory of God.

Verses 22–31 describe wisdom's role in creation. It is an important part because it sets the stage for the relationship between wisdom and the world. This passage could be divided into three parts: the birth of wisdom (8:22–26), wisdom's part in creation (8:27–29), and the joy of wisdom (8:30–31).

Wisdom is claiming to be the first principle of the world ever created and the pattern by which the world was created (8:22–26). The point here is that wisdom is the oldest of all principles in the world. As such, she holds to a superior position in the world and should be valued higher than creation itself.

Critical Observation

It is important to note the fact that wisdom existed before the dust of the ground (8:26). Mankind came from the dust of the ground. Therefore, humans, as dust, are part of the created world and cannot live contrary to the order by which the world was created. People who reject wisdom, therefore, reject something that is more powerful and wiser than they could ever hope to become. This is why every human needs to order his life by the wisdom of God.

Wisdom was present at two very significant points in creation, namely, the making of the heavens and the placing of restraints over the power of the sea (8:27–29). This is a powerful statement with direct implications. These two moments shaped creation. If humans are to live in this world in harmony with the world, then they must live according to the wisdom that shaped this world.

In the development of the world, wisdom found great joy (8:30–31). The creation of the world was in harmony with the logic of wisdom. Wisdom is an artisan, and the principles of wisdom are woven into the fabric of the created order. Thus, to truly understand the world around us, we need the wisdom of God.

Verses 8:32–36 are a fitting ending to this chapter. Since the whole world is embedded with wisdom, then it is very important to listen to wisdom. Those who listen become wise, but those who neglect to listen will suffer. In short, to have the blessing of God is to seek His wisdom. To fail to seek wisdom means that we will end up hurting ourselves and gaining destruction and death.

📖 9:1–18

TWO WAYS TO LIVE

The first major section of the book of Proverbs closes with a simple appeal: Will we walk in the way of wisdom or the way of folly?

Demystifying Proverbs

Proverbs 9 strongly emphasizes the notion of the two ways, a concept developed most completely in Proverbs and Deuteronomy. Either a person is with God and has life or rejects God and His ways and gets death. There is no neutrality—one is either on the side of life or death, and that is it.

The simple point of the passage is that if we enter wisdom's house, we will have life. Yet this point is made in some complex ways. The nature of wisdom's house of seven pillars is uncertain (9:1).

Wisdom has sent out a servant to invite everyone to her banquet (9:2–6). What this means is that the message of wisdom has been shouted around the entire world. The feast wisdom provides is illustrative of life, health, and celebration. It contrasts with the banquet of the dead behind folly's door (9:18).

The warning against trying to instruct mockers in verses 7–9 is common in Proverbs. Even though the call goes out to everyone, it always recognizes that there are some who will never listen. This reality appears even in 1:7, the theme verse of Proverbs.

Fear of the Lord is at the heart of being wise (9:10). To fear the Lord is to love what God loves and to hate what God hates. It is to have a heart of reverence for God that seeks glory to Him and Him alone.

The promise of life and statement of individual responsibility in verses 11–12 are a fitting conclusion to the call of wisdom. The joy and blessing that she offers is for the taking. Yet if someone rejects this message, he will bear the consequences of his folly all by himself, without help.

Verses 13–16 outline the way of folly. Like the adulteress (7:11), folly is loud, careless, and seductive. The parallel of verses 14–16 to verses 3–4 is obvious, but folly sits and accosts those who pass by as would a prostitute or a criminal in ambush.

Folly's promise of stolen water and food eaten in secret (9:17) is important to understand. Stolen water looks back to 5:15–18, where sexual relations are described as the drinking of water. Food eaten in secret is literally "bread of secrecy." It refers to the criminal conspiracies that tempt the young man to easy money, as in 1:11–14; 4:14–17; and 6:12–15. Folly entices one to sexual sin and to easy gain through immoral and illegal means. This is what folly appeals to—the basic instincts of our sin nature.

Verse 18 looks back to the two tempters—the man who draws the youth into a life of crime and the woman who draws him into promiscuity. Both are in the house of folly, and both draw more victims to the banquet of the dead. In short, everyone that joins in this way is dead spiritually. We cannot have life in this context. The only way to have life and blessing is to walk according to wisdom. We either walk in life by seeking the wisdom of God, or we walk in death seeking our own folly and walking and living among the spiritually dead.

PROVERBS 10:1–15:33

SOLOMON'S WISDOM, PART I

Setting Up the Section

This chapter marks a change in the way the book of Proverbs is written. Chapter 10 begins the part of Proverbs that most people think of when they encounter this book: short pithy statements of wisdom.

📖 **10:1–32**

CONTRASTING WISDOM AND FOOLISHNESS

In verses 1–5, the first theme emerges: that of the wise son versus the foolish son. The theme of these first verses is that a family will flourish if the children are diligent in their work but will fall apart if they are lazy or resort to crime.

A simple point emerges in verse 1: The behavior of children helps shape the happiness of the parents. If children are wise, parents find joy; if they are foolish, parents are grieved. This is a warning both to parents, to instill wisdom in their children, and to children, to recognize that their actions have a direct impact on their parents' hearts.

Verse 2 contrasts two possible paths for a young adult. If he gains wealth through immoral means, that wealth will be limited to this life only. If he gains success through the right means, he will have more than just earthly prosperity; he will have eternal life.

Demystifying Proverbs

Material wealth was often seen as a sign of divine blessing in Solomon's culture, and Proverbs 10:4 holds up wealth as a reward for hard work. But Proverbs 10:2 makes it clear that wealth by itself has no redeeming value. To pursue wealth through immoral means is to do nothing but find emptiness in life, and death in the end. For this reason, it is important to pursue righteousness rather than wealth.

Verse 3 unfolds the security that comes to the righteous. God cares for His children. He is their provider and thus there is no need to lie, cheat, and steal to get money. At the same time, God works against the wicked. If they think that fame, success, money, freedom, and material things are going to make them happy, they are chasing a shadow. God will not allow them to have the happiness they think those things will give them.

The focal point in verse 4 is work ethic. The person who does not work hard will be sowing the seeds of poverty in his or her life. Many people turn to God for a quick path to riches, but God has made it clear that work is to be the primary means through which one acquires possessions and resources.

Critical Observation

Verse 3 says that God promises to care for His children, but verse 4 says that a lazy person will sow the seeds of poverty. Does this seem contradictory? The reality is that the one who seeks to serve God and trusts in God has the heart and the desire to do the work God has provided. A heart for God causes people to love what God loves, and one of the things that God loves is when His children work diligently. It is the means that God uses to provide.

Verse 5 points out that a person who works when he is supposed to work will bring honor to his parents and ultimately bring glory to God. A lazy person will bring shame to his family.

The contrast between a righteous person and a wicked person is common in Proverbs. Solomon wants his son to understand this difference, so here he sets out to explain it using six contrasts.

First, wicked people can be identified by their deceitful speaking; they try to hide what is truly in their hearts. The righteous, however, are known by the evidence of God's favor upon their lives (10:6). This blessing does not necessarily mean monetary blessing. In fact, when God blesses people, usually money is not the central piece. Usually blessings encompass a whole life that is touched by God.

Demystifying Proverbs

In the book of Proverbs, *righteousness* means the holiness of God carried out in life. It is the justice of God, the goodness of God, the equity of God put in action in the world. Thus the righteous one is the one who puts into practice the very character of God.

The second contrast deals with the legacy of a person (10:7). When God works in and through a person, he is remembered for what God did and thus has a great legacy—a legacy that continues to bless. When a wicked person dies, his name will not just be forgotten, but it will be run through the mud and he will be remembered for who he really was—a wicked man.

Demystifying Proverbs

Whenever the notion of a person's name is mentioned in the Old Testament, it refers to more than just a person's title. It refers to one's character, the way that a person is understood. The simple point in Proverbs 10:7 is that the character of a person will be made known for generations to come.

The third contrast is in how a person receives wisdom (10:8). A righteous person is humble and is able to learn from anyone; he is teachable. The wicked person here is called a babbling fool. The idea is that of a person who does all the talking and is not able to learn from anyone. The inevitable result is to fall flat on one's face.

The fourth contrast in verse 9 has to do with integrity—being the same on the inside as on the outside. A person with integrity walks in this world secure because he has nothing to hide and is free from the fear of being caught. In contrast, the wicked have no real security in this life because their sin and depravity will eventually come to the forefront, and all will see it.

In verse 10, the fifth contrast highlights the trouble that comes from the deceptiveness (winking the eye) of wicked people. Righteous people, in contrast, are peacemakers.

Critical Observation

Proverbs 10:10 has been translated in two different ways. Some follow the Hebrew text: "Whoever winks the eye causes trouble, but a babbling fool will come to ruin" (ESV). Others follow the Greek version of the Old Testament: "People who wink at wrong cause trouble, but a bold reproof promotes peace" (NLT). Those following the Greek version argue that a copyist accidentally recopied verse 8 instead of verse 10—a mistake that was corrected in the Greek version.

The sixth comparison (10:11) contrasts the speech of the righteous and the wicked. In the Hebrew culture, the mouth was considered the window to the heart of a person. What a righteous person says reflects a heart that has been refreshed by the righteousness of God. With words of encouragement, rebuke, and so on, a righteous person passes that refreshment on to others. In contrast, the purpose of wicked people's speech is largely to cover up the wickedness that is in their hearts.

Jesus confirms that one's words reflect one's heart in Luke 6:45.

The proverbs in verses 12–17 outline how righteousness would look lived out in contrast to wickedness lived out. If wickedness is the driving motivation in life, then strife will be the fruit; the one who is righteous will not attack an offense but will cover that offense with love (10:12). The wise use their tongues carefully, but fools bring suffering on themselves by their words (10:14). Verse 13 gives a graphic example of that suffering.

In general, life is easier for the rich than for the poor, but wealth that is wrongfully gained will bring a person to ruin and death (10:15–16). A sinful person who is seeking righteousness will listen to correction, while the one who rebels against wisdom leads others down the road to destruction (10:17).

Proverbs 10:18–32 is set up in what is called *chiastic* fashion. A topic is introduced—in this case the tongue, which is destructive in a wicked person and positive in a godly person (10:18–21). Then a second topic is talked about—in this case the stability of the righteous over the wicked (10:22–25). Then a third topic is introduced—in this case laziness (10:26). Then the second topic is revisited—the stability of the righteous (10:27–30). Finally the first topic is revisited—the tongue (10:31–32).

Demystifying Proverbs

The *chiastic* pattern used here and in other places in Proverbs sets parallel ideas in mirror image to each other. If one thinks of the first topic as labeled A, the second as B, and the third as C, the chiastic structure would arrange the topics ABC CBA.

WHAT THE LORD HATES

God hates fraud, pride, and dishonesty (11:1–3). Riches gained by the unrighteous will not help them on the Day of Judgment (11:4). Their dishonesty and ambition will be their downfall, while the godly will be rescued—to the delight of those watching, because they know that godly people make good fellow citizens, while a bad neighbor goes around gossiping (11:5–13).

A nation will flourish when its leader pays attention to trustworthy advisors (11:14). But because so many people are untrustworthy, it's foolish to cosign a loan with a stranger (11:15).

Ruthless people may get rich, but they can't buy the respect that is due to someone gracious and kind (11:16–18). Ultimately, all that their ill-gotten gain can buy them is eternal death, because God hates people with crooked hearts (11:19–20, 13), but He rewards the godly with eternal life (11:19–20). According to verse 21, even the children of the godly benefit.

Tucked in almost as a sidenote is a warning that beauty is no more a guarantee of a good life than is wealth. Beauty without character is like fancy jewelry on a pig (11:22).

Verses 25–28 elaborate further on the role of material wealth: It is to be shared with the needy. When money becomes too important to a person to share, it will trip the person up (11:28).

People's wickedness doesn't affect only the people themselves; it affects family and friends (11:29–30). If that is apparent already in earthly relationships, think how significant it will be in eternity (11:31).

📖 12:1–4

A GOOD MAN

Proverbs defines a good man as one who loves discipline, obtains favor from the Lord, is steady in the righteousness of the Lord, and has an excellent wife.

The man who loves the discipline of the Lord (12:1) is the man who loves knowledge, because he understands that, on his own, his thinking is depraved. Thus, when God reproves him and instructs him in the way he should go, he is excited because he can walk in this world the right and proper way. The one who hates reproof is the one whom the Bible calls stupid. Any person who wants his own folly over the wisdom of the Lord is not thinking right.

The good man is the one who obtains the favor of the Lord (12:2). He will obtain this favor because he seeks God's wisdom. God blesses the one who lives for Him and condemns the one who pursues evil. God does not show His favor to those who spurn Him.

The good man also does not seek to establish himself by wickedness (12:3). This means he will not seek to find his way in the world by manipulation. Instead, he seeks to establish himself in the righteousness of God. By doing this, he gives his life a sure and steady root upon which to grow.

Finally, the good man is the man whose wife becomes his crown (12:4). What this means is that the wife who is truly righteous has such an impact on a man that it makes him better and more respected in the world. The wife who is not righteous not only has to contend with her own wickedness but she is equated as rottenness in his bones.

📖 12:5–8

STABILITY AND RESPECT

The next three proverbs flow together in a way that makes a significant point. Observe the progression: The righteous make plans that are just, but the wicked scheme with deceitful counsel (12:5); the wicked attempt to ambush the righteous with their lies, but the righteous are delivered by their integrity (12:6); the wicked are totally destroyed, but the righteous stand secure (12:7). The heart of this passage is that the righteous will stand secure in this world because they are established in the righteousness of God. Whatever comes against them will not uproot the security that they have in God.

With this stability comes respect. Solomon wants his son to understand that respect is not given by accomplishments alone; respect is gained by wisdom. If a person has the good sense to walk according to the wisdom of God, he will earn respect from those around him. On the other hand, to follow his own sense of twisted wisdom will lead to not only his own destruction but to being ridiculed by the world (12:8). The key to being respected is to walk in the wisdom of the Lord.

📄 12:9–15

A HUMBLE WORK ETHIC

This section opens with a reminder that a lifestyle of moderate comforts is far more desirable than the pretense of wealth (12:9). Verse 10 builds on this by saying that a good man cares for those who provide for him, even if they are only animals. The wicked take advantage of everyone and everything. This builds to a key point in verse 11: True success comes by hard work rather than by looking for the get-rich-quick scheme.

Solomon now broadens the topic of work and payment to make a powerful point about the wages that come to the wicked and those that come to the righteous. Wicked people are not repulsed by the wickedness of others but actually covet the spoils that others have managed to steal for themselves. They are never satisfied and are constantly wanting more. In contrast to this is the righteous man, who continues to prosper without stealing or defrauding people (12:12).

The evil man who walks down this road becomes ensnared by his lips. The lies that he tells will catch up to him, and he will be brought down by his own depravity. The righteous do not need to fear this kind of trouble because they walk in integrity, and integrity will not allow a man to become ensnared (12:13).

Verse 14 sums this up by saying that words are like labor. A person who uses his words with integrity will enjoy the fruit of that integrity. For what comes from the mouth reflects what is in the heart, and a righteous heart is satisfied with good words. The wise person is also ready to listen to words spoken with integrity, while fools are so sure of themselves that they never seek advice (12:15).

📄 12:16–22

THE RECKLESSNESS OF LYING AND THE VALUE OF TRUTH

The characteristics of fools described in this text are:
1) They react thoughtlessly to everything they hear and hurt others with thoughtless words (12:16–18).
2) They are liars and will incur the wrath of God (12:17, 19, 22).
3) They plot and scheme but in the end only bring trouble on themselves (12:20–21).

In contrast, characteristics of the wise are:
1) They respond with patience in the face of trials and insults (12:16, 18).
2) They bring healing with their words (12:16, 18).
3) They are honest and gain long life and divine favor (12:17, 19, 22).
4) They seek the well-being of others while gaining it for themselves (12:20–21).

The tongue of the wicked brings destruction, while the tongue of the righteous brings healing.

Critical Observation

Verses 16–22 use a form of repetition to make a point about the value of truth and the reckless-ness of lying. The issue of reckless words emerges two times (verses 16 and 18). The issue of honesty and lying emerges three times (verses 17, 19, and 22). Two times the issue of trouble for the wicked and peace for the righteous are addressed (verses 20 and 21). The parallels are not exact parallels, but instead they are loosely connected themes expressing similar ideas from slightly different points of view.

📖 12:23–28

A LIFE OF WISDOM

The final six proverbs of chapter 12 describe the characteristics of a life of wisdom.

According to verse 23, wise people are slow to speak and slow to share what they know. In addition, they seek to help their friends and be a source of assistance rather than lead-ing them astray (12:26). In contrast, foolish people talk a lot and thereby proclaim their folly (12:23). In their talking, they also lead their friends astray rather than help their friends along (12:16).

Wise people know the value of hard work. Again we see how much God values hard work and blesses the diligent (12:24, 27). Slothful people, however, will be forced into work against their will and will not be able to feed themselves (12:24).

Wise people also know the value of good words. Correctly used, words can build up a person weighted down by the stress of life (12:25).

The culmination of all of these dictums is that there is true life in righteousness (12:28). To walk in the righteousness of God means to find true life.

Take It Home

The only way to walk in the righteousness of God is to exchange your sin for God's righteous-ness. This occurs through bringing your sin to Jesus Christ (2 Corinthians 5:21). Once a person is walking in the righteousness of God, death will have no sting. In the righteousness of God there is life in abundance.

📖 13:1–11

WORDS AND ACTIONS

The theme of the mouth reemerges in chapter 13. The wise son listens to what his father says, while the wicked son does not listen but instead uses his mouth to mock his father's instruction (13:1). When a person uses good words, it is like eating a good meal (13:2). Good words nourish a person and cause a person to become healthy and strong. Those who guard their mouths avoid trouble. Those who do all the talking come to ruin (13:3). The talker is symbolic of those who do not listen to rebuke and speak out of their own arrogance. People like this will find themselves coming to ruin because of their pride.

Again the issue of a work ethic emerges—a common topic in Proverbs. The point to be drawn here is that, as a principle, lazy people will not get what they desire, because what they desire is gain without effort. Diligent people, on the other hand, want to reap the results of hard work, and generally they do (13:4).

Solomon wants his son to understand that the person who walks in integrity is protected by that integrity. Problems emerge for those who do not love righteousness and truth. Yet those who love righteousness and truth have the great privilege of finding protection from the consequences that befall those who hate righteousness (13:5–6).

Verses 7–11 deal with wealth and its deceptive nature. There is more to verse 7 than just pretending to be rich or poor. The bigger point is that things are not always what they seem. One person may appear to be rich but in fact is not, and on a more fundamental level has nothing. This is illustrated in verse 8: The rich may be able to pay a ransom, but the poor don't have to worry about being kidnapped in the first place. Verses 9–11 reiterate one of the central issues of Proverbs: A person who pursues wisdom will gain a reward far more lasting than the person who pursues money at all cost.

📖 **13:12–19**

HOPE AND DISAPPOINTMENT

Verses 12–19 follow the chiastic pattern of parallels that is used in 10:18–21. Outlined, it would look like this:

A. Hope fulfilled or deferred (13:12)
    B. Advice received or rejected (13:13)
        C. Reliable vs. unreliable instruction (13:14)
            D. Good sense vs. foolishness (13:15)
            D. Good sense vs. foolishness (13:16)
        C. Reliable vs. unreliable instruction (13:17)
    B. Advice received or rejected (13:18)
A. Hope fulfilled or deferred (13:19)

To receive the tree of life is to have an abundant life that cannot be taken away. To gain that abundant life, one must practice obedience, learn from people worthy of respect, and not act rashly (13:13–16).

Critical Observation

The tree of life is first mentioned in Genesis 2:9. Adam and Eve's sin puts the tree of life out of reach; they are banished from the garden where it grows. The book of Revelation tells of regaining the right to eat from the tree of life (Revelation 2:7; 22:14). Proverbs is the only other book of the Bible in which the tree of life is mentioned (Proverbs 3:18; 11:30; 13:12; 15:4).

A messenger is an example of a person charged with a serious responsibility (13:17). Just as an envoy is charged with representing someone and speaking the words of the one he represents, so too the faithful child of God must represent the wisdom of God and take it seriously. There are consequences for not being faithful.

📄 13:20–25

RELATIONSHIPS

Verses 20–21 speak of choosing friends wisely. Just as good friends have good influences, a friend who gets into trouble generally gets his friends in trouble with him.

Verses 22–25 present a worldview of the family. A wise family provides for the next generation in both physical and spiritual ways. God sets the pattern for this provision. Ultimately, God will use the wealth of the wicked for His children (13:22). A truly righteous person is satisfied. He is not seeking to get more and feeling the sting of consumerism. But a wicked person is never satisfied; he wants more and more (13:25).

Take It Home

The underlying point of this verse is that parents who spoil their children aren't providing a strong foundation of character for their children's future. They are taking the easy way out. It's more work—and wins fewer popularity votes—to consistently pay attention to your child's behavior, encouraging positive actions and disciplining negative actions. It is also the way a loving parent behaves.

📄 14:1–17

FOOLS

The book of Proverbs continues to make the point that there are two paths in life: the path of those who fear the Lord (in other words, the wise, since according to Proverbs 1:7 the fear of the Lord is the beginning of wisdom) and the path of the foolish, who despise the Lord (14:2). The following verses give examples of this principle.

If a woman is wise, her home grows and gets better and better, but a woman who is foolish will bring pain and destruction upon her home (14:1).

Foolish bragging leads to painful consequences in a man's life, whereas the wise will speak the words that bring healing and hope to their lives (14:3).

Some people seek the ease of avoiding work (illustrated by the clean and empty stable), but a wise person knows that those who take the burden of work (here illustrated by caring for an ox) also get the reward that comes from the work (14:4).

Yet again the mouth is brought into the conversation. The way that a person speaks reflects the condition of his or her heart. It is wise to avoid liars and mockers, because their language reveals the foolishness of a heart that does not fear the Lord (14:5–7).

Those who fear God understand what they are doing and why they are doing it. In contrast, foolish people will be seeking to hide the true intentions of their hearts (14:8).

A foolish person will sin and find no need to make things right before God, but a wise person seeks the path that God established to deal with guilt, and thus enjoys the forgiveness and acceptance that comes from having guilt wiped away (14:9). Everyone knows the real state of his or her own heart, so when the wicked deny their need for forgiveness, they lie to themselves and to God (14:10).

Even though wicked people may amass things on this earth, destruction will come. Even though righteous people might not gain as much, in the end they will know the security of being right with God (14:11). The way that seems right to wicked people is not really right at all. They might look at the world around them and feel as if they have everything, but in the end they will have nothing but destruction (14:12). They may seem to have fun, but the reality is those who live without God do not have the fun and excitement that they appear to have (14:13). When they leave the charade of fun and acknowledge their real condition, they will find that they chose the wrong path (14:14).

Critical Observation

The idea of the backslider in verse 14 is not the contemporary one of a Christian who progressively falls away from God. In this passage, the idea is that of people who eventually cannot keep up the external face of everything going well and begin to walk in their sin without a facade of goodness.

Wise people will think about what they hear and weigh what they are being asked to participate in, while foolish people jump at everything (14:15–16). Wise people understand that they must follow God. Foolish people think of nothing because God means nothing to them. Those who are quick to anger will make one foolish decision after another (14:17).

📖 **14:18–27**

THE REWARDS OF THE HEART

Solomon wants his son to understand what will happen to the wicked and the righteous on this side of heaven. Those who do not pursue wisdom will inherit folly; they will have to deal with the fruit of their wickedness. Eventually foolish people will bow down before the wise. They will not have honor in this world. The only way to have honor is to seek to honor God (14:18–19).

Verses 20–22 acknowledge that no one wants to be poor, and the poor do not garner the respect in the world that the rich do. But those who show kindness toward others, regardless of their social and economic standing, are blessed by God.

While it is true that many people are poor despite their best efforts, verses 23–24 make clear that this is no excuse for not working. The principle remains that the fruit of real work is reward, but people who hate work and only talk a good game get nothing.

The proverb in verse 25 appears to have the notion of legal proceedings as its theme. Honesty in court is not a mere fine point of law; people's lives depend upon it. This is why many legal systems have a moment where those giving testimony are called to give an oath that they are telling the truth.

Verses 26–28 give more examples of the benefits that accrue to those who fear the Lord. Fearing the Lord provides security from the storms of life and a kind of early warning system against the moral traps that wait. Thus, fearing the Lord is not just a religious or ceremonial act but a path of security in the world.

📄 **14:28–35**

WISDOM AND THE NATION

The health and well-being of a nation depends upon both the ruler and the governed. A ruler must be fair and, above all, must respect the rights of his people. The people, on the other hand, must have virtue in their lives or they will bring society into chaos. No government can succeed without the people, and no people can thrive if corruption and evil abound.

Without people there is no nation to govern (14:28). Thus, every leader must realize that the people he leads are also the people he needs. He must honor and serve those whom he has been entrusted to rule.

Verse 29 stresses the importance of patience. In this context, an impatient king may lose his people (14:28), and a headstrong servant of the king may lose his place before the king (14:35). Thus, patience must be a ruling virtue for both king and subject. Patience is essential for a healthy life as well (14:30).

Verse 31 stands as a warning to rulers not to trample upon the rights of the poor. The king who ignores this advice will soon find himself without a nation. God takes it personally when people disrespect the needy and hurt them for the purpose of personal gain. To honor God is to care for those who cannot care for themselves.

Wicked people will be overthrown, not by their enemies, but by their own evildoings. Yet those who pursue righteousness have hope, even on their deathbeds (14:32). This hope does not come from power; it comes from walking in the fear of the Lord—true wisdom (14:33).

Wisdom is not just for personal gain—there is a national aspect to it as well. A nation's political health depends to a great degree on the moral integrity of its people (14:34). For this reason, political leaders are better served by people of integrity (14:35).

📄 **15:1–17**

THE TONGUE AND THE HEART

The ability to avert quarreling and to live in harmony with others is a virtue of wisdom. A wise person knows how to speak gently, appealingly, and truthfully (15:1–4). He both listens to and gives good advice, and the prayers he speaks are pleasing to God (15:5–8). But God hates the religious practices of the wicked. What pleases God the most is not religious ceremony but a heart that pursues righteousness all the time (15:9).

God will allow a fool to have the complete consequences for all of his actions. And those who do not repent under this discipline and continue to reject it will die (15:10–11). This death could refer to spiritual death alone, but Proverbs makes it clear that both physical and spiritual death are included in the consequences. How foolish it is to reject correction (15:12)!

Demystifying Proverbs

Some versions of the Bible use the words *Sheol* and *abaddon* in verse 11, while others use the words *death* and *destruction*. *Sheol* refers to the place of the dead. *Abaddon* refers to the experience of destruction for the wicked. The point is that God has the power to bring death and destruction to those whose hearts are set against Him.

Verse 13 reminds the reader that the focal point should always be the heart and nothing else. A person cannot control his experience with this world from the outside in; it has to be from the inside out. A wise person seeks to understand the world from God's point of view, which brings joy to the heart (15:14). A happy heart has a continual feast (15:15). In fact, to have a heart feasting on the joy, fear, and love of the Lord is better than a literal feast (15:16–17).

📖 15:18–33

TWO ROADS

The remainder of chapter 15 outlines a series of contrasts between the wicked person and the righteous person in relation to anger (15:18), laziness (15:19), relationships with parents (15:20), joy (15:21, 30), taking advice (15:22, 31–32), speech (15:23, 28), prudence (15:24), protection (15:25), intentions (15:26), greed (15:27), and prayer (15:29).

The summation of all these contrasts is that the ultimate starting point of wisdom is the fear of the Lord (15:33).

Take It Home

These proverbs were written with the intent of helping the king's son become a better leader. While you might not have a kingdom to oversee, you may have equally important areas of responsibility as a parent, household provider, office manager, committee chairman, or so forth. What advice from these proverbs can you apply to your own "domains"?

PROVERBS 16:1–22:16
SOLOMON'S WISDOM, PART II

Setting Up the Section

In this ongoing segment of the proverbs of Solomon (10:1–22:16), this particular section begins a minor shift. Chapters 10 through 15 made a lot of contrasts between righteous and unrighteous behavior. Chapters 16 through 22:16 contain fewer contrasts and instead begin to focus more on the value of righteous behavior.

▤ 16:1–15

THE HEAVENLY KING AND EARTHLY KINGS

Chapter 16 begins with a reminder that God is sovereign. If Solomon's son were to truly rule in peace, he must first acknowledge that he did not have ultimate control over the world. Everything he did must be submitted to the ultimate will of God.

Verses 1 through 3 are a reminder that *all* human plans are subject to the will of God, who will have the final say as to what will actually happen. This is not meant to discourage people from planning, the importance of which is emphasized in other parts of scripture (see Luke 14:28–33), yet it is important to remember that God's will is the ultimate trajectory of life. The Lord knows people's hearts and understands why they desire what they do. If He overrides someone's plans, it is because He knows what drives those plans. The more a person fears the Lord, the more his or her plans will be in accordance with the will of God.

God is intimately involved in this world and has made everything for His purposes (Proverbs 16:4). Even nonbelievers, as they eventually suffer the consequences of their actions, reveal God's righteous judgments. Verse 5 affirms that wicked people will certainly not go unpunished. People can live entire lifetimes being prideful and powerful, appearing to be in charge and getting their way. But in the end, they will be humbled in the judgment of God.

Avoiding the problem of pride is a simple matter of fearing the Lord (16:6). God is a God of mercy and truth who has made atonement for the sin of the proud (Isaiah 53:5). People can be forgiven of their sin and learn to walk right with God if they submit to Him in fearful reverence. Not only will they begin to avoid evil, but they will also see positive changes in the everyday circumstances of life (Proverbs 16:7).

Critical Observation

The promise in Proverbs 16:7 is a general principle. The writer does not mean that a godly person will not have enemies. However, when God's favor shines on a person, he or she is much less likely to experience opposition from others.

After someone develops a fear of the Lord, his or her perspective shifts (16:8). The person begins to understand that it is more preferable to have only a little in this world while remaining righteous than to acquire much without justice. Verse 9 echoes verse 1: People make their plans, but God ultimately directs their steps.

While these insights are valuable for anyone, they are especially relevant for human leaders. Solomon's son would be next in line for royal leadership, so it was important for him to understand how a king was to act.

To begin with, a king should remember that his words are not just for himself, but that he speaks decrees for the entire nation (16:10). He is not to use the role of "oracle" for his own personal purposes. The word metaphorically describes the king as having deep spiritual wisdom allowing him to become the channel for the plan of God.

Justice is another crucial criterion for a godly king. While verse 11 does not directly mention the king, it is in the context of kingly instructions. Justice is derived from God, and human leaders do not have the authority to suspend or violate the principles of fairness. King and subjects alike should honor honesty and justice.

If a king uses his position for personal profit, he ignores the justice of God and commits an utter abomination. Kings should acknowledge and reward those who speak the truth (16:12–13). In return, people should show proper respect for their king. The king controls the power of the nation, and the sword may fall on anyone who incites his wrath. It is far wiser to appease the king than to antagonize him (16:14–15).

16:16–33

A DISCIPLINED LIFESTYLE

Life is a series of choices, which is why Solomon yet again emphasizes the importance of wisdom (16:16–17). People see the value of tangible things like gold and silver, yet wisdom and understanding are far more valuable. Choosing positive but intangible qualities over the riches of the world requires humility, as Solomon explains in verses 18 and 19. Those who take pride in their riches are destined for destruction.

A person's words reflect his or her inner motives. Wise words are instructive (16:20), pleasant (16:21), and life-giving (16:22). A wise heart guides one's speech. Wise words are as exciting and pleasurable as candy to a child (16:24).

The choice of "ways" in life is the issue of verse 25. Imagine a person committing to a particular road that looks just fine, yet when he comes to the end he discovers that death lies before him no matter which way he turns. The image suggests that anyone left to his own natural thoughts will end up pursuing a path to destruction.

Honest people work in order to eat (16:26). In contrast, some people seek easier, less demanding ways to make money. They create evil schemes to acquire wealth unethically. Verses 27 through 30 expose the motives of the crook, the wicked person, and the violent person. Such people bring nothing but pain and misery on themselves and others.

Making good life choices can be difficult, but it is ultimately rewarding. A person who lives a righteous life is more likely to live longer (16:31). Controlling one's temper reflects great inner power—more than that of a victorious military leader (16:32).

Verse 33 concludes the chapter as it had begun, with a reminder that the sovereignty of God directs all human activity. People have a number of ways to decide how to proceed in life, but they should be thankful that God is the One whose will is ultimately accomplished.

Demystifying Proverbs

A *lot* (16:33) was like a die or dice thrown to help leaders ascertain God's direction (see, for instance, the Urim and Thummim of Exodus 28:30). God would control the piece(s) and make His will known. The casting of lots is found throughout the Old Testament and the Gospels, culminating with the selection of a disciple to replace Judas Iscariot (Acts 1:23–26). But after the coming of the Holy Spirit, the casting of lots was not mentioned again in scripture.

📖 17:1–28

THE PAIN OF FOLLY

Proverbs repeatedly makes it clear that peace resulting from the blessing of God is far preferable to acquired wealth that creates problems and suffering. Solomon had untold riches at his disposal, yet he understood that the simple essentials of life with "peace and quiet" were better than great wealth accompanied by strife (17:1).

Verse 2 was a profound point for the son of a king to consider. Wisdom would allow one's ability and character to overcome any disadvantages of birth, and those born to advantage could forfeit their position through immorality and sloth. Choosing wisdom is not always as simple as it might seem. God will sometimes "test the heart" (17:3), bringing out the true nature of a person.

People often have little choice of whether or not they *hear* gossip and slander, but they can always choose whether or not to *believe* it. Those who thrive on taking gossip seriously are malevolent and hate the truth (17:4). Similarly, those who mock or celebrate the sufferings of others display a cruelty that will certainly be punished. The offense is not only against their fellow human beings but also against God (17:5).

Some people like to revel in their individuality, but they are not as independent of others as they might like to think. Verse 6 puts things in perspective. Older adults derive a sense of honor from their descendants, while children depend on their parents for a sense of self-worth.

People's words should reflect their true natures. It quickly becomes evident when a foolish person attempts to be arrogant or when the leader of the nation is telling lies (17:7).

Proverbs 17:8 is what some scholars call an observational proverb. Its intent is not to promote offering bribes. The point, rather, is to show that those who give gifts often receive special favors and are treated differently from those who hoard their wealth.

The section that follows shows the pain and destruction that come from foolishness and why it is of extreme importance that people of God not associate with fools. To begin with, the foolish people who keep harping on the offenses of others are unable to establish lasting friendships (17:9). "Covering" an offense includes not only forgiving the wrongdoing but also refusing to bring it up again. Fools, however, keep dwelling on the mistakes of their peers.

However, that doesn't mean people are always to "look the other way" when someone sins. Verse 10 continues the thought and clarifies that the wise person's pursuit of truth will include a willing acceptance of well-intentioned rebukes for things he or she has done wrong.

Fools, on the other hand, tend not to be swayed no matter what happens. One hundred lashes would not turn foolish people from their corrupt ways (17:10). Such obstinacy makes it dangerous to be near fools (17:12). People who refuse to accept constructive criticism create chaos for all of society.

The rebellion of foolish hearts has consequences, according to verse 11. Rebellious people are repeatedly sought out to receive imposed justice. They will never escape problems in their lives. And those who repay good with evil will soon find themselves plagued with evil (17:13).

Conflicts cannot always be avoided, yet they can be controlled. Starting a quarrel is more dangerous than it may seem. . .not unlike breaching a dam. It's much easier to keep the water from overflowing to begin with than to try to stop it once it begins to gush. Wise people are quick to respond to contention with kindness, directness, and forgiveness (17:14).

With no desire for wisdom, foolish people acquit the guilty and condemn the innocent (17:15). They can collect money for schooling, but without a genuine desire for wisdom, the money goes to waste (17:16). No one wants such people around during difficult times. That's when people seek the help of true friends (17:17). A real friend is more than just someone who vouches for another (17:18); a genuine friend is there around the clock. But those who never resist the tendency to sin are quick to quarrel, and they will eventually fall hard, like an oversized gate in a city wall (17:19).

Folly is particularly painful within households, yet people with perverse hearts and deceitful tongues (17:20) affect those close to them as well as outsiders. Verses 20–22 imply that the greatest source of a crushed spirit is trouble in the family. Foolish children create much pain for righteous parents (17:21, 25). Such foolish behavior circumvents the happy hearts that are key to full and healthy lives (17:22).

It seems that some people literally "lose sight" of wisdom (17:24). They accept bribes to punish the innocent and/or allow the guilty to go free (17:23, 26).

A wise person uses few words (17:27). According to verse 28, even fools can appear wise if they keep their mouths shut. By paying attention over time to what (and how much) a person says, one can determine whether that person is wise or foolish. Words are the fruit that reflect the quality of the heart.

📖 18:1–24

WISE AND FOOLISH WORDS

The selfish pursuits of foolish people result in the frequent expression of their personal opinions (18:1-2). In the absence of wisdom, they are drawn to vanity and narcissism.

The contempt and shame associated with foolish and wicked people are usually accompanied by verbal insults. In contrast to such shallowness, wise people are described in verse 4 as a fountain—not only deep, but refreshing and life-restoring as well.

Foolish words can be harmful to others when innocent people are deprived of justice and wicked people get away with their corrupt behavior (18:5). But those same words are also harmful to the people who speak them, resulting in potential physical violence and spiritual defeat (18:6-7). Similarly, gossip may be considered "tasty" by some (18:8), yet consumption of those morsels of gossip results in conflict and eventual destruction.

Gossip and inappropriate speech are not the only problems among wicked people, of course. Laziness is another common factor (18:9). Such people also tend to depend on their wealth for security, while wise people know that God is the only reliable refuge (18:10-11). Lessons of humility come too late for the wicked, who learn only after a disaster that their self-reliance is insufficient.

People who "answer before listening" (18:13) reflect an arrogant spirit not concerned with truth. They reject instruction and are unwilling to hear others' opinions, which is both a folly and a shame. Their words can have powerful effects, even to the extent of crushing a person's spirit (18:14).

While many people adopt the behavior of the wicked, others see its limitations and commit to seeking wisdom instead (18:15). The gift that opens the way for the giver, mentioned in verse 16, may be a reference to the gifts God gives people that allow them to help others, or its meaning may be along the lines of 17:8, suggesting that bribes are an effective means to prompt people to respond as one wishes.

Wise people do not respond too hastily to the words of others. Someone presenting his case may make quite a persuasive argument, but it is always valuable to hear the other side of the issue before reaching a final decision (18:17). When disputes arise, it is wise to seek God's mind in the matter—which was the purpose of casting lots. If the nation were to continue to function smoothly, it would be important for the people to settle their controversies quickly and justly (18:18-19).

While words can be misused in any number of ways (18:21), when used properly they can edify others. Verse 20 suggests that just as food satisfies one's hunger, well-chosen words can be an equally pleasurable source of contentment. Wise people take their words seriously.

From words, Solomon turns to relationships. The book of Proverbs has much to say about the importance of avoiding the wrong women and forming relationships with spiritually strong females. In this case, the emphasis is on the favor God will bestow on the husband of a good wife (18:22).

A person's financial status can affect his or her attitudes toward justice. The poor have no other recourse than to plead for mercy. Those who are rich, however, may tend to rely more on their status and respond harshly—to dictate terms rather than beg for forgiveness (18:23).

Finally, the choice of one's friends is a matter of wisdom versus folly as well (18:24). Those with many friends have little time for intimacy with any of them, and such people may be led astray by some of their many acquaintances. True friendships, however, can be much closer than family relations.

📖 19:1–29

PRIORITIES FOR THE BEST POSSIBLE LIFE

This section concludes the extensive "Proverbs of Solomon" that began in 10:1. What Solomon has been doing, and continues to do, is to help his son think through some important priorities for life. Many people try to get ahead by lying, cheating, and stealing, but there is a better way.

Honesty and integrity are crucial ingredients of the best possible life (19:1). Impulsiveness should be avoided. Hard work in itself is not enough because people should have an awareness of what they are doing and why (19:2). A respect for wisdom should underlie one's pursuits. Too often people go through life doing whatever they want to do, and then when things don't work out they are quick to blame God (19:3).

The proverb in verse 4 may say more than it appears to at first reading. Of course, wealth attracts friends more than poverty does, but what does that say about those "friends"? Genuine friendship should be the same between poor people as between rich ones. Wealth, then, seems to attract gold diggers and fortune hunters in the guise of "friends." The other side of this issue is reinforced in verse 7. The brutal truth is that many people don't necessarily like to associate with their poor friends and relatives, so what kind of "friendship" is that? In order for poorer people to have the best possible life, they need to find satisfaction in God. And wealthy people who truly love God will reach out to the poor.

Honesty is important at all times—not just when it is convenient. Witnesses need to speak the truth, even if they might profit in some way from a lie or half-truth (19:5). Similarly, in trying to impress rulers or people in power, the tendency is to tell them what they want to hear when truthfulness would serve a better purpose (19:6).

Rather than attempting to curry favor with influential people, it is far better to seek wisdom and find satisfaction with one's own life (19:8). The sense of satisfaction should be enough in itself, but it also prevents eventually being judged and punished for lying (19:9).

Verse 10 makes a simple, but astute, observation. People who seek wisdom and work hard to accomplish something of their lives can truly appreciate blessings and rewards when they come. But foolish people who somehow are plunged into luxury are no more able to enjoy life than a slave who somehow is promoted to rule. Neither is ready to appreciate the position that a wise person would be grateful for.

Those who walk in wisdom learn to control their emotions. Patience and slowness to anger are frequent challenges throughout Proverbs as well as the rest of scripture (19:11).

This is particularly true for leaders (19:12). The power that kings hold can easily be misused if they do not control their anger, but leaders set memorable examples when they are gracious and forgiving.

Contentment within the home must be a cooperative effort. One person can create misery for all the others, such as a foolish child or quarrelsome spouse (19:13). One aspect of wisdom is seeking God's direction in choosing one's lifetime mate (19:14).

One person's laziness has an effect on others as well, whether those others are family members or a wider community (19:15). It is difficult to effectively relate to people who would rather sleep than work or eat.

Two themes reoccur throughout Proverbs: obeying parental instructions and keeping the commandments of God. According to verse 16, such obedience is actually a matter of life or death more than people may realize. Children are not naturally wise and need to be trained in wisdom. Parents who love their children will discipline them lovingly and properly (19:18).

Verse 17 explains that the kindness shown toward other people is not only noticed by God but is also counted as if He were the recipient of such actions. Poor people may not be able to repay loans, but God certainly can. . .and will.

Critical Observation

Jesus would later make the same point as Solomon (19:17; Matthew 25:31–46). Whatever people do to "the least" of humanity is perceived as their attitude toward God.

The reason discipline is important at an early age (19:18) is to prevent problems such as the one described in Proverbs 19:19. When people fail to control their emotions, anger issues are not easily resolved. It can become a full-time job for someone to repeatedly "rescue" an angry friend or family member.

Wisdom comes from acknowledging and obeying God's instructions. A person's plans eventually come into alignment with God's plans for him or her. Poverty becomes less troublesome than loss of integrity in the search for unfailing love. With an ongoing, unyielding focus on obeying God, the rewards of life are great, including contentment and freedom from trouble (19:20–23).

As parents pass along God's instructions to their children, they may need to address common problems such as sloth, mocking, blatant dishonesty, and even violence. Discipline can turn children from such problems and teach them prudence and knowledge. Failure to address the problems, however, is likely to result in shame and disgrace for the entire family (19:24–26).

Sometimes parents do all they can do, and the children still don't respond. So Solomon follows with some specific warnings for those who ignore what they have been taught, beginning with his own son. An ongoing refusal to respond to the teachings of God and one's parents will surely result in evil, penalties, and punishments (19:27–29).

PRIORITIES FOR BECOMING THE BEST POSSIBLE HUMAN BEING

It is difficult enough to avoid conflicts in life under the best of conditions, so it is the essence of wisdom to minimize problems whenever and however possible. One way is to avoid intoxication that might otherwise lead to brawling. Another is to keep from provoking those in power. People who avoid conflict are seen in a positive light because any fool can pick a fight (20:1–3).

A wise person knows when to take action. In Israel's agricultural society, the seasons for planting and reaping were determined by the weather. Someone who refused to plant in the proper season would not be able to do so later, and such sluggards would be empty-handed at harvest time (20:4).

Solomon realized that many people claimed to be wise and righteous but never actually demonstrated it. Most people have deep feelings, but only a truly wise person will sort through those feelings and "draw out" significant truths about himself or herself. Once someone is able to learn to live in righteousness, however, his or her children receive the positive effects as well (20:5–7).

Verse 8 is another reminder that Solomon's mind is on the role of the nation's king. It is easy for those with much power to become corrupt, but a king with integrity has the power to "winnow out all evil." He just needs the determination to do so. Integrity is a challenge for everyone, from kings down to the children in the kingdom (20:8–11).

Demystifying Proverbs

The challenge of personal integrity is greater when society as a whole is corrupt. Solomon provided a number of clues as to the widespread problem of fraud in his nation. In 20:10 he cites "differing" weights and measures—tools used by unscrupulous merchants to cheat their customers. But lest we feel too sorry for the customers, they are shown in verse 14 loudly complaining about poor quality (no doubt to secure a lower price) and later boasting of the great deal they got.

Just as children are taught to look *and* listen before crossing a street, Solomon challenges his son not only to listen to a person's claims of wisdom and righteousness but also to see for himself if the person lives up to what he says (20:12). Remember, many people claim things that are not necessarily true (20:6). Sometimes all it takes is for a slothful person to stop lazing and stay awake. Before long he will see the results of his work (20:13).

One problem is that people don't tend to acknowledge the real value of wisdom. Solomon reminds his son that wisdom is a precious commodity even rarer than gold and rubies (20:15).

Wisdom involves doing certain things and *not* doing other things. Vouching for someone's debt, particularly that of a stranger, is usually not smart. Defrauding someone in order to eat ends up leaving a bad taste in a person's mouth. Rushing into major commitments without the advice of others is foolhardy. Talking too much and revealing sensitive information will lose friends. Cursing one's parents is a direct violation of God's law. Quickly squandering an inheritance will prevent enjoying it. Hasty revenge is not as satisfying as waiting for God to act. Dishonesty in business dealings both offends one's associates and angers God. Vows made without adequate thought can become problematic (20:16–25). Although many of these actions seem commonplace and natural, the wise person will exhibit patience and see better results.

Critical Observation

Clothing served as a sort of IOU for debts in the ancient world (Deuteronomy 24:10–14). Solomon warned to be careful whose debt one assumed (Proverbs 20:16).

God created human beings. They belong to Him and He has their best interests at heart. Yet even when He leads them where He wants them, it can still be confusing. People make plans, and many times those plans coincide with God's will for them. When the plans don't mesh, however, wisdom dictates that people follow God's path rather than their own (20:24).

When wickedness is rampant, a wise leader will use insight and understanding to discern the problem and mete out appropriate consequences. The image of the threshing wheel rolling over the wicked in verse 26 referred to separating the valuable seeds of grain from the worthless chaff. Winnowing, then, involved tossing up the product of threshing so the seeds would fall back to the ground while the chaff blew away. Yet even as kings address problems of wickedness, they should display love toward others and faithfulness to God (20:28).

Verse 27 suggests that people owe everything to God. He is the source of light and life. He knows everything about every person, and no one can hide anything from Him. Consequently, those with wisdom realize the importance of living before God in openness and honesty.

People are blessed with different gifts at different phases of life. Many bemoan losing the strength of youth when, in fact, they should rejoice at the accumulation of wisdom that comes only with age (20:29). Wisdom helps people understand and endure the painful experiences of life. In time they see how their sufferings work to keep evil at bay and make them stronger individuals (20:30).

📖 21:1–31

ASSORTED PROVERBS FOR LIVING

The proverbs in this section reinforce many great themes that were established in previous chapters—themes such as righteousness, hard work, self-control, and the sovereignty of God.

The sovereignty of God becomes evident from the beginning. Even Solomon, with all his wealth and power, realized that a king was like water that God could direct anywhere He wished. Indeed, *all people* need to weigh their feelings and understanding of the world in light of God's wisdom. It is not enough to do as one wishes and offer God the occasional sacrifice; what God desires from people is consistent righteousness and justice (21:1–3).

Verse 4 recalls 6:16–19, but the language there was even stronger. God *hates* haughty eyes and a wicked heart. Pride and arrogance are at the root of any number of other sins.

There are right ways and wrong ways to accomplish most things. In seeking to make a living, for instance, planning and diligence are usually rewarded with success. Getting in too big of a hurry is detrimental, lying to get ahead is downright deadly, and unprovoked violence is never the right course of action (21:5–7). Sometimes it appears that wicked people are prospering, and others are tempted to emulate them. But that path always has an abrupt and destructive end. Upright conduct will yield much greater rewards (21:8).

In home situations, an argumentative spouse is a continual source of tension. It is better to withdraw than to argue endlessly or to be an ongoing target of verbal abuse (21:9). If a corner of the roof doesn't provide enough distance, another option is to move to the desert (21:19). Wicked neighbors are no better than contentious spouses. Such neighbors quickly lose the respect of others and find themselves alone after pushing away everyone they encounter (21:10).

Demystifying Proverbs

Homes in ancient Israel had flat roofs that could provide additional housing if needed. The image of Proverbs 21:9 is not as awkward (or comic) as it might appear in a modern neighborhood of steep, sloped roofs.

Verse 11 restates 19:25. Seeing a wicked person punished is an encouragement to faithful people. Wise people need not get to the point of punishment. They will learn from positive instruction and/or an occasional rebuke that keeps them on the right track.

The identity of "The Righteous One" in verse 12 is debated. Some people believe the term refers to righteous people in general. More common, however, is the belief that the phrase refers to God. Proverbs repeatedly makes clear that God will oppose and judge the wicked.

Everyone is in need from time to time. People who ignore the needs of others usually discover in their own time of despair that no one responds (21:13). Appeasing someone with a gift can help minimize potential anger. The "bribe" issue arises again in verse 14, as it did in 17:8 and 18:16. In this case, the focus is on the importance of peacemaking and justice; the passage does not endorse the use of bribes to circumvent fairness (21:15).

The choices of life do not include a "neutral" path. People must choose either the road of understanding and life or the path of wickedness and death (21:16). Many of the habits of the wicked and foolish are evident: living only for pleasure, overindulgence in alcohol and fine food, gluttony, and more (21:17–20). Equally apparent are the behaviors of the righteous and godly: disciplined accumulation of life's necessities, long life, prosperity, honor, success in the struggles of life, control of one's words, and so forth (21:20–23).

Negative emotions and behaviors, left unchecked, lead to even more problems. Pride and arrogance result in mocking. Sloth results in craving for more and more things that working could easily provide. Attempting to appear godly (offer sacrifices) with a wicked heart is a spiritually detestable act. Lying can result in offering false testimony, which is harmful in a number of ways. Perhaps one of the worst resulting sins is hypocrisy. A wicked person usually doesn't want to *appear* wicked to others, so he or she puts up a "bold front" (21:24–29).

How much better (and more effective) it is to acknowledge and seek the superiority of the wisdom of God. No other "wisdom" can approach God's wisdom (21:30). It is fine to plan and prepare for success, yet no one succeeds without God's help. No matter what kind of battles people fight, "victory rests with the LORD" (21:31).

📖 22:1–16

WHAT GOD VALUES

This closing section of the proverbs of Solomon provides some critical observations about what God values and what He hates. Verse 1 underscores a key theme in Proverbs: the fact that integrity is integral to being a child of God. Given the choice of a good name or great wealth, people should always choose the former. Sadly, many are quite willing to sacrifice their reputation for financial gain. People make distinctions based on wealth, but God doesn't (22:2). He created all people, and He does not prorate His love according to personal bank accounts.

Sometimes wisdom is displayed in simple common sense. When danger approaches, prudent people use their heads and seek protection, while naïve people plunge ahead and suffer the consequences. The "danger" (22:3) may be a physical threat, but it is just as likely a spiritual temptation that wise people avoid while foolish ones get caught up and trapped. This seems clear from verse 5, which describes the "thorns and snares" on the path of the wicked. More than merely avoiding danger, those who humbly fear the Lord receive wealth, honor, and life (22:4).

Verse 6 is probably one of the most quoted from the book of Proverbs. Like many others, this proverb is true in a general (not an absolute) sense. When parents fear God, seek wisdom, get their priorities straight, and attempt to instill the same things in their children, those children have a much better likelihood of learning to make good decisions on their own. Still, many will stumble and fall. Some will rebel and succumb to various temptations. But most will appreciate the solid training they received and carry it with them into their adulthood.

Verses 7 through 9 are a series of general observations rather than insights. Most people can look around and confirm that the rich rule over the poor, that borrowing money makes the borrower beholden to the lender, that those who act wickedly are in for trouble, and that those who are generous to others will be blessed with satisfaction.

Those who suffer because of quarrels and insults need to eliminate the source. Conversely, gracious speech has a positive effect, even attracting the ear of the king. God values truth, and those who attempt to distort truth will ultimately be frustrated (22:10–12).

People who dogmatically resist seeking wisdom come across looking pretty foolish at times. The sluggard of verse 13 is a master of lame excuses to avoid going to work. The men who fall prey to the lure of the adulteress in verse 14 are certain to suffer consequences later on. And those who attempt to impress the rich with gifts until they spend themselves into a level of poverty are perhaps the most pathetic of all (22:16).

Critical Observation

The "rod" mentioned in 22:15 referred to a shepherd's tool used to guide the sheep away from a dangerous direction. It was not used in a harsh manner. Any discipline conducted in anger is improper.

In his conclusion of this section, Solomon once again emphasizes the importance of disciplining children. Acting foolishly is not only potentially embarrassing but frequently harmful as well. Loving parents will dedicate themselves to helping their children get beyond the allure of folly to discover the true joy of godly wisdom (22:15).

Take It Home

In your own circle of acquaintances, can you differentiate between people who display genuine godly wisdom and those who can only attempt to emulate that wisdom with a "bold front" (21:29)? How are their lives different? Do you relate to the two groups in the same way, or is there a difference? Can you think of any ways to ensure that your own wisdom is genuine and godly, and not merely the product of human training and techniques?

PROVERBS 22:17–24:34

SAYINGS OF THE WISE

Setting Up the Section

Proverbs 10:1–22:16 contains proverbs of Solomon, and more follow in 25–29. But this section is made up of "Sayings of the Wise." The unknown writer lets his readers know that he has provided thirty sayings of counsel and knowledge. Like Solomon, he is focused on the perfect wisdom of God that brings nothing but the best results for those who find it.

📖 **22:17–24:22**

THIRTY SAYINGS OF COUNSEL AND KNOWLEDGE

Verses 17 through 21 are an introduction to this segment of Proverbs. The writer attests that his words are true and reliable, yet he wants his readers to respond not to him but rather to the wisdom of God. He begins with a series of warnings, most of which are clear. The poor and needy already have trouble enough, so we must not add to it by exploiting or pressuring them. We are to avoid relationships with easily angered people, or risk becoming one ourselves. And we are not to be too hasty to cosign loans for others, or we may soon find ourselves impoverished (22:22–27).

The warning in verse 28 is a bit more obscure. Land in Israel was very important for survival. The ancient landmarks established boundary lines, and moving them was a subtle method of stealing property that belonged to someone else.

The proverb in 22:29 shifts to a positive example. People who are skilled at what they do, and who do their work without complaining, will succeed. Soon they will be recruited to serve before kings.

It's important to understand the context of 23:1–3. Eating before a king required tact and proper etiquette. A visitor would want to acknowledge the honor and show appreciation for the splendid meal, yet to overeat and appear to be gluttonous was likely to incur the king's wrath. It was a delicate situation, to be sure.

Verses 4 and 5 reinforce a point that runs throughout Proverbs (and the New Testament as well): Although God can use money and although money can bring some temporal benefits, it should never be a primary pursuit of one's life. Wealth is a temporal entity.

The warning in verses 6–8 is about avoiding a stingy person. God loves a generous heart that sacrificially cares for others. Stingy people can't enjoy personal relationships because they are always focused on the cost. Wise people will not waste their time and expose themselves to such pain.

Verse 9 stands on its own as a proverb yet echoes a frequent theme of this book—the actions of a fool. There is no reason to try to argue or reason with a fool because he wants nothing to do with wisdom.

Verses 10 and 11 begin the same way as 22:28, but the proverb here is more specific. Moving ancient landmarks literally changed the boundaries of a piece of land. Here the intent was not just to expand one's own land; in doing so the person intentionally wanted to steal the land of widows and orphans, the socially powerless and vulnerable.

Critical Observation

The reference to a *redeemer* or *defender* in verse 11 carries a double meaning. Certainly God is the Redeemer of the disenfranchised. In addition, a custom in the ancient Israelite world allowed a family member to redeem the land a widow or orphan might lose after the death of the family patriarch. In either case, the warning in 23:11 is that while one might perceive a widow or an orphan as defenseless, a defender might actually be nearby.

Verse 12 encourages a posture of learning. This challenge leads well into the admonition of verses 13 and 14 regarding parental discipline. Training and instructing a child are essential in helping that child differentiate between wisdom and foolishness. Parents who fulfill the role of training preserve the lives of their children. Those who neglect it bring harm upon their children. Verses 15 and 16 reflect the joy that comes from seeing a child who values wisdom.

Sometimes it is easy to envy someone who seems to get away with wrongdoing. Verses 17 and 18 are a reminder to continue to obey God. Walking in the fear of the Lord brings true and lasting hope, life, and peace.

Verses 19–21 are a call for a son to wisely avoid a life of excess—specifically regarding food and drink. The call continues in verses 22–25, this time as a reminder that the way the son lives affects the joy of the parents.

Critical Observation

The concept of *buying the truth* in verse 23 means that the truth is so important that it is worth any sacrifice to acquire and keep.

And in verses 26–28, the warning shifts to the illusive allure of a prostitute or wayward wife. Such women are outwardly attractive to young men, yet they will draw the man into a trap from which he cannot easily escape.

The final verses of Proverbs 23 are a warning to stay away from the seduction of wine (23:29–35). The painful symptoms of overindulgence are listed in detail. Alcoholism affects one's body, causing the person to become disoriented, lose control, and disregard wisdom.

Those who are involved in various sins may seem to get what they want and are sometimes even objects of envy. Yet it is wrong to be jealous of wickedness. Behind the facade of success is a heart devoted to violence and troublemaking (24:1–2).

Just as a house is constructed and then filled with goods that make it livable, a commitment to wisdom builds up people, and ongoing knowledge edifies them and allows them to function together (24:3-4). Wisdom also makes people powerful because knowledge provides strength that goes beyond the physical. A group of wise people can achieve victory in whatever they do (24:5-6). Foolish people find that they cannot attain wisdom. Without it, they attempt public discourse and discussion yet have nothing of substance to offer. Instead, they exhibit only a desire to scoff and hurt others. The folly of such people alienates them from the community (24:7-9).

Endurance is essential when trials and problems arise. Being strong allows someone to pursue justice and rescue others who are treated unfairly or even being led to their death. God, who knows what is in each heart, will judge those who neglect to stand up for what is right (24:10-12).

Wisdom's effect on the soul is comparable to honey's sweetness in one's mouth. Those who feast on wisdom will never lose their hope for the future (24:13-14).

Verses 15 and 16 serve a twofold purpose: to both warn the wicked and encourage the righteous. It is foolish for the wicked to try to overpower the righteous because godly people have the strength and wisdom to endure difficult times. The wicked, lacking strength in God, will be worn down by trials. It is important to remain humble even when one's enemies suffer the consequences of their sin (24:17-18). Another person's judgment is no occasion to gloat or rejoice.

The righteous should not desire to be like evildoers, who have no future (24:19-20). Sin and wickedness lead to death, so it is foolish to envy people involved in such things. Verses 21 and 22 issue a call to fear both God and the king—to respect those in leadership, both divine and human. Associating with people who rebel against authority is wrong and dangerous.

📖 **24:23-34**

A FEW ADDITIONAL SAYINGS

A series of final instructions—additional sayings of the wise—begins in verse 23. First is an admonition to be fair in judgment. People see how others respond to evildoers, and they judge those actions and attitudes accordingly (24:23-25).

The one who tells the truth does something that is right and pleasurable (24:26).

One should first commit to his "outdoor work" (source of income) before starting to build his house. In other words, all things should be done in the wise and proper order (24:27).

Verses 28 and 29 caution against creating trouble for one's neighbor without a reason and add a warning against deception. When one is offended by another, it is wrong to automatically respond with an equally offensive action. Forgiveness is far preferable to retribution.

The final caution is against laziness, a problem more severe than it might appear at first (24:30-34). The writer realizes that the eventual outcome of laziness is poverty, although it comes so gradually that the person is caught unaware. It might seem a small matter to value sleep over work, but laziness is as effective as a bandit in stealing everything a person has. Sloth leads to destruction.

Take It Home

This section of Proverbs warns of many things that can prevent or impede success in life: greed, drinking too much, cheating others, callous attitudes, laziness, and more. Looking back over your own life, which of these (or other) problems have you struggled with? How can you prevent such things from robbing you of the wisdom and contentment that are available?

PROVERBS 25:1–29:27

SOLOMON'S WISDOM, PART III

Setting Up the Section

Chapter 25 begins a new section of the book of Proverbs. Chapters 1–9 provide a more narrative approach to the value of wisdom and the importance of shunning evil. Chapters 10–22:16 present the first collection of the words of Solomon. Chapter 22:17 through chapter 24 contain another section of Proverbs that was probably added later. Chapters 25–29 return to the wisdom of Solomon with a series of unrelated proverbs.

📖 25:1–28

PROVERBS FIT FOR A KING

The collection of proverbs contained in chapters 25 through 27 was either compiled or rediscovered by King Hezekiah (25:1). The collection begins with a series of proverbs about kings. While the king needs to search things out to understand them, God does not (25:2). Similarly, a king's subjects cannot fully understand the king (25:3).

Demystifying Proverbs

The proverbs in chapters 25 through 29 may have been locked away some two hundred years after Solomon's reign, when King Ahaz closed the temple (see 2 Chronicles 28). When Hezekiah succeeded Ahaz as king, he reopened the temple and recovered many of the temple objects (2 Chronicles 29). Quite possibly these proverbs were among them (see Proverbs 25:1).

Just as the dross needs to be taken away from silver before it can be used to create something, so too wickedness needs to be removed from the kingdom in order for it to be justly established (25:4–5).

It is foolish to try to exalt ourselves to make us known before the king (25:6). If the king does not feel the same way, we will be publicly humiliated and cast down to a lower position than where we started (25:7).

Verses 7–8 warn against bringing people too hastily into court. If we respond out of emotion, we may be made a fool of in front of all. The best thing to do is to bring our problems to our neighbors directly (25:9). There is a pragmatic reason for this: In the course of a trial, our own sins and failings will be brought to light (25:10).

Words spoken at the right time have extreme value (25:11). The focal point of this proverb is that saying the right thing at the right time is what is important. The comparison with a golden apple is a bit difficult to understand. The most likely meaning is that it refers to some type of a precious stone. When the stone is in the right setting, its beauty is seen. So, too, the right setting for words enhances the beauty of the words. Even reproof needs to be done at the right time to benefit the one hearing it (25:12).

Take It Home

One of the critical lessons that Proverbs teaches is that not only should we say the right thing but we must say the right thing at the right time. Understanding our environment is of critical importance when we speak. Just as an apple of gold by itself is enhanced by the right setting, so too are words spoken in the right setting.

We could restate verses 13 and 25 this way: A faithful messenger brings comfort to his boss in the same way an air-conditioned tractor refreshes a farmer on a hot summer day. The person who over-promises and under-delivers frustrates many people (25:14).

Tough leaders are won over not by a show of force but through patience. All a fight does is embolden the ruler (25:15).

The proverbs in verses 16–17 and 27–28 deal with having too much of a good thing. Too much of any of the pleasures of life is a bad thing.

The one who would sell out his neighbor for his own personal gain is a deadly person to be around (25:18), and placing faith in such a person will only bring pain and complications (25:19).

Blithely overlooking someone's grief produces a reaction in that person in the same way that vinegar and soda react (25:20).

In ancient Middle Eastern cultures, revenge was a way of life. The proverbs in verses 21 and 22 offer another way of dealing with the enemy—serve him and meet his needs. The point of pouring burning coals on the enemy's head is not to wreak vengeance but to shock him with this response.

A person with a loose tongue is a storm of problems (25:23).

Verse 24 repeats the proverb found in 19:13 and 21:9.

CHARACTERISTICS OF THE FOOLISH

Chapter 26 focuses on the characteristics of four kinds of people who do not pursue wisdom: the fool (26:1–12), the lazy person (26:13–16), the maddening person (26:17–22), and the hypocrite (26:23–28).

A fool never deserves honor (26:1–3) and should never be encouraged to think his ideas are valid (26:4–5). Putting confidence in a fool is suicide (26:6). Wisdom is useless to a fool—he cannot use it (26:7–9); it would be pointless to expect anything from him (26:10). Despite consequences, a fool will do the same foolish thing over and over again (26:11).

Yet, the worst thing in the world is not to be a fool—it is actually to be a prideful person. Pride is so destructive that there is more hope for a fool than the prideful man (26:12).

The lazy person is condemned just like the fool. The lazy person is worthless for a variety of reasons: He makes excuses (26:13), he loves sleep over work (25:14), he is too lazy even to feed himself (26:15), and he is extremely prideful (26:16).

Critical Observation

The fact that *seven* wise people are mentioned in 26:16 is no doubt symbolic; seven is the number representing perfection. In other words, when a lazy person is presented with perfect wisdom, he will pick his lazy attitude every time.

Some people are simply maddening. They meddle in problems that they have no reason to be involved in (26:17). They cover their lies by saying they were only joking (26:18–19). They start quarrels and keep them going with their gossip (26:20–21), savoring the rumors they spread (26:22).

The final verses expose the deception of hypocrites. Like a glazed ceramic, the words of the hypocrites seem good at face value, but in reality they mask malice (26:23). These people use their lips to hide their hearts (26:24–25), but in the end they will be exposed for the liars that they are (26:26). This is why the warnings of verses 27–28 are important: Any harm we plan for others will come back to hurt us in the end. God knows that the lying tongue is out to hurt others (26:28); people who utter lies will face their own self-inflicted destruction because hypocrisy cannot stand before God.

AN ATTITUDE ADJUSTMENT

Chapter 27 deals with right and wrong attitudes. One's attitude determines how one will respond to everything in this world.

A boastful attitude is a foolish attitude, whether one is boasting about himself or what he will do in the future (27:1–2). Resentment and envy are two attitudes that foster dangerous conflict (27:3–4).

Critical Observation

Proverbs 27:1 provides the foundation for the warning found in James 4:13–16.

A real friend is willing to tell the truth and say the tough things. Those who receive a rebuke should receive it as a sign of love, not of hate (27:5–6). But the context of a person's life—whether he is "full" or "hungry"—determines *how* he hears what he hears (27:7). When tough things have to be said, it is more dangerous to leave and ignore those tough words than to stay and endure them (27:8). Through friendship people are challenged, changed, refreshed, and supported (27:9). Friendships already established in the family are worth trusting in and ministering to (27:10).

Solomon wants to know the joy of his child's obedience and the honor that comes from wise children in the community (27:11). Some marks of that kind of wisdom include anticipating and avoiding trouble (27:12), not being an easy target for swindlers (27:13), and saying the right thing at the right time (27:14). If Solomon's son marries a contentious woman, it will be a great annoyance in the home (27:15–16).

Godly friendships, as earlier proverbs have said, exhort and motivate people to be godly (27:17). In a similar way, mutual respect between boss and worker benefits both (27:18).

The last set of proverbs in this chapter deals with issues of the heart. The heart of someone is who that person really is (27:19). The desires that are in the heart are never satisfied (27:20). Verse 21 can be understood to mean that what people say about a person reveals his character, or that how a person responds to praise and flattery reveals his character. In either case, if foolishness has taken over the heart of someone, then that foolishness will be impossible to remove (27:22).

This chapter ends on a practical appeal: to have a shepherd's heart for the resources that God has entrusted to us (27:23–28).

📖 28:1–29:27

PRACTICAL RIGHTEOUSNESS

In chapters 28 and 29, we see righteousness played out in practical terms for both the king and his subjects.

The boldness of the righteous is equated to the boldness of a lion—which is a courage that stands up against any foe. What one gets when walking in the righteousness of God is the ability to stand up for what is right regardless of the foe (28:1).

If a leader takes advantage of his people and operates in an unfair manner, then they will rise up and there will be a conflict between leaders in the nation. The ruler who realizes this and pursues a righteous approach to leadership will rule over a stable land for a long time (28:2). Under a bad leader, poverty becomes so widespread that the poor even prey on one another (28:3).

Individuals, as well as leaders, contribute to how society functions. A person who breaks the law is in essence endorsing all lawbreakers, while obeying the law is a blow for justice (28:4–5).

In most cultures around the world, being rich seems to be the best of all possible achievements. But if being rich causes someone to lose integrity, then it is much better to remain poor and maintain a good reputation (28:6). Similarly, overindulgence is a shame to be avoided (28:7), as is charging excessive interest (28:8).

Demystifying Proverbs

The law of God forbade one Israelite to charge a poor Jew interest (Exodus 22:25). They were to show kindness to those in need and not to make a profit off of them.

Practical righteousness involves joining prayer with obedience (28:9), setting a good example (28:10), and having the right perspective on success (28:11–12). It means taking responsibility for one's actions (28:13) and consciously choosing right over wrong (28:14). For a ruler, it includes governing with integrity and compassion (28:15–16). The consequences of unrighteousness—whether it be disregard for human life (28:17) or any other crookedness—are fatal (28:18).

As a general rule, the trustworthy, hardworking person does better than the person chasing a get-rich-quick scheme—especially at the expense of others (28:19–22). Without honest accountability (28:23), it is far too easy for greed to lead to conflict within the family and beyond (28:23–25). It is wiser to abandon a self-centered perspective and use what one has to help others (28:26–27). That way of life is better for everyone (28:28–29:2).

Again Solomon returns to some key themes: the impact children's behavior has on their parents (29:3), the importance of just rulers for a stable society (29:4), and the dangers of flattery (29:5). He again emphasizes the consequences of actions (29:6), the importance of caring for the poor (29:7), and the trouble a loose tongue can cause (29:8).

He repeats his warning about the futility of taking a fool to court (29:9), how differently good and bad people react to the innocent (29:10), and the wisdom of keeping one's temper (29:11). Rulers are again warned against listening to bad counsel and reminded that rich and poor are equal in the Lord's eyes (29:12–14).

Solomon concludes his proverbs with a review of how children's behavior reflects on parents (29:15, 17); the impact of those in authority (29:16, 19, 21); the importance of taking correction (29:18); the dangers of thoughtless speech, temper, and pride (29:20, 22, 23); and the foolishness of aligning oneself with lawbreakers (29:24).

This final section of Solomon's wisdom ends by affirming that ultimately God's judgment trumps any judgment human beings may offer (29:25–27).

Take It Home

You may notice that Solomon keeps coming back to the same themes he feels are important. Sometimes parents, church leaders, business managers, and so forth may feel they are "harping" on an issue if they feel a need to repeat it more than once or twice. Yet essential issues may bear repeating. Think through the things in life you feel are absolutely the most important, in any areas over which you have influence, and try to formulate some ways to restate them so that others might respond more readily to your passion and enthusiasm.

PROVERBS 30:1–31:31
WISDOM FROM THE MASSAITES

Setting Up the Section

Chapter 30 marks the beginning of the final section of the book of Proverbs: the sayings of the Massaites. Massa was a clan from the line of Ishmael that lived in north Arabia. The two men whose wisdom is recorded here were contemporaries of either Solomon or Hezekiah and probably were influenced greatly by the theology of Israel. Some have speculated that Agur (chapter 30) was a leader of the Massaites and that Lemuel (chapter 31) was probably the king of that region.

30:1–17

PEOPLE IN RELATIONSHIP TO GOD

Agur, whose words are recorded in chapter 30, begins by acknowledging the frailty of humanity. He is weary. He feels stupid. He doesn't understand life. He lacks wisdom. All this is for one simple reason: He does not know God (30:1–3).

To highlight how little he knows, he asks a series of rhetorical questions (30:4):

Who has ascended to heaven or come down from heaven?

Who has gathered the wind in His fists?

Who has wrapped up the waters in a garment?

What is His name—and His Son's name?

The great news is that there is an answer to Agur's questions in 30:4: Jesus Christ—the very wisdom of God.

Agur is in awe of the complete trustworthiness of the Word of God and the total danger that would be involved if someone added or subtracted from it (30:5–6). He then makes two requests of God: (1) that God would remove falsehood and lying from his life, and (2) that God would give him neither poverty nor riches (30:7–8). He wants enough food to eat so that he will not profane God for not having enough, but he does not want so much that he forgets about God and lives only for himself (30:9).

It is important to Agur that truth be held high. He describes ways that deceit and falsehood are expressed in the world: by slandering a worker to his employer (30:10); by dishonoring parents (30:11, 17); by self-righteousness (30:12); by arrogance (30:13); and by cruelty (30:14).

The reason there is such deceitfulness and falsehood is that the human heart is wicked and never satisfied. It is like a leech that continually sucks the blood of its victim and is never satisfied (30:15). To describe this even further, Agur lists four more things that are never satisfied (30:16):

1) Sheol—or death. Every moment of every day someone dies, and this will never end on this side of eternity.

2) The barren woman—nothing will satisfy a woman who wants a baby and cannot have one.

3) Dry land—when a place is very dry, it seems that no matter how much it rains it is never enough.

4) Fire—fire keeps burning as long as there is fuel to keep it going.

📖 30:18–33

PEOPLE IN RELATIONSHIP TO EARTH

Next Agur sets forth a series of wonders about the world around us: an eagle in flight, a serpent slithering on a rock, a ship on the high sea, and a couple in love (30:18–19). Agur responds to each of these with a sense of awe. He wonders how anyone who sees what God has made can act as if God's laws have no validity (30:20).

Agur next outlines a series of things that would throw his world into disarray: political, moral, marital, and domestic chaos (30:21–23). The point here is that certain structures are essential for society to function. There is a need for order, and this drives us to our need for God.

Agur next extols the great virtues of wisdom by picking some of the smallest and most vulnerable creatures from the animal world to illustrate the great power of wisdom (30:24): hardworking ants (30:25), small rock-dwelling mammals (30:26), hordes of locusts (30:27), and lizards that live even in the richest homes (30:38).

Four more examples identify creatures that demonstrate a certain authority (30:29): the head of a pride of lions, the rooster that dominates the henhouse, the nimble male goat, and the commander-in-chief of an army (30:30–31).

Agur's point is that fools who have tried to present an impressive image or do harm need to stand quiet before God (30:32). To persist in their foolishness will inevitably cause problems (30:33).

📄 31:1–9

THE WARNING

Chapter 31 contains lessons that King Lemuel's mother taught him (31:1). A king must hold himself to a high standard. Playing around with adulterous women brings nothing but pain and misery to a king and his kingdom (31:2–3). Nor is a partying lifestyle appropriate for a king (31:4). Drunkenness is a dangerous thing. It can lead a king to make decrees he knows nothing about and do things to hurt people and not act out of justice and righteousness (31:5). Strong drink should be provided for people who are dying so that they can have some comfort and forget their pain (31:6–7). Rather than opening his mouth for debauchery, a king should speak up for those who cannot do so for themselves (31:8–9).

📄 31:10–31

WISDOM PERSONIFIED

This final section of Proverbs is an acrostic poem. Each of the twenty-two verses begins with a consecutive letter of the Hebrew alphabet.

Critical Observation

At one level, the poem in Proverbs 31:10–31 appears to be about a godly wife. On another level, when this chapter is taken in the context of the book of Proverbs, it could also be seen as a personification of wisdom. It is probably not intended to be a checklist for a woman to evaluate her worth. Instead, this is no doubt the expression of how wisdom would act if wisdom were a wife. All of the virtues adorned in the book of Proverbs are mentioned in this chapter: work, wise use of money, wise use of time, caring for the poor, planning ahead, respect for one's spouse, wise counsel, and fearing God. Both men and women can learn from Proverbs 31:10–31.

The wife of noble character is a rare jewel (31:10). This echoes the description of wisdom in Proverbs 8:11. The question, "Who can find such a woman?" does not suggest that such women are nonexistent but that they should be admired, and the husband who finds such a woman should be ecstatic.

The noble wife's husband has confidence in her. He trusts her completely because she is wise (31:11). Her careful management of the home enhances their family's living. He lacks nothing of value within his home because of her hard work (31:12).

This kind of woman is an asset, not a liability, because her motives are to do good to her husband and her family. She is not defined by what she gets but by what she gives (31:13–15). She works hard and with gusto and energy. Her wise business dealings are profitable (31:16–18).

Critical Observation

Because women were not permitted to buy land at the time Proverbs was written, some have concluded that verse 16 shows that the poem is not about a woman but about the personification of wisdom. However, a wife, even though she might not be the one actually buying and selling, could just as easily give the instructions for the purchase.

The noble wife is also selfless and generous. She understands that it is the desire of God to care for the poor, and therefore she does it with all of her heart. At the heart of wisdom is a love for the poor (31:19–20).

Her preparedness has provided her entire family with all that they need (31:21). She even makes her family's bed coverings so that they can sleep in comfort. She also takes care of herself and her appearance (31:22).

A noble woman enhances her husband's standing among those who transact legal and judicial affairs at the city gate among the elders. Though she is obviously proactive and competent, she functions in a way that honors her husband's position in the community (31:23–24).

At the end of the day, when people look at this woman it will not be how she is dressed that will matter; it will be her strength and dignity. She can face the future confident that she is walking in integrity and that, no matter what happens, she will respond with faith in God and faithfulness to her family (31:25).

The book of Proverbs speaks a lot about controlling one's tongue. This woman has such self-control. She is praised for her wisdom and faithful instruction. She speaks with the intention of being wise and building others up (31:26).

Her children honor her for her hard work and loving care for them and call her blessed. Her husband praises her. He realizes that there are others who have done much, but he tells her that she has surpassed all other women in the world. (31:27–29).

At the heart of this woman is godly character. Even though she might be physically charming and beautiful, those qualities do not last. The key to her godly wisdom is the fact that she fears the Lord (31:30). This is the key application of the entire book of Proverbs (see 1:7).

The writer urges his readers to recognize and praise the faithful work and kindness of this woman. She deserves public recognition for her fear of God and faithfulness to her family (31:31).

Take It Home

As you review this section of Proverbs—and the book as a whole—consider what goals you might want to set for yourself in the future. For example, have you ever prayed (like Agur in 30:8) for neither poverty nor riches? Or how would your personal demonstration of wisdom-in-action compare to the woman described in 31:10–31? The book of Proverbs holds up some lofty goals, all of which should inspire us to be better people.

ECCLESIASTES

INTRODUCTION TO ECCLESIASTES

The book of Ecclesiastes is considered part of the Wisdom Literature of the Old Testament. Contained within its verses are proverbs, teachings, stories, reflections, and warnings about a myriad of topics. But the underlying pursuit of the book as a whole is the meaning of life. The author explores the purpose of life and, more importantly, asks what humanity's purpose is as a creation of a sovereign God. Verse by verse through the book of Ecclesiastes, the author answers that question. The purpose of life, meaningless though it may feel, is to fear God and obey His commands.

AUTHOR

The question of authorship of Ecclesiastes is a debated subject. The author does not directly identify himself, but he does state that he is the son of David and king in Jerusalem. Traditional scholarly opinion is that Solomon is the writer of the book, and early church testimony supports this view. A few passages that support this view internally include 1:1, 12; 2:4–9; and 12:9. Solomon was known for his wisdom and dedicated most of his life to its pursuit. He also wrote most of the books of Proverbs and Song of Songs. With Solomon in mind as the author, many of the teachings of the book seem to have a direct correlation to the events of his life.

It wasn't until the 1700s that Solomon's authorship came into question. The chief argument against Solomonic authorship is rooted largely in debates over the original Hebrew, which is a different dialect than that of Solomon's other writings and seems to reflect a later version of Hebrew. Furthermore, the writer refers to himself as *Qohelet*, or *the teacher*, a pseudonym that scholars argue would be unnecessary for the king. As far as internal evidence against Solomon's authorship is concerned, in 1:12 the writer seems to allude to a time when Solomon was alive following his reign, but no such time exists. It should also be noted that after chapter 3, the references to Solomon taper off, and many of the proverbs and teachings that follow seem to contradict those in Proverbs.

Within this commentary are included some of the opposing views and relevant points that support each view, and the author will be referred to by the generic title *Qohelet*. It should also be noted that there is an unmistakable narrator present in 1:1–11 and 12:8–13, who is likely the author of the book. For those who favor Solomonic authorship, this is an elder Solomon reflecting back on the pursuits and teachings of much of his life—the body of the work within the frame. Those who take a non-Solomonic view, however, believe this to be the voice of the author. The switch to first-person in 1:12, then, begins the quotation of the unidentified Qohelet.

PURPOSE

The main purpose of the book of Ecclesiastes is threefold. First, it paints a picture of a sovereign God who controls everything in the world. Second, Qohelet's teachings highlight the meaninglessness of life apart from fearing and obeying the sovereign God. And lastly, the book provides wisdom and counsel for future generations rooted in the things Qohelet learned throughout his life's pursuit of meaning.

OCCASION

The date of Ecclesiastes depends heavily on which view of authorship one holds. Most scholars who deny Solomonic authorship agree that Ecclesiastes should have a date in Israel's late history, anywhere from 450–250 BC. Because the book doesn't contain any direct internal evidence that helps date it, the date is based largely on the style of the Hebrew it is written in, which most agree is similar to a later Hebrew style. On the other hand, for those scholars who hold to Solomon's writing, the book must have been written during his reign, which covers a span anywhere from 971 BC to 931 BC.

THEMES

Ecclesiastes contains several proverbs and teachings, but they all center on just a few main themes. These themes include: wisdom, the sovereignty of God, the limitations of humanity, and death. Throughout the author's quest for meaning in life, he returns again and again to the meaninglessness of everything, a reality based on humanity's smallness in the face of God's great sovereignty and control.

CONTRIBUTION TO THE BIBLE

Many of Qohelet's teachings seem to contradict teachings in other parts of the Bible. However, one cannot deny that Qohelet's reflections on life paint one of the most realistic pictures of the fallen world in which we live and humanity's purpose within that world. As God's sovereignty is acknowledged again and again throughout the book, one can't help but look forward to the coming of Jesus Christ and His redemptive work on the cross. Ecclesiastes paints a picture of a fallen world and the impact of sin, but knowing the promises that have been fulfilled post-Christ make the realities of this world bearable. Christ is the meaning to all the meaningless Qohelet observes, and the death that he fears takes on a new hope for all who believe in Christ.

OUTLINE

ECCLESIASTES 1:1–11

QOHELET'S OPENING THOUGHTS

As is common with many books of the Bible, Ecclesiastes begins with a superscription introducing what will follow as the words of Qohelet, son of David as scribed by the unknown narrator. It is this opening line that draws the initial correlation between the speaker and King Solomon.

Verse 2 sets the tone for everything to follow. The declaration that everything is meaningless is repeated in 12:8, forming the bookends for everything that will be read in between. With the critical understanding of the book riding on this single phrase, it is important to understand what the author means by the use of the Hebrew *hebel*. The concrete meaning of hebel is "breath" or "vapor," and it can either be understood metaphorically as "meaningless" or "transient." *Vanity* is an old English word that means the same as meaningless.

Having stated the mantra for the book, in verse 3 the author poses a rhetorical question to engage the reader and further emphasize the meaninglessness of life. If everything is meaningless, then the obvious answer to the question posed is that people do not profit from their hard work.

Critical Observation

It is interesting to note that the Hebrew word *yitron*, translated here as *profit*, occurs nine times in the book of Ecclesiastes, but it does not occur anywhere else in the Bible (2:11, 13; 3:9; 5:9, 16; 7:12; 10:10–11).

Verses 4–11 illustrate the meaninglessness of humanity's toil by appealing to the cyclical, unchanging world in which we live. Although time is progressing and generations come and go, nothing else is changing (1:4). Verses 5–7 provide specific examples from nature of these repetitive patterns of the world. When viewing the cycles of nature in such a way, it's no doubt that the writer's tone is one of pessimism and weariness—his life exists within this repetitive cycle, where there is always more to see and hear (1:8).

From nature the narrator now turns to history as another example of the futility of everything. Although time passes and generations change, history seems to be on the same cyclical pattern as nature (1:9–10). The human condition remains the same—meaningless. The narrator closes the prologue by noting that not only has history proven to repeat itself but the pattern will not be broken in the future.

Take It Home

Reading through Ecclesiastes, it is repeated time and again that everything about life is meaningless. This can be overwhelming and may illicit a variety of responses, but above all it should encourage us to fear God and seek to live in obedience to Him.

ECCLESIASTES 1:12–2:23

EVERYTHING IS FUTILE

Setting Up the Section

Verse 12 notes the shift from the narrator's voice to the voice of Qohelet, who will be the speaker through 12:7. While the narrator (or the elder Solomon) establishes the tone and theme in the prologue, it is Qohelet's first-person reflections that form the bulk of the book.

📖 1:12–18

THE FUTILITY OF WISDOM

Qohelet briefly introduces himself in verse 12 and then moves into his initial reflection on his quest for wisdom. Qohelet points out that he isn't just trying to gain some additional insight into the world around him but that he has been tasked with trying to gain all the wisdom under heaven. In verse 13, he describes this as a burdensome task given him by God.

Having searched for all the wisdom in the world and studied everything under the sun, Qohelet came to his conclusion: It's all meaningless (1:14). Qohelet quotes a proverb in verse 15, supporting his idea that what is wrong with the world cannot be righted by mankind. The crooked imagery attests to the perversity of the human condition. Because of the fallen world and sin's presence, the human heart knows only evil unless affected by God. It is interesting to note that the prophet Isaiah uses this same imagery when he talks about the coming Messiah (Isaiah 40:4). The reflection in verses 13–15 is repeated in verses 16–18, with verse 16 reemphasizing Qohelet's quest, verse 17 again noting the meaninglessness—here of folly in addition to wisdom—his quest uncovers, and verse 18 including a second proverb that supports his frustration.

Demystifying Ecclesiastes

This passage in the opening chapter of Ecclesiastes is one of the key texts used to argue Solomonic authorship (1:1; 3:1–8; 8:2–6; 12:9–12). Whether Solomon is the author or not, the comparison is important because it raises the question, if the most wise person in the world finds everything meaningless, what hope does anyone else have to reach a different conclusion?

📄 2:1–11

THE FUTILITY OF PLEASURE

Qohelet's pursuit moves from wisdom to a selfish pursuit of pleasure, but he doesn't leave the reader guessing of his quest's findings—this also proves to be meaningless (2:1). Among the ways he pursues meaning in pleasure are drinking and folly (2:3); building mansions and expansive grounds (2:4–6); employing servants and amassing animals, treasures, singers, and concubines (2:7–8).

Verses 9–11 summarize Qohelet's reflection on the endless pleasures he pursued. While his pursuits were greater than those of anyone around him, he was able to maintain his wisdom throughout, since the pleasures were a part of his greater quest for the meaning of life (2:9). In his pursuit of worldly pleasures, he didn't hold back from anything he desired, but it was all in vain, because he reached the same conclusion that his pursuit of pleasure was meaningless with no profit (2:10–11).

📄 2:12–16

IN THE END WISDOM AND FOLLY ARE FUTILE

This section of Qohelet's thoughts is set apart from the reflections on wisdom in 1:12–18 by the emphasis on death being what renders both wisdom and folly futile. It seems to be Qohelet's impending death that is forcing him to reflect on his life's pursuits and draw the conclusion that they have been meaningless. Qohelet makes this comparison personal in verse 15, when he refers to himself as a wise man who will encounter the same fate as any fool. Not only do both the wise and the fool face the same fate but their deaths render them one in the same—forgotten (2:16). Such futile thoughts leave the writer hating all he has worked for in his life, and he again closes with the mantra that everything under the sun is futile (2:17).

Critical Observation

Contrasting wisdom and folly is not unique to the writer of Ecclesiastes, as it is a common characteristic of proverbial writings. What stands out in Qohelet's comparison, however, is that he concludes that the lives of both the wise and the fool result in the same fate (death), thus nullifying the importance of wisdom.

📄 2:17–23

THE FUTILITY OF WORK

Verse 17 leads Qohelet from wisdom and folly into a reflection on the meaning of work. But again, the thought that work might provide some semblance of meaning is negated by the fact that in death his life's work will be passed on to someone else, and he'll have no control over who receives it (2:18–19). However, Qohelet doesn't simply stop with the conclusion that work is rendered futile in death. Because one's work holds no long-lasting value, all the present pain, toil, and sleepless nights it creates are futile as well (2:20–23). In Qohelet's observation, these two factors—the present and future futility of work—support his conclusion that work, also, is meaningless.

Take It Home

A single refrain is heard echoing throughout the early sections of Ecclesiastes: Everything is futile. Qohelet has searched for meaning in wisdom, selfish pleasures, and work, only to maintain the same sense of defeat at the end of each pursuit. With a foreboding sense of his life's finiteness, Qohelet's quest has left him empty-handed thus far.

ECCLESIASTES 2:24–3:22
GOD'S PURPOSE AND TIMING

Setting Up the Section

Having presented his initial observations of life and its futility, Qohelet now shifts gears—be it ever so slightly—from reflection to instruction. In the following verses, Qohelet presents the reader with advice gleaned from his life's pursuit.

📖 **2:24–26**

THE SMALL PLEASURES OF LIFE

This section, which marks a notable shift in Qohelet's tone, is the first of several passages that give advice on how to find fulfillment in one's day-to-day life amid the foreboding sense of meaninglessness. Qohelet's advice? Find a way to enjoy the small pleasures in life—namely to eat, drink, and enjoy one's work. What is critical to this advice, however, is the understanding that apart from God, enjoyment of daily pleasures is impossible (2:24). God enables a person to enjoy these things because they are not looking for ultimate satisfaction in them; that satisfaction is found in God alone (2:25).

Verse 26 points out that there are two different types of people—those who please God and those who offend Him. Qohelet observes that it is up to God to determine who will have the ability to enjoy these small pleasures. But Qohelet finds even these pleasures of God to be meaningless in the grand scheme of things (2:26).

A TIME FOR EVERYTHING

Ecclesiastes 3:1–8 contains several verses that support the line of thought that Solomon is the author of this book and is speaking out of personal experience. The overarching theme in this passage is the sovereignty of God, whose hand controls everything. Humanity's limitations and futility are made most evident in comparison to God's sovereignty. Part of what frustrates Qohelet about the futility of life is that everything is out of his control. In this passage, he employs the literary device of a poem to further this idea that there is a time and a season for everything (3:1).

Critical Observation

Included in Qohelet's poetic verses are several stylistic elements. Among these literary devices are rhyme (lost on us in the translation but present in the Hebrew), repetition of the phrase "a time to" that begins each line, and antithetical parallelism in which each verse contains a pair of opposites that illustrate a parallel meaning.

Included in the body of this poem are fourteen different pairs of opposites, each supporting the idea that everything on earth functions within its predetermined time frame (3:2–8). The poem breaks down as follows: Verses 2–3 illustrate that everything has an already established beginning and end time, whether it be life and death or construction and destruction. In verse 4, Qohelet observes that we experience our varying emotions at their predetermined times. The time when things will be excluded and included has already been set (3:5), as has the time for obtaining and ridding oneself of possessions (3:6). Even experiencing strong personal emotions, and the way those emotions manifest themselves in relation to others, is out of one's control (3:7–8).

GOD DETERMINES THE TIME FOR EVERYTHING

In verse 9, Qohelet returns to the rhetorical question of what profit might be gained from work in such a structured world. Qohelet establishes in 2:24–26 that it is in God alone that someone can find purpose in daily life, even in the simple things like food, drink, and work. He mentions God again here in response to his rhetorical question (3:10). In a statement almost identical to 1:13, Qohelet observes that searching for meaning in such a structured world is a burden.

Demystifying Ecclesiastes

Verse 11 seems to stand in opposition to the burdened feeling of verse 10. The first line of the verse reflects on the beauty of God's timing and the eternal perspective He brings. However, the second part of the verse, as well as the context of the verses surrounding it, attests to the frustration Qohelet feels at being unable to understand God's plans and His timing.

In verses 12–13, Qohelet returns again to the conclusion that because everything is orchestrated in God's timing, humanity is resigned to settle with enjoying those lesser pleasures of daily life mentioned in 2:24. Furthermore, Qohelet concludes that the timeline God has set in motion cannot be altered, a testimony to why God is worthy of being revered (3:14).

But Qohelet doesn't stop there with reasons why God is to be feared. At this point in his observations of the world, he brings up the idea of God's justice, which has been established within the ordered world He has created (3:15–22). When he observes the world around him, Qohelet can't find any justice—only wickedness and injustice (3:16). So he adds justice to the list of things that God will bring to pass in His timing, at which point He will bring justice to both the wicked and the righteous. This idea of future judgment directs Qohelet's thoughts toward death, which as noted previously is a terrifying concept to him. Chief among God's sovereignty is that in His time He will bring glory to His name and enact His judgment on the world.

Verses 18–21 include his reflection that in death there is no difference between humanity and the animals, because both eventually end up dead.

Take It Home

Qohelet's lack of understanding regarding the afterlife is made evident by verses 20–21, wherein he questions the shared fate of humans and animals. If there is no afterlife, when will God right all of the world's wrongs? Once again Qohelet concludes that finding pleasure in the small things, namely work, is all humanity can count on (3:22).

ECCLESIASTES 4:1–12

THE BURDENS OF LIFE

Setting Up the Section

Qohelet's search for purpose moves from the role of justice in the world to the heavily burdened people he has seen around him, including the oppressed, those who labor in vain, and the friendless. For each he concludes the same thing—this, too, is meaningless.

📄 **4:1–3**

OPPRESSION

In the same vein of the injustices in the world and the reign of wickedness, Qohelet now laments the oppression he sees everywhere he looks. The chief problem he observes in regard to oppression is the powerlessness of those being oppressed (4:1). But like many of his other observations, he simply resigns to that powerlessness and concludes that in lieu of such oppression it would be better to be dead (4:2). And beyond that, it would be better still to have never been born and never exposed to the wicked world (4:3). Qohelet feels crippled in the face of oppression and hopeless to bring about any change.

Critical Observation

Verse 2 contains the first in a series of "better than" statements that Qohelet will make over the succeeding verses (4:3, 6, 9, 13; 5:5; 6:3). In each instance, Qohelet emphasizes the negativity of something by comparing it favorably to something else.

📄 **4:4–6**

LABOR

Having already spent some time on the meaninglessness of work, Qohelet returns to that observation in verses 4–6. Here he draws an additional conclusion—both toil and success come from the envy of one's neighbor (4:4). It is Qohelet's conclusion that humanity is motivated by jealousy, which is yet another reason that all of humanity's toil is futile. To support this conclusion, he then states two proverbs that present three differing types of workers. The first is the lazy person who doesn't work at all, who the proverb deems a fool (4:5). The second is the person who works some as needed but also knows how to rest, while the third is the person who knows only work and no rest (4:6). Of the three, the only one Qohelet seems to approve of is the second, whose combination of rest and work is better than the other two, if for no other reason than their life isn't dominated by something Qohelet has already concluded to be futile.

📄 4:7–12

FRIENDLESSNESS

If a life spent toiling away in vain isn't meaningless enough, Qohelet goes on to state in verses 7–8 that the one who labors away *alone* is even worse off. Thinking about loneliness leads Qohelet to form another "better than" conclusion in verse 9: Having a friend is better than being alone. He then lists four practical reasons why the one who has a companion lives a less-burdened life than a lonely person (4:9–12). The final image of the passage—that of a three-strand cord—summarizes why companionship is better than loneliness: There is strength in numbers (4:12).

Take It Home

While all three of the aforementioned situations—those who are oppressed, whose labor is motivated by jealousy, and the lonely—seem very different, the unifying theme is that all are living lives that seem to be utterly meaningless.

ECCLESIASTES 4:13–6:9

EVERYTHING IS FUTILE

Setting Up the Section

Having paused to voice his thoughts on the predetermined structure of time and those who live burdened lives, Qohelet returns once again to his subject of futility. While the meaninglessness remains the foundation for his conclusions, verse 13 picks up where 2:23 ends.

📖 4:13–16

POLITICAL POWER IS FUTILE

The themes of wisdom and folly return in this passage, as Qohelet ponders the meaninglessness of political power. To illustrate this, he compares two very different characters in verse 13. One is poor, young, and wise; the other is king, old, and foolish. It is also pointed out that the king is foolish because he ignores the advice of others. Wisdom is better than foolishness, regardless of the circumstances (4:14). The tone in verses 15–16 is reminiscent of 2:12–17, and again wisdom is no better than folly and power is no better than being powerless. Furthermore, because each share the human condition of imperfection, it is highly likely that the young ruler will become like the older one in time.

📖 5:1–7

GOD'S HOLINESS *IS NOT* FUTILE

Amid his discourse on futilities, Qohelet includes a word of caution. God's holiness is not among the meaningless; therefore enter into the place of worship with caution. In this passage, wisdom most certainly trumps folly, and Qohelet gives three examples of worship wherein caution is key: sacrifice (5:1), prayer (5:2–3), and vows (5:4–6).

Critical Observation

The speaker includes another "better than" statement in verse 5, as it relates to taking vows. Because vows are not a mandatory part of worship, Qohelet warns that he who never makes a vow is better off than he who cannot keep the vows he makes. Jesus makes a similar warning in Matthew 23:16–22. Vow-making is no longer a part of our worship today because the ultimate vow was made—and kept—on our behalf when Christ died on the cross.

Verse 7 reiterates the point made in verse 2, that in worship one is to speak little and listen much. Qohelet then gives a command that will be reiterated throughout the rest of the book: Fear God. The point has already been made that God, who is in heaven and separate from mankind on earth, controls the timing of everything. Mankind is dependent and powerless, therefore God is worthy of humanity's fear and awe.

📖 5:8–6:9

THE FUTILITY OF WEALTH

Next Qohelet enters into a discourse on the meaninglessness of wealth. But he begins by warning that while God's divine authority is to be feared, human authority is by nature corrupt and therefore worthy of caution (5:8-9). The drive for profit controls one's desire for power, the perfect segue into Qohelet's observation on the futility of wealth.

It is not surprising that Qohelet finds the accumulation of, and attempt to enjoy, wealth utterly meaningless. To present his observations, Qohelet begins with three proverbs that illustrate the inability to find pleasure in money. Qohelet determines wealth meaningless because one never has enough of it (5:10); the more you have the more others are collecting (5:11); and having much leads to many sleepless nights—whether from worry or a lack of hard work (5:12). However, the implications of these verses reach beyond just wealth and shine a light on the insatiable nature of lusting after things.

In verses 13-17, Qohelet presents two scenarios that illustrate his conclusion that wealth leads to evil. The first scenario is the evil of hoarding all of one's wealth (5:13). No pleasure can come from money that is hoarded. The same can be said of losing one's money (5:14). If a person depends on money for happiness, then when it is lost the person has nothing and can pass on nothing to his offspring. Just as death renders wisdom and folly futile, it does the same for wealth (5:15-16). Whether one's riches are hoarded or stolen, in the end it makes no difference.

Demystifying Ecclesiastes

Earlier in his writing, Qohelet observes that because all of life is meaningless, one must seek pleasure in the simple things such as eating, drinking, and enjoying one's work (2:24–26; 3:12–13, 22). When wealth is involved, however, even those small pleasures aren't possible. The blind pursuit of wealth nullifies even the simplest of pleasures.

The only exception to the futility of wealth is when it is a gift from God. Just as some are able to find pleasure in their work because God allows it (2:24-26), so a special few are able to find pleasure in their wealth (5:19-20). Qohelet considers these people to be a fortunate few, especially in consideration of the fact that to others God gives wealth and does not let them enjoy it (6:1-2).

Verses 3-6 contain another "better than" statement, in this case that a stillborn baby who has never known anything of the unfairness of the world is better off than the rich man who can't enjoy his wealth. And, as he has concluded several times before, isn't the fate of the stillborn baby and the rich man the same?

Qohelet closes his section on the futility of wealth with a final series of proverbs that conclude that neither the desire for wealth nor the attainment of it lead to any real satisfaction (6:7–9). In the end, the pursuit of riches for pleasure is meaningless, too.

ECCLESIASTES 6:10–12:7

QOHELET'S WISE COUNSEL

Setting Up the Section

These three brief verses (6:10–12) are a pivotal point in Ecclesiastes. Now, halfway through his discourse, Qohelet turns his attention from his observations to wise counsel for how others should live.

📖 6:10–12

THE SMALLNESS OF HUMANITY

In verse 10, Qohelet reiterates his "there is nothing new under the sun" mantra with a reminder that humans are dependent on One who is stronger, presumably God. In such a world, mankind can only understand so much, so an increase in words is an increase in meaninglessness. The two rhetorical questions that close this section focus on two thoughts that plague the writer: the uncertainty of the future and of death (6:12). Only God knows the certainty of such things, and coming to this conclusion has been the long, arduous journey of pursuits Qohelet has relayed in prior verses.

📖 7:1–8:1

A LIST OF PROVERBS

Qohelet begins his section of wise counsel with several pieces of advice written in the form of proverbs. This pattern will continue throughout most of the verses that follow. The use of the literary style of a proverb is just one of the elements of Ecclesiastes that attest to Solomonic authorship.

Verses 1-14 function as Qohelet's response to the rhetorical question of 6:12: "Who knows how our days can best be spent?" (NLT). Qohelet includes a series of proverbs—

many in the "better than" structure—to present some of the values he has found in an otherwise meaningless life. Two dominant themes are prevalent in verses 1–12, and neither theme is new to Ecclesiastes: death (7:1–2, 4, 8) and the wisdom/folly relationship (7:4–7, 9–12).

Verses 13–14 conclude the preceding list of proverbs with the counsel to consider what God has done. In verse 14, Qohelet advises that they should make the most of their days, whether good or bad.

The second section of proverbs, verses 15–22, focuses on the limitations of humanity as established in the two preceding verses. Qohelet warns against the extremities of life, especially when it comes to pursuing righteousness and wisdom (7:16) or wickedness and folly (7:17). It is Qohelet's advice that people should search for balance in life.

Righteousness and wisdom don't guarantee a longer life than the wicked or the foolish. And furthermore, no one is perfect, so the endless pursuit of perfection will leave one empty-handed (7:20). Qohelet's final point, the fact that no one can escape sin, is demonstrated in verses 21–22.

Critical Observation

Verses 23–24 are an interlude in which Qohelet reminds the reader of the pursuit of meaning he has been on for much of his life. These two verses also serve to set up the counsel that will follow, in which the action of seeking and finding, or more often *not* finding, is of utmost importance.

The final portion of this set of proverbs centers on the sub-par view of humanity Qohelet develops during his quest for meaning (7:25–8:1). While we know from the previous six chapters that Qohelet's quest does not lead to the answers he had hoped for, he does learn at least three things about humanity. First, a manipulative woman is more bitter than death (7:26). Second, a virtuous man is rarely found, and no woman is upright (7:27–28). And lastly, God may have created humanity pure and sinless, but humanity has strayed from that state (7:29). Qohelet wraps up this initial list of proverbial reflections with rhetorical reminders to the reader that his quest for wisdom has proven that indeed no person can attain it (8:1).

📖 **8:2–9:16**

MISCELLANEOUS COUNSELS

At this point in his discourse, Qohelet shifts his focus to several points of counsel that seem unrelated. However, each point, from how to act in the presence of the king to the shared fate of all, further supports the aforementioned conclusion of Qohelet's pursuit: God alone is in control of everything that happens in the world.

Qohelet has repeatedly noted that God alone controls everything that happens in the world, from the timing of everything to the administration of justice. However, that does not negate the power the king has been given. Just as a person is expected to obey God, the same expectation goes for obeying the king (8:2–3). In verse 4, Qohelet gives the impression that people should be obedient to the king because, regardless of his demands, he has the power to do as he wishes. Generally speaking, those who act in obedience to the king will avoid the trouble that opposing him will bring about—this is an example of acting wisely (8:5–6). However, Qohelet gives the caveat that because of the corruption of the world, there is no guarantee that obeying the king will keep someone out of trouble, again pointing out the limitations of wisdom in the grand scheme of things (8:7–9).

Demystifying Ecclesiastes

One's view of the authorship of Ecclesiastes determines how Qohelet's insight in this passage is to be interpreted. If Qohelet is not Solomon and not a king, then he is speaking from one subject of the court to another. However if Solomon is the author, then his advice stems from his personal experience as king and how he expects a king to be treated.

Qohelet returns to the concept of justice for the wicked, which he previously mentions in 3:16–22. It seems evident from his quest that the wicked are not receiving the punishment they are due (8:10). And even worse than that, Qohelet concludes that the lack of justice is simply encouraging people to continue acting in evil ways (8:11). The only hope one has is that in the end God will enact His justice (8:12–13). Even though Qohelet includes this statement, it is difficult to be convinced he believes it based on his tone throughout the book. Again he looks around and only sees meaninglessness and a lack of justice (8:14). It seems that the best advice Qohelet can give is to trust that in the end divine retribution will make up for the lack of justice in the world. Verse 15 repeats the now familiar refrain that all one can do is take pleasure in the small things of eating, drinking, and working.

Pondering such things leads Qohelet to once again summarize the quest for wisdom and meaning he has been on (8:16). But again Qohelet concludes that the work of God in the world is beyond human comprehension (8:17). We will never be able to fully grasp God's sovereignty.

Critical Observation

It has now become evident that mankind's inability to understand God and the way He chooses to work in the world is one of the main themes of Qohelet's discourse. For the other instances when he makes this point, see 3:11; 7:25–29; 9:12; and 11:5.

Chapter 9 elaborates on a point Qohelet has made several times prior: In death everyone and everything is rendered meaningless. Piggybacking on the point he makes in 8:10–15, Qohelet reiterates that being righteous and wise doesn't mean one is in control of his or her fate (9:1). To support this point, he lists five pairs of opposites in verse 2, all of whom share the same fate—death (9:3). Verses 4–5 include a slight note of hope that life may be a little better than death, and then in verse 6, Qohelet reveals that the ability to have strong emotions is something to be missed in death. Inasmuch as the wicked and righteous share the inevitability of death, God's sovereign judgment is still pending, and it is in that judgment that the difference between the wicked and the righteous will be seen in the end.

In light of this unavoidable death, Qohelet's advice in verses 7–10 is to seek pleasure in the little things of life, like eating and drinking, being pampered, and enjoying one's wife. Qohelet encourages his audience to do each of these things, because they will all be impossible after death. While he reminds them that in these things they won't find ultimate purpose, he implies that some pleasure will be gained from enjoying them. And the enjoyment of such things is necessary, since no one knows when hard times might come (9:11–12).

Take It Home

Qohelet closes this section of miscellaneous advice with a short story demonstrating that in the end everything is futile (9:13–16). The subject of the story is a poor man, but he is wise. He saves an entire city of people, only to be forgotten, along with the wisdom he shared. This story sums up Qohelet's underlying point that in the end everything, including wisdom, is meaningless.

📄 9:17–11:6

A SECOND LIST OF PROVERBS

To bring his discourse to a close, Qohelet dedicates the final chapters of his work to a series of proverbs that cover a wide range of topics. Though these proverbs may seem random, they center on the same few themes: wisdom versus folly, dealing with the king, seeking pleasure in the small things, uncertainty of the future, and impending death.

Verses 9:17–10:3 include five different proverbial examples of why wisdom is superior to folly. Present in these verses, however, is Qohelet's undeniable skepticism that folly carries some weight because of its ability to taint wisdom. The proverb of verse 4 is Qohelet's counsel on how to handle an angry superior, presumably the king. His answer? Stay calm.

The following verses (10:5–7) make up a story that demonstrates what Qohelet means in the proverb of verse 4. Just as folly wreaks havoc among wisdom, so a foolish decision in leadership leads to a messed up world.

The next set of proverbs addresses seemingly unrelated illustrations, each of which proves an argument Qohelet has been making throughout his teaching: Life is unfair, even for the wise. But if there is any doubt that wisdom has some value, the next proverbs erase it. Verses 12–15 provide several illustrations that support the undeniable truth that wisdom must trump folly, even if just barely.

Critical Observation

If the proverbs of 10:12–15 sound familiar, it may be because they are more closely related to those in the book of Proverbs than to Qohelet's other sayings. See Proverbs 10:8, 21; 15:2; and 18:7 for these comparisons.

Again Qohelet mentions the king, this time making a statement about how contagious leadership is, regardless if it is foolish or wise (10:16–17). The king sets the standard that others follow, which is why it is all the more important he rules with wisdom. Qohelet will readdress the king in verse 20, but he pauses momentarily to offer two bits of seemingly random advice: Don't be lazy (10:18), and sometimes money leads to happiness by paying for the things that bring enjoyment (10:9). The latter seems a contradiction to the earlier section on the meaninglessness of wealth. The final piece of advice Qohelet has in dealing with the king, and any superior for that matter, is to always be wise and cautious in dealing with them (10:20).

Verses 1–2 of chapter 11 return to Qohelet's previous teaching that with the future comes uncertainty. While it is uncertainty that earlier frustrates Qohelet in his pursuit of wisdom, he does not use it as an excuse for inactivity, as is seen in the following verses. He uses several images from nature to support the idea that the future is out of human control and in the control of God (11:3–6).

📄 11:7–12:7

REFLECTIONS ON YOUTH, OLD AGE, AND DEATH

The reflections of 11:7–12:7 build from the enjoyment of youth (11:7–8) to the inevitability of death (12:7). Ecclesiastes 11:7–8 includes the most hopeful tone Qohelet displays in regard to youth, but he quickly brings the reality of youth's fleeting nature to view. The pattern of verses 7–8 (enjoy your youth, but death is coming) is repeated in verse 9, with the addition of judgment accompanying death.

Demystifying Ecclesiastes

Verse 10 is a frustrating verse in true Qohelet fashion. He seems to have been praising youthfulness and encouraging his readers to enjoy it because of its carefree state. But then in the same breath he calls youth meaningless. These discontinuities in the text are not unusual to Qohelet's thoughts and further the notion that Ecclesiastes covers more questions than answers, as the writer wrestles with the meaning of life and God's sovereign work in the world.

For his closing reflection in 12:1–7, Qohelet turns to rich symbolism to illustrate old age and the destruction of the body it brings, all culminating in death. God is in view as the main subject of these verses, because He is the controller of time.

Take It Home

The metaphors end with the symbolism of man returning to his state as dust in the ground—a reversal of man's beginning as described in Genesis 2:7 and 3:19. Thus concludes Qohelet: Death is the end.

ECCLESIASTES 12:8–14
EPILOGUE

Qohelet's message is summarized in verse 8: Everything is meaningless. While this conclusion dominates the text of Ecclesiastes, it is verses 13–14 that summarize the overarching message of the book: Fear God and keep His commandments. This is the punch line of the whole book. Even in light of the futile elements of human life, we are to live in the reality of God's presence and judgment. We will give account to Him for what we do with our journey, though disillusionment may be inevitable. While we may call something "meaningless," we will not truly understand what matters and what doesn't until God reveals that in His judgment of life. He has the final word.

Demystifying Ecclesiastes

The switch to the third-person narrative voice in verse 8 marks the end of Qohelet's discourse and the beginning of the conclusion. For those who hold to the Solomonic authorship, these closing verses are from present-day Solomon, wise and repentant in his old age and reflecting back on the pursuits that dominated his youth. Those who do not hold to a Solomonic authorship argue that this shift in perspective closes Qohelet's discourse and returns to the voice of the narrator.

SONG OF SONGS

INTRODUCTION TO SONG OF SONGS

Song of Songs (or Song of Solomon), for the most part, is a book of poems about romantic love.

AUTHOR

The title "Song of Songs" suggests that it is the greatest of all songs. There is disagreement among scholars as to whether Solomon wrote Song of Songs, but he is mentioned in the book and many credit him with part of its authorship, if not all.

PURPOSE

The Song celebrates sexuality in its proper context. While some apply it as an allegory of spiritual truths (for example, the relationship of God and Israel or of Christ and the church), here it is treated as poetry that describes a love relationship between two people.

OCCASION

The Song of Songs represents the courtship of a man and a woman, both young, probably just coming to maturity. In ancient Israel, marriage took place in the early or mid teen years. Many define the major sections of the book as courtship (1:2–3:5), wedding and honeymoon (3:6–5:1), and lasting marriage (5:2–8:4). Others, however, consider this book a collection of love poems that don't occur in any chronological kind of order.

SONG OF SONGS 1:1–2:17
THE TRANSFORMATIONS OF LOVE

Setting Up the Section

In this first section of the Song of Songs, we learn about the joys and difficulties of love.

1:1–17

THE BEGINNING OF LOVE

While the majority of Song of Songs is love poetry, verse 1 serves as a superscription, describing the contents of the book. This verse mentions Solomon, who is mentioned seven other times in the book. While there is disagreement as to Solomon's authorship, this may indicate that he wrote some of the poems included here.

The poetry begins with verse 2, when the woman takes the initiative to ask for a kiss (1:2–4). The woman also invites the man to get away with her to a private place; the words used in this case refer to an inner chamber. While this is the first entreaty of this kind, it is a theme that appears again.

Demystifying Song of Songs

In verses 5–6, the woman addresses not the man but the daughters of Jerusalem. Throughout the rest of the book, the poems will go back and forth between the perspectives of the man, the woman, and this chorus of women. This chorus is sometimes the audience of the man and the woman who affirm their relationship, and sometimes they are the disciples of the woman.

In verse 5, the woman complains that the sun has made her dark, which she considers unattractive. This has nothing to do with race, but social class. She attributes her dark complexion to the vineyards she is forced to work in. She also uses the word *vineyard* in a more allegorical sense, perhaps meaning that she hasn't tended to herself or her own beauty.

Addressed once again to the man, verses 7–8 open with a kind of tease, or a request for a location where the woman can meet him.

Critical Observation

The mention of a veil in verse 7 highlights the fact that the Israelite women didn't always wear veils. They were for special occasions, such as weddings. Some attribute the veil to the clothing of a prostitute, but there is nothing else here that points to any kind of impropriety. If anything, she may not wish to be mistaken as a prostitute.

Verses 9–11 reveal the man's admiration of the woman's physical beauty. He refers to her as a mare among chariots. This relates to a military strategy. Stallions, not mares, pulled chariots. When chariots were bearing down on their enemy, one could defend oneself by loosing a mare in heat as a red herring. The stallions would then change their target and chase the mare instead. Likewise, the beloved is a distraction with her stunning beauty.

In verse 10, the man admires only the parts of her body that are visible. This reflects the stage of their relationship. In verse 11 the use of *we* doesn't indicate that the man will have a hand in creating the jewelry, but rather that he will only enhance her beauty with these gifts of jewelry.

Verses 12–14 constitute a responding poem of admiration toward the man, but in verses 15–17 the two have a back-and-forth dialogue. The beloved's eyes are compared to doves. While it is obvious that this is a flattering statement, we can't be sure what trait of an ancient dove relates to a woman's eyes, whether it is the color, the softness, or the fact that doves are known for faithfulness to their mates. The trees mentioned—cedar and fir—were known for their fragrance.

🖹 2:1–17

THE DIFFICULTIES OF LOVE

Verse 1 begins a poem building on the symbols of flowers and trees. The following verses, while continuing this theme, are also good examples of poetic parallels. In verses 2–3, a simile opens the verse and is interpreted in the second part.

The thorns, mentioned in verse 2, are unattractive and invite anything but intimacy. So in this description, the man is clearly raising his beloved above her peers.

Whereas in chapter 1 the woman is described as having been forced to work in the direct sunlight, which damaged her skin, here in verse 3 she is privileged to rest in the shade of her beloved. The banner she describes in verse 4 is a public declaration that she belongs to him.

Demystifying Song of Songs

The raisin cakes and apples mentioned in verses 5–6 were used in pagan fertility rites and were viewed by some as aphrodisiacs. Because both fruits have many seeds, they were associated with fertility.

Verse 6 is a description of an embrace, while verse 7 is a strong warning to the woman's peers to not rush their journey to love (repeated in 8:3–4).

In verses 8–17, the woman describes her beloved in his eagerness. The description in verse 9 (repeated in verse 17) of the man as a buck or gazelle implies someone swift, powerful, and beautiful.

Critical Observation

Winter in Palestine runs from October to April, the only time rain falls. Since these rains end in April, the timing for the occasion of this poem is probably around May. The woman notes the end of winter and the beginning of springtime in many ways: The rains have ended, the flowers have blossomed, singing has begun, and the turtledove (known to return to Palestine in April) is cooing (2:10–13).

Verses 14–15 are probably a continuation of the woman quoting the man rather than a switch of voices. Lacking confidence, she hides metaphorically in rocks to make herself feel secure. The foxes in that part of the world were notoriously cunning and destructive. When they were small, they were even more undetectable. Here, they represent obstacles to new love.

Verse 16 is repeated in 6:3 and 7:11. Verses 16–17 are full of images which can be interpreted a variety of ways. Lilies somehow seem to represent the woman herself or some element of her womanhood. The stag and gazelle are mentioned again, but differently. The mountains are seen by some to symbolize her breasts. These images are clearly meant to be expressions of desire.

SONG OF SONGS 3:1–5:1

THE JOY OF LOVE

Setting Up the Section

The opening of chapter 3 is a poem about yearning. Absence and longing always lead to search and discovery in the Song.

📖 3:1–11

THE CELEBRATION OF LOVE

The scene changes throughout verses 1–5. What is described here may be more like a dream sequence rather than an experience unfolding in a chronological way. Verse 2 begins the woman's search for her love—something that happens again in chapter 5.

While in some of the previous poems it is left to interpretation where a poem ends or begins and how much connection exists between them, verses 6–11 are clearly a section unto themselves. The only other marriage poem in the Bible is recorded in Psalm 45.

Critical Observation

Solomon's name appears several times in this passage (3:7, 9, 11). Some believe that Solomon is the author of this whole book and is in fact the man, and later groom, mentioned throughout. Others hold that this reference to Solomon is a poetic way of painting a picture of opulence and luxury—often considered a young woman's ideal marriage scenario.

The images and fragrance in verse 6 emphasize wealth. In verse 7, Solomon's portable couch is a *palanquin*, which was an enclosed couch carried on the shoulders of men by poles.

It is noteworthy that sixty warriors surround the couch. This is double the number that accompanied Solomon's father David during his ceremonial travels (2 Samuel 23:18–19, 23). These sixty warriors are friends of the groom who will provide safety for the wedding party (Song of Songs 3:8).

According to verse 9, the carriage is made from timber from Lebanon, known to be the highest quality. It was probably aromatic cedar and represented beauty, luxury, and excellence. Silver, gold, and purple wool or cloth all indicate royalty (3:10). The incense and the couch were very expensive—weddings, as they still are now, are a time to show off one's worth.

The *daughters of Zion* (3:11) is a unique phrase to this book, but it is clearly an alternate for the often used *daughters of Jerusalem*. It is not clear, however, whether the crown mentioned in verse 11 pertains to a coronation crown or if it is a special wedding crown reserved for this occasion.

📖 4:1–5:1

THE INTIMACY OF LOVE

The words in verses 1–7 are affectionate: *Beautiful* appears several times as the groom describes his bride's hair, teeth, lips, neck, and breasts.

The man undresses his new bride, beginning with her head and working his way down to her breasts. This differs from his earlier description in 1:15, which is repeated in the first half of 4:1. Here, he comments on everything he sees.

Chapter 4 can be divided into several poems, but thematically they are tied closely together. In verses 1–7, the man declares the woman beautiful. In verses 8–9, he draws her to him, proclaiming his love. Then from verse 10 through the first verse of chapter 5, the poetry focuses on the image of a garden.

Demystifying Song of Songs

Verse 8 mentions several mountains. Hermon is perhaps the most well-known. It lies in the northern region of Israel. Amana and Senir are part of the Lebanon range that connects to Hebron in northern Israel. The groom is inviting his bride closer. He wants her close to him and safe from threats, here described as lions and leopards (or panthers).

In verses 10–11, the groom calls his love his *sister*. In the ancient Near East, *sister* was at times an affectionate term for one's wife.

In verses 12–15, the man continues working his way down her body as she undresses for him. She is a virgin—a locked garden, inaccessible (4:12)—and he is praising her for it. And in her garden are the choicest exotic spices. This exaggeration in number and variety of spices is a form of flattery. Verse 15, while confirming the man's satisfaction with his wife, introduces a new image associated with her body—a well or fountain.

Verse 16 is the woman's invitation for her groom to enjoy her virginity. She invites him in, using symbolic language with openly sexual overtones. Though the language here is sometimes used in modern culture to imply oral sex, that is not the intent here. These words refer to the satisfaction of one's sexual appetite.

The first verse of chapter 5 documents the man's satisfaction after the couple's first sexual experience. He claims with highly sexual overtones to have entered his bride. The last part of this verse is attributed to the daughters of Jerusalem. It is an invitation for the couple to enjoy their sexual partnership with gusto, drinking their fill of love even to the point of intoxication.

SONG OF SONGS 5:2–8:14

THE ENDURANCE OF LOVE

Setting Up the Section

The remainder of chapter 5 makes up a poem that actually spans through verse 3 of chapter 6. Rather than the symbolic language as in the poems of chapter 4, the woman seems to be telling the women of Jerusalem about an actual experience.

📖 **5:2–16**

LOVE'S ANTIDOTE

The woman is awakened by the abrupt knocking at the door by her lover. He calls her four terms of affection: *sister, darling, dove, flawless one.* While getting ready for bed was more involved in the ancient world (dirt floors, less sophisticated door locks), the woman's hesitation to answer the door costs her the opportunity to be with her lover.

The mistreatment she experiences in verse 7 doesn't even seem to faze her. In contrast, she had previously been assisted in her search by the watchmen (3:3). In this case, it is likely that the watchmen represent the social difficulties which the woman works her way through in order to get to the object of her desire.

In the first part of this chapter, her focus is exclusively on herself and her own comfort, but in verses 8–16 her focus is exclusively on the man. He had earlier described the woman as he addressed her; here the woman describes the man, but she is addressing the daughters of Jerusalem. In ancient Near Eastern literature, such physical descriptions of one's lover were almost exclusively male descriptions of females.

The comparison to gold in verse 11 implies great value, especially since gold had to be imported to Palestine. Verse 13 indicates that his cheeks smell of cologne. In verse 15, his legs are described as marble, signifying strength.

It was common to describe another's physical characteristics from top to bottom, but after working her way down, she goes back up to his lips once more. This, along with 1:2, suggests that she is particularly attracted to his mouth—both with his kisses and his sweet words. She concludes by calling him her friend (5:16).

📖 6:1–13

THE LEISURE OF LOVE

While chapter 6 continues the poem begun in 5:2, in verse 1 the daughters of Jerusalem respond to the woman, offering to help her find her missing groom. Then, in verse 2, the bride seems to know where her groom is. Keep in mind that this is poetry, not to be understood as a linear story line.

Note that verse 3 is the same as 2:16 but in reverse order.

Verses 4–9 are written from the man's perspective; then he is joined by the chorus in verse 10. He compares his bride's beauty to two famous cities in Israel—Tirzah and Jerusalem (6:4). Tirzah was captured by Joshua and, following the split of the nation, was named the capital of the northern kingdom (1 Kings 16:8–9, 15). The compliments offered in verses 5–7 are similar to those offered to the bride on her wedding night in 4:1–3.

Critical Observation

Verse 8 mentions three categories of women in a royal harem: queens, concubines, and young women. These form concentric circles of relationship to the king—which especially pertain to how their offspring might or might not be considered in line for the throne. The sons of queens are in direct succession to the throne. The sons of concubines are not, unless the king specifically appoints them. Young women have either not yet been presented to the king or not borne children—in which case theirs is a temporary label, and they will become either queens or concubines. The mention of these women here makes the point that this one woman is worth more to the king than all the others.

Some disagree as to who is speaking in verses 11–12. Most likely the woman is talking, and the man invites her to turn to him in verse 13. Verse 12 may be the most confusing verse in the book. The wording varies widely among the different Bible translations. There are two things that most commentators agree on, however. First, the difficulty of the text. And second, that it reflects passion so powerful that someone gets carried away with it.

📖 7:1–13

THE DEPTH OF LOVE

In verses 1–10, the man expresses his admiration for his bride (4:1–15; 6:4–8; 7:1–9). This passage in chapter 7 is considered even more intimate than that of their honeymoon (4:1–15).

He begins with her feet, perhaps because she is dancing. While his comparison of her navel to a mixing bowl and her belly as a mound of wheat does not sound flattering from a modern perspective, these descriptions show how his wife satisfies him (7:2).

In verses 4–10, the man comments once again on his wife's eyes, comparing them to Heshbon, which is a beautiful area to the east of the Dead Sea. He also compares her to a palm tree. In verse 8, his desire to climb the tree and take hold of its fruit indicates his desire to be intimate with her and enjoy her breasts.

In verses 11–13, the woman initiates physical intimacy with her husband, speaking *to* him rather than about him (as she does in 1:2; 2:6; 4:16). She invites him to be with her in the vineyards.

📖 8:1–14

THE POWER OF LOVE

The first four verses of chapter 8 describe a yearning for love. In the ancient Near East, public displays of affection were culturally frowned upon unless the person was a relative. This is the reason the woman wishes that her husband was her brother—so she could dote on him without receiving stares. This also speaks to why she constantly invites him away from public view to isolation and intimacy—she isn't even supposed to kiss him in public. This section ends with the same warning that appears, at least similarly, in 2:7 and 3:5.

Verses 5–7 provide comment on the very nature of love. The first part of verse 5 is attributed to the women of Jerusalem, but the remainder is credited to the woman. Verse 6 may be the most powerful in the book. The seal and signet indicate ownership and personal identification. The first seal—the cylinder—was more common in Mesopotamia, and it was rolled across clay to leave an impression. The second seal—the signet—was more common in Palestine, and it was simply pressed into clay to make an impression.

While there is some disagreement about this, verses 8–9 are attributed to the woman's brothers, mentioned earlier as having forced her to work in the fields, thus darkening her skin. They represent her as the little sister they remember—undeveloped. In verse 10, however, the woman clarifies the reality—she is a fully grown woman.

While Solomon appears in chapter 3 in a positive light, in verses 11–12 he appears in a negative light. Baal Haman, the site of his vineyard, is an unknown location. Earlier, the *vineyard* is used as an image for the woman's beauty or for a place of intimacy. While this poem is puzzling, it is clear that the woman is claiming herself, someone whose love cannot be purchased, perhaps comparing the significance of her relationship with her beloved with the anonymity of Solomon's harem.

Verses 13–14 make up the final poem of the book, one last interaction between the man and woman. After the man calls out to the woman, her words are reminiscent of earlier images—the gazelle or stag (see 2:9, 17). And she finishes the book in a familiar way—by calling him away to solitude and intimacy.

🏠

Take It Home

The book ends abruptly in mid-story, open-ended. In these poems, however, God does more than endorse marriage; He endorses physical love within the context of marriage.

CONTRIBUTING EDITORS:

Dr. Stephen Leston is pastor of Kishwaukee Bible Church in DeKalb, Illinois. He is passionate about training people for ministry and has served as a pastor at Grace Church of DuPage (Warrenville, Illinois) and Petersburg Bible Church (Petersburg, Alaska).

Rev. Stephen C. Magee, MBA, MDiv, is pastor of Exeter Presbyterian Church in Exeter, New Hampshire. He has preached through all of the Old Testament as part of daily worship at the Exeter Church. He also writes an online devotional series at www.epcblog.blogspot.com.

Jeff Miller holds a ThM degree from Dallas Theological Seminary and has been in ministry for nearly ten years. Jeff is coauthor of the *Zondervan Dictionary of Bible and Theology Words* and has written *Hazards of Being a Man* (Baker Books). He is currently working on a Greek-English dictionary (forthcoming with Kregel Publications). Jeff lives in Texas with his wife, Jenny, and two daughters.

Stan Campbell has an MA from Wheaton College and has been a freelance writer for 25 years, overlapping with ten years in Christian publishing and 18 years on staff as a church youth director. Among his almost three dozen books are *The Complete Idiot's Guide to the Bible* and *Bible to Go: Genesis to Revelation in One Hour.*

CONSULTING EDITORS:

Tremper Longman is the Robert H. Gundry Professor of Biblical Studies at Westmont University. He has taught at Westmont since 1998 and taught before that for 18 years at the Westminster Theological Seminary in Philadelphia. Dr. Longman has degrees from Ohio Wesleyan University (BA), Westminster Theological Seminary (MDiv), and Yale University (MPhil; PhD). He has also been active in the area of Bible translation; in particular he serves on the central committee that produced and now monitors the New Living Translation.